THE FINAL STRUGGLE

"Ian Easton's *The Final Struggle: Inside China's Global Strategy* is a must-read for anyone who cares about freedom's future. It's a convincing and in-depth study of the CCP's unbridled ambition for global dominance."

—Mike Pompeo, former CIA director and U.S. Secretary of State

"Ian Easton, a key member of a new generation of scholars with the chops to analyze internal Chinese documents, obliterates the idea that Beijing's strategic plans are obscure. *The Final Struggle* shows, using the regime's own words, how Beijing's aspirations aren't regional—they're global, with grave implications not only for democracy, but for the centuries-old principle of national sovereignty."

—Matt Pottinger, former Deputy National Security Advisor, chairman of the China Program at the Foundation for Defense of Democracies

"What are the Chinese Communist Party's goals and how does it intend to achieve them? Ian Easton's new book seeks to answer these important questions by examining a wide variety of Chinese language sources, including both official statements and previously untranslated documents intended only for internal circulation. Easton's conclusions are grim and will be controversial, but they deserve to be considered and debated."

—Aaron L. Friedberg, Professor of Politics and International Affairs at Princeton University, author of *Getting China Wrong*

"In this rigorous yet accessible study, Ian Easton delivers the definitive and often chilling account of China's ambitions to supplant the existing global system. Drawing extensively from authoritative Chinese-language sources, he lets the Chinese Communist Party speak for itself about its quest for supremacy. Easton skillfully weaves in riveting vignettes that are sure to keep readers turning pages. *The Final Struggle* is a wake-up call for the policy community and the citizenry alike to meet China's challenge on the world stage."

—Toshi Yoshihara, Senior Fellow at the Center for Strategic and Budgetary Assessments, coauthor of *Red Star over the Pacific*

THE FINAL STRUGGLE

INSIDE CHINA'S GLOBAL STRATEGY

IAN EASTON

Published by Eastbridge Books, an imprint of Camphor Press Ltd

83 Ducie Street, Manchester, M1 2JQ, United Kingdom

www.camphorpress.com

Cover design by Michael Cannings.

ISBN   978-1-78869-275-5 (paperback)

          978-1-78869-276-2 (hardcover)

The moral right of the author has been asserted.

Set in 11 pt Libertinus Serif.

For Mia, Kelly, Grace, and Katie

CONTENTS

LIST OF ILLUSTRATIONS

NOTE ON TERMS

The Chinese Communist Party (CCP) has many policies and ideas that it knows the average thinking person might consider ugly and sometimes terrifying. So it has mastered the art of using euphemisms instead of clear language to speak to the people of China and the world. Euphemisms are bland, bureaucratic, or pleasant-sounding words substituted for those things considered too offensive or embarrassing to address plainly. For example, Chinese officials refer to the largest campaign of forced abortion, sterilization, and infanticide in human history as the "One-Child Policy."

It is common for American observers of China to adopt the euphemisms used by the authorities in Beijing. Many of the world's most distinguished journalists, scholars, and statesmen do it. They will talk about the worst manmade famine of all time using the Chinese Communist Party's term for it: the "Great Leap Forward." They will call Mao Zedong the "Great Helmsman," or simply "Chairman Mao," and not mention the fact that he murdered more people than Adolf Hitler.

It says something important that so many professionals choose to apply euphemisms to the subject of their work instead of more honest terms. After all, these are men and women who are highly educated and trained to be critical thinkers, experts at using the spoken and written word, the kind of people with doctoral degrees. They would never use some upbeat Nazi nomenclature to describe the Holocaust. When it comes to China, however, bizarre wordplay happens all the time.

Perhaps China specialists self-censor to demonstrate their progressive credentials and political awareness. Intelligent people try to conform with the linguistic expectations of their colleagues, making groupthink and group talk commonplace in any professional community. Or maybe they are motivated by greed: they want the money that comes from being an accepted Beijing insider with access to the Chinese market. Or maybe they are simply afraid of getting on the wrong side of a regime whose red lines they only vaguely understand. Whatever the reasons, it must be acknowledged that the corruption of language is sinister. It leads to the destruction of human thought. George Orwell's warnings on this point are as important today as they were in the 1940s, when he penned them.[1]

A good linguist can tell you exactly what a Chinese government or military document says word for word. But an even better one knows that direct translation is confusing, often to the point of making language meaningless. To overcome possible misunderstanding, they will attempt to tell you what the source actually means. They will analyze and interpret and explain. They will decode and untangle strange phrases. When there are multiple ways to translate a term or concept, as is generally the case, they will make tough judgement calls.

In this book I will strive to translate the jargon used by CCP sources into clear, plain English, while also letting you know how they are commonly translated. And when I quote euphemisms, I will tell you what I think they actually mean.

AUTHOR'S NOTE

This book is about the Chinese Communist Party's global strategy and, more precisely, its plan for world domination. But in the case of China, that emotionally charged term, "world domination," doesn't mean what you might think it means. When we hold those two words in our minds, they tend to cast alight mental scenes of vast armies goose-stepping into fallen capital cities. We see a series of military invasions, hordes of tanks, and fascist storm troopers swarming across the map. Or we imagine communist paratroopers descending upon sleepy American towns like they did in *Red Dawn*.

To be sure, China is preparing to conquer the island nation of Taiwan that way – with bold surprise attacks and old-school brute military force. But that's not how the CCP plans to take over the rest of the world. That could never work, and China's rulers know it. Anything so obvious as a sweeping campaign of military invasions, no matter how carefully and quietly the plot was laid, would undoubtedly be exposed. That, in turn, would give armies around the world time to unite for a countervailing war of resistance. No matter how fast China's People's Liberation Army might strike, the United States and its allies could rally, fight back, and win.

Beijing's plan is much more sophisticated than anything seen in a World War II documentary or Hollywood film plot. The CCP calls it "the final struggle," a protracted campaign of silent invasions to replicate on a global level what it sees as its own superior system. In theory, it could actually work. By the time you finish reading this book you might be convinced that Xi Jinping and his comrades are brilliant, even diabolical. You might believe that, barring major change, China could actually be on track to winning. If we remain ignorant and smugly complacent, one day we (or perhaps our children) could wake up and find ourselves in a world turned upside down, a world in which it is impossible to wriggle free from the grip of tyrants. And we will scarcely understand how it happened.

I began writing this book because I wanted to understand China's strategy for long-term competition against the United States, and especially what official Chinese government and military documents had to say about it. What began as an academic interest, a mere point of intellectual curiosity, grew over time into something altogether different. As the research advanced and the individual pieces of information coalesced, an entirely new scene emerged, leaving an indelible and uneasy impression.

While my understanding of Chinese strategy is still a work in progress, this research has opened my eyes to a baleful vista of future possibilities, a totalitarian world order stalking us just over the horizon. It's a scary story, far darker than I expected it would be when I began writing. Today, as I gaze out my office window at the leafy suburbs of Washington, DC, it seems unthinkable that the American experiment with democracy could catastrophically fail and careen off into the shadows. Nonetheless, China's rulers have a different view.

FOREWORD

The supreme strategic challenge of our time is now clear. For the United States and our allies and friends, the People's Republic of China is a threat like no other. Never before in modern times has a totalitarian one-party dictatorship exercised so much power and influence on the world stage. Thanks in part to favorable trade arrangements with the West, and in part to a colossal campaign of state-driven espionage, China has far surpassed the former Soviet Union in economic and scientific strength.

Unfortunately, the Chinese Communist Party has demonstrated little interest in harnessing the wealth that the people of China have built to create a more just and prosperous society that protects their civil rights and cherishes their diversity. Instead, we are reading with distress and shock about the pitiless ill-treatment and persecution of millions of individuals solely on the basis of race. And we are watching as China's rulers engage in the largest peacetime military buildup the world has witnessed in over a century.

When we learn of how the CCP worsened the COVID-19 pandemic for everyone via a system of deliberate cover-ups and disinformation, we cannot help but hope that the "China Model" never finds purchase in any other country. Make no mistake, we are in a war of ideas with the Chinese Communist Party. As this book shows, the Party is on an ideological quest to destroy the free and open international order and replace it with a centralized regime made in its own image. While the power and latent advantages of the United States are vast, it is not clear that we are winning the fight against the spread of authoritarianism. True victory, at this point, is not even on the minds of most Americans.

As this goes to print, China's government is investing staggering sums in nuclear arms, militarizing the global commons, and committing genocide. Beijing is supporting Moscow's invasion of Ukraine, and the Chinese military is coercing Taiwan. Chairman Xi Jinping, for his part, is wrapping himself in a fanatical cult of personality, all while attempting to control the future of the Internet. Yet there is still no Washington consensus when it comes to our ends, ways, and means. Even an overall theme for our strategic competition with China remains elusive.

In any healthy, liberal society one would expect more surface area for critical thinking and a growing appetite for knowledge as the stakes go up. Precisely the opposite seems to have happened with China. From Hollywood to the Ivy League, and from Silicon Valley to Wall Street, Americans are in the presence of a growing pressure toward conformism, censorship, and subtle thought control. This book reveals the extent to which we need a rigorous examination of the CCP's plans, intentions, and activities. Enormous intelligence gaps exist that could become lethal if left unaddressed.

It is axiomatic that the best antidote to the erosion of freedom and democracy is sunshine. In that sense, this volume will serve to advance public education, inform policy deliberations, and guide decision makers toward a future in which universal values and individual liberty can flourish at the expense of collectivized power.

Randall G. Schriver
Chairman of the Board
Project 2049 Institute

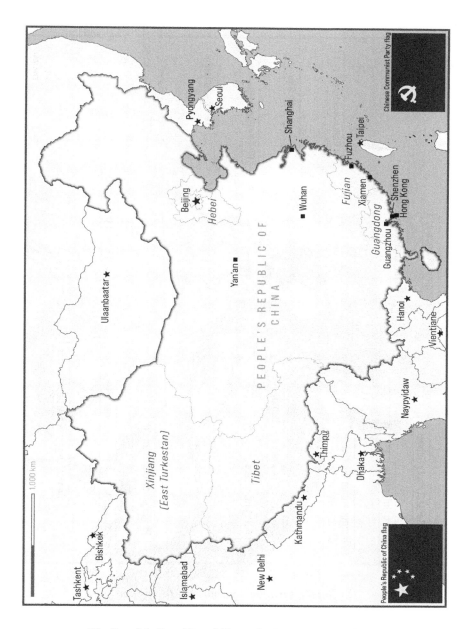

The People's Republic of China, by Louis Martin-Vézian

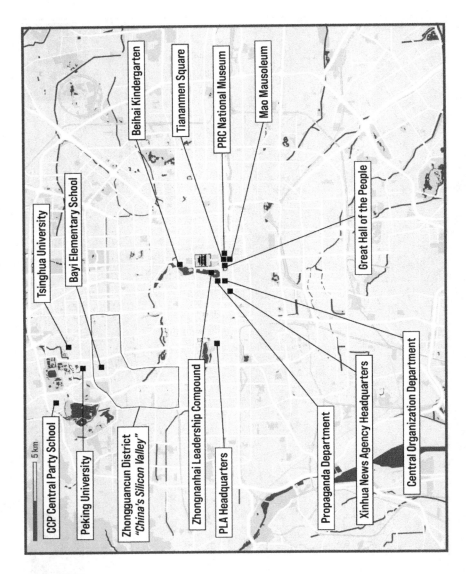

Xi Jinping's Beijing, by Louis Martin-Vézian

THE FINAL STRUGGLE

1

WREATHS & RADIOS

> Here then was one of the great secrets of the war and
> of the world.... But hardly anyone would believe it ...
> and almost all the great responsible authorities stood
> gazing at it with vacant eyes.[2]
>
> —Winston S. Churchill

IT was the ultimate display of American patriotism. On December 7, 2019, the largest veterans' parade in the United States began. The date was a memorable one. It was the seventy-eighth anniversary of the surprise attack on Pearl Harbor.

A prayer service was held at daybreak in the small windswept town of Lubec, Maine, the easternmost settlement in the country. Soon after, a long caravan of powerful Chevy trucks decked out in American flags and filled with thousands of memorial wreaths began a week-long journey, rumbling south to Washington, DC.[3]

The parade wound its way through six states, stopping at high schools, veteran sites, war memorials, fire departments, American Legion posts, and shopping malls. For those involved, their mission was threefold. First, to remember the bravery of past generations of fallen American heroes. Second, to honor the present generation of Americans who defend and serve the nation. And third, to teach the next generation of young Americans the value of freedom.

Wherever the parade stopped, ceremonies were held. Stories were told. Prayers were whispered. Memories were sparked. Pride was felt.[4]

The national president of the Gold Star Mothers, Mona Gunn, led the caravan as grand marshal. For her, the coming days would be deeply meaningful. She was on her way to Arlington National Cemetery, where her son was buried.

Her son, Cherone Louis Gunn, had been born on Valentine's Day and raised in Virginia Beach. Known for his warm and lovable personality, Cherone followed in the proud footsteps of his father and his grandfather and joined the Navy. When his training was complete, Cherone became a Signalman Seaman, a job he learned to perform with distinction aboard one of the fleet's best ships.[5]

After a series of exercises at sea, first in the Gulf of Mexico and then off the coast of North Carolina, Cherone deployed with his shipmates on an overseas mission that must have made many of his friends envious. On paper, it looked like every sailor's dream come true: a late-summer cruise in the sparkling Mediterranean Sea. And, for a while, that's exactly what it was. Until suddenly it turned into something altogether different.

The Final Voyage

On October 12, 2000, at 11:17 a.m. local time, Cherone's ship was docked at a foreign port and refueling. The floating steel fortress he served on seemed invincible. It was a guided-missile destroyer. That meant the ship was capable of raining Tomahawk cruise missiles down on America's enemies from over one thousand nautical miles away, demolishing them at an incredible range with God-like precision.

If you took out a map and asked the ship's strike officer to hit a particular enemy building, he would almost certainly ask you which window you wanted the missile to enter and what effect you wanted the warhead to have once it did.

Of course, launching Tomahawks was just one part of what the ship could do. It was armed with air-defense missiles, anti-ship missiles, anti-submarine rockets, torpedoes, chain guns, and an imposing naval artillery gun. If those somehow failed to cut, shred, or blow the enemy to pieces at a respectable distance, there were two Phalanx "sea-wiz" systems aboard: fully automatic Vulcan cannons mounted on swiveling bases like killer robots (in fact, the Phalanx close-in weapons system is nicknamed R2-D2, after the *Star Wars* droid).

The ship's armaments were every bit as intelligent as they were lethal. Rivers of data rippled across their circuits from databanks located inside the Command Information Center (CIC). This was the ship's brain: a secretive war room hardened to withstand nuclear, biological, and chemical attacks. It was a place where officers could study real-time intelligence reports and updates coming in from classified satellites, radars, sonar arrays, and listening stations.

The ship had other defenses too. It could smash aggressors with particles beamed out from the CIC's electronic-warfare terminals. It had chaff, decoys, and torpedo countermeasures to further confuse attackers. And, when required, the ship could sprint out of harm's way. Unlike most other large warships, this one ate jet fuel and could tear through the waves at well over 30 knots.[6]

But on this particular day and at this particular hour neither the ship's amazing speed nor its high-tech defense systems afforded any protection. The ship was at anchor, and the enemy was already too close to engage with smart weapons. Had there been any warning, the best defense would probably have been a man on deck armed with a machine gun.

Hungry American sailors were lining up for lunch in the galley, chatting and eyeing their options. Those who had been working topside that morning would have been thirsty. The air was dry and heavy with a smell that clung to harbors everywhere: sea salt, dead fish, and diesel fuel. Ice-cold "bug juice" (military-grade Kool-Aid in communal jugs) is a staple refreshment aboard U.S. Navy vessels the world over. It must have been a welcome sight to those going on break.

A tiny fiberglass boat approached the floating steel fortress. Two local men were at the wheel. They smiled and waved reassuringly at the puzzled American sailors eyeing them from above. A fraction of a second later, the men disappeared in a fiery flash. And, a fraction of a second after that, the ship's galley vanished into the void.[7]

The men were suicide bombers. Cherone's ship was the USS *Cole*.

The Road to Arlington

Just over a week after the attack, Cherone was laid to rest in a resplendent flag-draped casket. Next to him was his shipmate Richard Costelow, a father of three who had been buried earlier that same day. The chemical eruption that ripped through the steel skin of their ship had cut short seventeen bright and promising lives. A volley of rifle shots rang though the warm autumn air. Cherone had dreamed of joining the Virginia State Police after getting out of the Navy. It was not to be.[8]

Nineteen years later, sharply dressed state troopers flanked the all-American caravan that his mother led. They represented a world of strait-laced order and discipline. Alongside them on heavy bikes rode seemingly unlikely allies: Patriot Guard Riders, Patriot Riders of America, and Rolling Thunder. These tough and rugged individuals helped the police ensure the safe transportation of all the participants and their precious cargo.

Many of the bikers were war veterans. Others bore scars from a lifetime of battles closer to home. Their uniforms were basic yet intimidating: blue jeans, T-shirts, and black leather jackets with American flags, military patches, and words like "Standing for those who stood for us" etched into them. You wouldn't want to tangle with these dudes. And, of course, we have no reports of anyone causing the parade trouble.

Wreaths Across America is a non-profit civic organization that coordinates wreath-laying ceremonies at thousands of graves and memorial sites around the nation, from Cape Canaveral, Florida, to Miramar, California. It started in 1992 as a pilgrimage made by a Maine wreath-maker, Morrill Worcester, who drove his truck to Arlington that year with five thousand wreaths as a gesture of thanks.

Over the years, Worcester's pilgrimage has grown into a national movement. On the same Saturday each year, ceremonies are held at cemeteries in all fifty states and several locations overseas. The escort caravan to Arlington National Cemetery is the main event. The culminating moment comes when a wreath is laid at the Tomb of the Unknown Soldier, where it remains under the safekeeping of armed Marines in dress blues.[9]

But this year something was wrong. Unbeknownst to any of the participants, every move the caravan made was being tracked by a technology company with ties to a hostile foreign power. The company had donated forty-five radios to Wreaths Across America, each of which was connected to a cloud-based server so that truck drivers, police officers, bikers, and staff members could talk to each other and coordinate on the road. According to its press release, the company's cloud-based server had software that tracked each GPS-enabled radio in real time as the escort traveled from Maine to Washington, DC.[10]

At first glance the company appeared to be an excellent fit for the parade. Any Patriot Guard Rider who visited its website would have liked what he saw on the homepage: an iconic image of the Chicago skyline at dusk fading into a picture of schoolchildren getting on a yellow school bus. Overlaid were the words "Better School Security Communications." Another image showed a map of the United States, with blooms of connectivity set against a digital radio set.[11]

The company, Hytera, had crafted its website with care, making itself look like all of its peers. It boasted of a global sales network, research labs, and regional offices. It proudly declared, "Hytera is the fastest growing radio communications company in the world.... From major events such as the Rio Olympic Games, the US Open, and the America's Cup, to oil rigs, utility companies, football stadiums, schools, hospitals and hotels across the country, Hytera's professional radio communications systems are exceeding the expectations of the modern workforce."[12]

It is easy to see why Wreaths Across America would welcome this company as a sponsor. Hytera's products were trusted by some of the best of the best. Hytera supplied first responders across the United States with a variety of high-tech communications equipment. Hytera products were employed by local and state governments, and could be found in the nerve centers of prisons, where radio communications and remote access controls are used by operators to move prisoners, lock doors, and maintain perimeter security.[13]

Two of Hytera's subsidiary companies, Norsat and Sepura, supplied the Pentagon and close allies, such as Her Majesty's government in the United Kingdom, with satellite communications and covert surveillance gear used by undercover units.[14] Another Hytera-owned company, PowerTrunk, served utility companies in Georgia, oil refineries in Minnesota, chemical plants in Texas, the New York subway, and the New Jersey transit authorities.[15]

Teltronic S.A.U., which had been bought out by a British company that subsequently went bankrupt and was sold to Hytera, now serviced the communications needs of public transportation networks in Toronto, Mexico City, Barcelona, and Nottingham (and, just for good measure, Malaysia's entire government).[16] All across democratic society, then, critical communications that could mean the difference between life and death ran on Hytera. But who actually was this sprawling technology company that so many governments trusted?

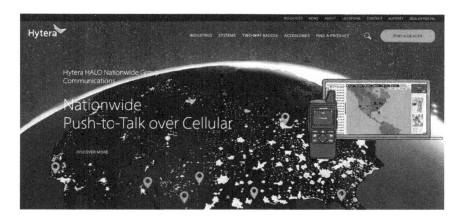

*Artistic rendering of Hytera's American
website, by Grace Young*

Twin Websites

For years I had lived just a few blocks from Arlington National Cemetery and had long wondered who put wreaths on the graves every Christmas. Then one day in early 2020, I came across Hytera's press release advertising its participation in the Wreaths Across America veterans' parade. I started reading and learning about the parade. At last, the mystery was solved.

But there was more. It turns out that lurking on Hytera's website, well outside the normal American's scope of need and interest, is a tiny box that opens up a drop-down language menu. Hytera has a Chinese website too. Because, of course, Hytera is a Chinese company. Here is its original name: *Hainengda* (海能达). Before long I had clicked my way into it, and a whole other side of the organization glowed on my display. Websites can change with a few finger taps on plastic, so after revisiting it several times to make sure I wasn't imagining things, I began saving screenshots. Then I revisited it again months later. It was the exact same: an unmovable feast of chilling digital detail.

Hytera's Chinese website showed that its English website had an evil twin. Part of the company might have been American and patriotic. Yet Hytera was tied to the world's largest and most powerful anti-American political organization: the Chinese Communist Party (CCP). It was a trusted supplier for China's military and internal security services.[17] Hytera was so trusted by the Chinese government, in fact, that the company was chosen by the Ministry of Public Security to build and operate critical segments of China's mass surveillance system.[18]

What I saw on Hytera's Chinese-language website was image after image of uniformed security personnel sitting in command centers, monitoring banks of computer terminals being fed streams of video captured, recorded, and processed by the company's big-data analytics equipment.[19] I was looking at a system that uses advanced technology to hunt human beings, women and men deemed to be enemies of the state. Many of those in China who are arrested by the regime's political police didn't commit a crime, or at least anything Americans would understand to be a crime.

In the People's Republic of China, one can commit a "crime" by doing something as simple as going to church on Sunday – especially if it's a church not registered and approved by the officially atheist state. One can commit a crime by practicing the wrong kind of taiji (the Falun Gong kind); by having a baby without authorization from the local family planning committee; by following the teachings of the Dalai Lama; by advocating for rule of law, or the right to free speech. The regime's enemy list is a long one. Write, publish, or sell a book like this one in China, and you'd probably find yourself on that list.

Artistic rendering of Hytera's Chinese website, by Grace Young

A Brutal System

What exactly is the CCP? As we will see, it is a totalitarian political organization with over 90 million members, most of whom are undercover. In recent years, it has carried out a secretive program to round up millions of Uyghurs (and untold numbers of Tibetans, Christians, and others), sending them into sprawling concentration camps constructed on a ferocious scale.[20] Entire towns have been emptied, with young children taken from their mothers' arms and placed in state-run orphanages where they learn to disdain their parents' native traditions.[21]

According to the U.S. State Department, the Chinese government has built a brutal system of repression through forced labor, brainwashing, systematic rape, sterilizations, invasive birth control, and other forms of cruel and unusual punishment.[22] A legal study found that Beijing is committing genocide and breaching every article in the United Nations' 1948 Genocide Convention.[23] While horrifying, the regime's crimes against humanity may actually have a back-to-the-future quality for many people in China. Throughout its history, the Communist Party has used murderous purges and mass movements against innocent groups, often targeted seemingly at random, as an instrument of broad social control. The campaign this time is different only insofar as it is part of a much larger machine of state terror and an indicator of a far-reaching transformation underway across China and around the globe. The authorities in China have made clear they are determined to succeed in a new type of social engineering, one enabled by technologies Mao Zedong could only have dreamed of.[24]

The current ruler of China's one-party dictatorship, Xi Jinping, is constructing a system that has the potential to do what his predecessors never could: use artificial intelligence technology to turn people into living robots. In theory, any individual freedom and autonomy of thought, no matter how small, could one day be made virtually impossible by China's increasingly sophisticated control complex.[25]

Elements of this Orwellian system are euphemistically referred to as the "Social Credit System," "Smart Cities," and "City Brain." Hyper-intrusive, China's government uses big-data analytics to chart a person's conformity to Marxist-Leninist ideology and loyalty to the communist regime. It monitors Chinese citizens and other persons of interest around the world (including in the United States) using video cameras and cutting-edge algorithms covertly embedded in popular apps, social media, computers, televisions, and even restaurant tables.[26] It pipes torrents of data into CCP-controlled server farms to be stored, fed, and processed by supercomputers.[27]

Hytera's Chinese-language website was proudly declaring itself to be a major player in a harshly repressive system and a valuable asset to China's state security apparatus. That is likely why, in 2019, Hytera was placed on a U.S. government "entity list" alongside CCP-controlled telecommunications and video surveillance companies Huawei, ZTE,

Hikvision, and Dahua.[28] The federal government designated Hytera and its subsidiaries and affiliates as a national security threat and prohibited their use "for the purpose of public safety, security of government facilities, physical security surveillance of critical infrastructure, and other national security purposes."[29] After further review, the U.S. Federal Communications Commission ordered American carriers to "rip and replace" Huawei and ZTE equipment used in their communications networks, offering taxpayer funds to reimburse them. The FCC declared that Hytera had been found to "pose an unacceptable risk to U.S. national security" and indicated the company might have its equipment authorizations revoked.[30]

Even though Hytera was barred from new federal government contracts, it still had access to the American commercial market and was able to maintain its offices and labs in California, Illinois, and Florida. These linkages continued to give it the ability to sponsor work visas and green cards for Chinese nationals and employ American technology experts, some of whom its U.S. competitor Motorola Solutions claimed were poached as part of commercial espionage operations.[31]

On February 14, 2020, after a marathon fourteen-week trial in a Chicago federal court, Hytera was found guilty in one of the largest technology theft cases in U.S. history. Motorola Solutions was awarded $764.5 million by the court, every dollar in damages it sought.[32] Brandon Brown, one of the litigators who represented Motorola Solutions, stated the following:

> The scale and scope of theft is truly without precedent –
> Hytera had tens of thousands of Motorola's confidential
> documents and millions of lines of source code in its
> possession while trying to develop a competing product.
> They used a lot of the code literally line for line, but
> also engaged in a systematic effort to obscure its theft
> by changing its code to "look different" than Motorola,
> so Motorola would never figure it out when it tested
> Hytera's radios.[33]

But Hytera was nothing if not resilient. Long after being sued and placed on an entity list, Hytera still sold its products to schools, small businesses, and factories across the country. And some of its loyal American customers were vocal in their support for the company, ignoring the guilty verdict and calling the federal government's actions "absurd."[34]

As for Hytera's wholly owned subsidiaries, it was not clear that they lost their access to government contracts. In the United Kingdom, for example, they were still supplying the "Airwave" network used by emergency services across the country.[35] The website of one Hytera-controlled company, Sepura, continued to state, "Our solutions are used globally by: organized crime investigations teams, counter terrorism units, military units, drug investigation teams, serious fraud investigation teams, and counter espionage units."[36] In 2021, Sepura won a major contract in Brazil to supply military, police, and border security forces with communications systems.[37]

For Hytera, any setback in the United States may have been only temporary. Prior to the onset of the COVID-19 pandemic, President Donald Trump seemed inclined to bring Chinese tech giants back in from the cold as part of a broader trade deal. Although it seems increasingly unlikely, President Joe Biden or a future president could still opt to do so.[38] And even if the U.S. government crackdown on Hytera continues, the company can still count on a vast global market and the support of powerful clients outside the United States.

But why had Washington placed restrictions on Hytera in the first place? Wasn't that xenophobic, anti-competitive, market-distorting behavior? Didn't that go against the tide of globalization that America long advocated for and benefitted the most from? Internal Chinese government and military documents reviewed for this book reveal that the U.S. government made an alarming mistake. Yet it wasn't a mistake driven by the national security community's paranoia.

Rather than overreaction, Hytera's case could be viewed as a remarkable study in government complacency. In retrospect, it seems surprising that a Chinese technology company such as Hytera could ever have been allowed to establish operations on American soil in the first place. Even more surprising was that whatever legal loopholes let them in were still left open long after it was discovered that Hytera and a large number of other Chinese entities had become embedded into the nation's critical infrastructure.[39] The fact that nothing was actually done by Washington to block Hytera's servers from tracking the Wreaths Across America veterans' parade might tell us something about the effectiveness of China's global strategy.

There are many reasons national security officials should have been more concerned about having technology companies from China inside the American market. To begin, let's look at some of the problems associated with the way China's government does business.

Shadow Companies

The published laws and regulations of the People's Republic of China force companies like Hytera to share their data with the CCP and the regime's secret police and intelligence services.[40] The PRC State Intelligence Law, for example, states that all Chinese companies (and indeed all citizens) must cooperate with the government's intelligence operations whenever asked. Moreover, the law demands Chinese companies keep their related activities secret so their customers and business partners – their targets of exploitation – never know they are being spied on.[41]

Companies in the PRC are not, and have never been, independent legal entities the way their American counterparts are. If the Chinese government or its secret agents order them to collect intelligence and share data, they have no legal way of refusing.[42] Chinese companies and Chinese citizens have no rights at all other than those granted them by the CCP, which sits above the law and uses the law to enforce its own will.[43]

From a legal standpoint, any separation between the Chinese government and private sector exists in name and imagination only. Chinese companies (and foreign companies operating in China) are controlled by Communist Party committees, which have the power to override decisions made by corporate boards. In fact, according to its own writings, the CCP is so powerful and all-pervasive that it is misleading to think of Chinese boards as if they wield real influence over company decisions. That's mirror imaging, projecting Western values and practices onto something very different.

In China, all business leadership teams are stacked with Communist Party members, most of whom are undercover and don't advertise their true affiliations. Indeed, *all* organized groups of human beings in China have to form political committees, which are made up of individuals who undergo background checks, have every detail of their personal lives monitored, and endure invasive screening their entire careers, long after that first initiation ceremony when they raise their right fist and swear eternal loyalty to the hammer and sickle.[44]

To put it quite simply, private companies in China are not actually private at all. CCP agents run their affairs and sit in their management offices, ensuring there is no internal conflict between business interests and regime interests. Chinese business leaders must serve the government first, not their shareholders or the capitalist god of profit.[45]

The Communist Party's grip on the Chinese market and its constant intervention into commercial affairs are not always good for individual companies. But that's beside the point. They are good for the regime, and what's good for the CCP is believed to be good for the state, the nation, and all society. Companies in China are expected to serve as the commercial arms of the government even if it costs them profits. Even if state intervention ultimately bankrupts them, Chinese companies must obey the directives of the authorities in Beijing. Disobedience driven by greed or by a belief in Adam Smithian principles is far from unheard of, but it can come with severe consequences.

Companies that cross the Chinese government can find themselves suddenly crushed by competitors or closed down altogether, the culprits (real or imagined) "disappeared" – imprisoned and tortured, pumped with mind-altering drugs, and sometimes executed. The Communist Party has limitless coercive leverage over all individuals and all companies in China.[46] This means that any American whose personal or sensitive information connects to Chinese electronic systems is at risk of having that data compromised and exploited by China's political police and intelligence services, harming not only the American user but also U.S. economic competitiveness and national security.[47]

Extraordinary Military Access

According to the laws and regulations of the PRC, Chinese communications companies must install hardware and software that allow their products to be accessed by the People's Liberation Army (PLA).[48] In recent years, companies across China that previously had no military ties have had to establish internal bodies to ensure their products are made to PLA specifications.[49] In practice, this likely means that ostensibly private companies must open up their doors to military liaison officers and do whatever they say.

The PLA is not a normal military. It's the armed wing of the Communist Party. Without it, the regime simply wouldn't exist. The military's job has always been to serve the regime, not the constitution or the people of China. It exercises extraordinary power in China and, increasingly, around the world because of its special status, which gives it vast political and commercial influence. With over two million active personnel, the PLA is the largest military on earth and probably the single largest and most sophisticated intelligence collector in human history.[50]

This all matters a great deal because any personal or sensitive information that connects to Chinese electronic systems is at risk of being compromised and exploited by the CCP to the detriment of not only the American user, who can be targeted for extortion or blackmail, but the U.S. military. In the words of a U.S. Department of Defense report to Congress, China has the ability to mobilize "all relevant aspects of its society and economy for use in competition and war;" China's Military-Civil Fusion means "there is not a clear line between the PRC's civilian and military economies."[51]

In a future war, then, the Pentagon could find itself under siege from cyberattacks coming from infected electronics across the American heartland. Imagine how that Patriot Guard Rider would feel if he discovered that his own handheld device had been enslaved by the Chinese military and was taking part in an attack on the men and women in his old unit. It may seem outlandish to some, but that is exactly the kind of power over foreign electronic networks Beijing aims to achieve and, in many cases, probably already has.[52]

Winners and Losers

The same laws and policies that allow the regime to take whatever data the military might need from companies in China also allow the Communist Party to decide which ones thrive, living in the spotlight, and which ones wither away.[53] According to internal documents, those state-owned enterprises and private "national champion" companies that the CCP favors receive massive no-compete contracts and cash flows from both central and local government treasuries. They get generous subsidies courtesy of the state on things like land, office space, water, electricity, and gas. They get tax breaks. They get coveted stock market listings in New York, London, and Hong Kong that are potentially worth hundreds of billions of dollars.[54]

In addition to monetary benefits, the CCP's commercial arms get top-tier international talent recruited by China's headhunting super agency, the Central Organization Department, which runs talent-acquisition offices in Silicon Valley, Boston, New York, Oxford, Tokyo, Taipei, and other centers of technology and finance around the world.[55] Chinese companies get advanced technology handouts, often acquired by the regime's intelligence services through illicit means, including bribery, blackmail, and espionage.[56]

Beijing's chosen elite get lavished by the Central Propaganda Department and feted by the Chinese media machine. You might see their CEOs interviewed by the *China Times*, the Xinhua News Agency, CGTN (the China Global Television Network), or, in the case of then Alibaba CEO, Jack Ma, at West Point lecturing on leadership.[57] You might notice opinion editorials in your favorite media outlet promoting them. You might see former U.S. senators lobbying for them in Washington.[58] You will definitely see their products featured in popular South Korean dramas such as *Crash Landing on You* and Hollywood blockbuster films like *Transformers: Dark of the Moon.*[59]

You see these companies' names advertised on the Internet, on roadside billboards, and on stadium walls at football games. You see their products on the shelves at Walmart, Target, and Best Buy on Black Friday, and on Amazon on Cyber Monday.[60] And you might wonder how the store can afford to sell such cool brand-name electronics so cheaply.

Of course, what you won't see is all that took place behind the scenes to make that company a titan of industry capable of flooding foreign markets with low-cost yet high-quality products. You won't see their secret committee meetings to work out state subsidies, their deals with the military, their liaisons with spies in China's security bureaus, their brutal treatment of factory workers, their illegal access to trade secrets, their exploitation of concentration camp labor, and their flouting of environmental protection rules.

To say that CCP-controlled companies have unfair advantages over American and other international competitors would be like observing that hurricanes can result in wind gusts. The truth is that China's commercial champions have illicit, extralegal powers that allow them to battle and undersell any competitor. They have an impressive track record of violating the commitments made by the Chinese government when it joined the World Trade Organization (WTO), while escaping punishment and penalties.

When the PRC joined the WTO in 2001, that organization was tasked with the mission of reforming the mammoth Communist economy, making it compliant with Western trade norms. Instead, the WTO enabled China's state-directed, predatory trade practices. Chinese companies have been allowed to flood the world with heavily subsidized exports while Beijing maintains a tight grip on China's domestic market. Foreign firms wanting access must agree to hand over their core technologies, relocate their production lines to China, and allow the CCP to monitor them from the inside with intrusive Communist Party committees. These arrangements are designed to bolster Chinese companies and undermine their competitors, allowing Chinese companies to infiltrate and destroy their American rivals, replace them, and take their market share.[61]

Just ask Motorola Inc., a formerly American telecommunications giant that was forced to split into two companies after losing billions of dollars to its rivals. Lenovo, a Chinese company founded and run by a Chinese military institute graduate and former government official, took over Motorola's mobile device business, making Lenovo one of the world's top smartphone vendors.[62] This deal allowed Lenovo to market its electronics to consumers in the United States with the trusted Motorola brand name and logo. (The Chinese-owned company's full name is Motorola Mobility. Motorola Solutions remains an American company.)[63]

Or ask IBM. In 2005, Lenovo bought out IBM's iconic ThinkPad brand and its personal computer business, making it the world's number one seller of PCs.[64] Lenovo continued to use the ThinkPad brand and, in 2014, acquired IBM's server business.[65] Or ask General Electric. In 2016, GE sold its century-old appliance division to its Chinese competitor, Haier, a PRC state-owned enterprise.[66] Instead of changing the company's name to reflect its new ownership, Haier calls its wholly owned subsidiary GE Appliances and continues to use the GE brand and logo.[67]

What are the implications of U.S. companies getting into the domestic Chinese market only to be taken over? And could companies like Lenovo and Haier be turned into arms of the PLA? If you want to get a sense of how pervasive the CCP intends for its militarization of Chinese companies to be, consider the PLA's official training manual on military-civil fusion. This internal document exhorts Chinese military officers to "Use a mix of education, propaganda, and other methods to flood society with the right concepts regarding military-civil fusion and national defense ideology.... Make these penetrate down into the bone marrow of all our ethnic Chinese people."[68]

So, when Americans purchase electronic systems made by companies in China, they are giving money to the commercial arms of a hostile power. They are buying from government and military-controlled corporations able to do things no normal business could ever consider. Many Chinese companies don't even have to make a profit, at least not in the near term, because they are arms of the state.[69] Once they undercut rivals, corner the market, and achieve global monopolies (or cartels with other Chinese giants), then the profits can and will come. And the Chinese government can take their profits and invest them back into the augmentation of other strategic companies and things like espionage and military hardware.

With the help of authorities in Beijing (and unwitting international customers), China's national champion companies are out-competing their foreign rivals in America and around the world. As you will see in the following pages, CCP-controlled electronics are deeply woven into the fabric of critical infrastructure everywhere, including in places you would never imagine, places like the radio network used in America's longest veterans' parade. That matters a great deal. Yet communications technology and commercial competition are just the tip of the iceberg. There's an even bigger problem lurking under the surface, one that rarely gets addressed but could decide the future of the world.

2

NEED TO KNOW

Capitalism is bound to die out and socialism is bound to win.[70]

—Xi Jinping

IN a foreword to the Defense Intelligence Agency's *2019 China Military Power Report*, General Robert Ashley Jr. wrote: "The Defense Intelligence Agency – indeed the broader U.S. Intelligence Community – is continually asked, 'What do we need to know about China? What is China's vision of the world and its role in it? What are Beijing's strategic intentions and what are the implications for Washington?'"[71]

These words would prove telling. In 2019, the U.S. government finally decided that the American people had a need to know about the national security threat posed by the Chinese Communist Party. More than that, the government decided the threat was so perilous that the public needed to be reminded of it again and again until the idea finally took root.

To help answer the questions penned by General Ashley, then Vice President Michael Pence and officials from across Washington began what was to become a remarkable public-education campaign – a coordinated information blitz on a scale not seen since the 1980s, the last decade of the Cold War. A storm of speeches, testimonies, and reports about what the government euphemistically termed the "China challenge" flooded the nation.[72]

Randall Schriver, the Pentagon's top Asia strategist, held a press conference in which he said, "China seeks to erode U.S. military advantages. And seeks to gain and maintain influence. And it backs these ambitions with significant resourcing, which translates into real capabilities and capacity." Schriver continued, "Our concerns are significant when it comes to the ongoing repression in China. The Communist Party is using the security forces for mass imprisonment of Chinese Muslims in concentration camps."[73]

In the following months, the national security advisor, the director of the FBI, the attorney general, the secretary of state, and the secretary of homeland security each took part in a series of historic China speeches.[74] The deputy national security advisor, Matthew Pottinger, gave two speeches in Mandarin on strategic competition with the CCP, both delivered from the White House and addressed to Chinese Americans and the broader Chinese diaspora.[75]

For decades, the U.S. government had dedicated itself to cooperating with China to integrate it into the global economy. Now Washington's top national security leaders were officially warning the American people that the previous policy of partnering with the CCP had failed. To protect the nation, they asserted Americans would have to treat the regime in China like the strategic rival it actually was. This was going to be a life-and-death contest, a matter of war and peace. The entire world order – even Western civilization itself – was on the line. And there was no guarantee that America would win.

This remarkable change in policy toward China led to an outpouring of intellectual resources dedicated to examining the historical, structural, and theoretical underpinnings of strategic competition between America and China. Yet significant uncertainties still exist about how PRC government officials view the issue and what their global strategy looks like.[76] How do Xi Jinping and the Communist Party elite view great power competition? What are their aspirations for China's future? Do they keep score? If so, how do they measure success? It appears increasingly likely that an open-ended strategic competition between the United States and the PRC will become the central story of the twenty-first century.[77] How that story unfolds will depend, at least in part, on the ambitions, plans, and perceptions of China's rulers.

The United States has a national interest in developing a deep understanding of the prevailing mindset in China's halls of power. One of the most difficult intellectual challenges facing Americans will be eschewing mirror imaging, the projection of our own assumptions onto an adversary with vastly different habits of mind and patterns of deed. Until that happens, we will struggle to empathize with and respond to Chinese actions, and a wise strategy will be beyond our grasp. We will be blind and at the mercy of fate. To prevail in what could prove to be the most difficult and dangerous foreign policy test the United States has ever faced, we must peer into the minds of our strategic rivals, seeking to understand how they observe themselves, how they perceive us, and how they see everything else.

We must attempt to learn how they think, how they feel, and how they might change over time. What deeply buried scars and desires control them? What points of leverage might be there to grasp? Where are they weak and vulnerable? What reservoirs of strength are lurking in areas best avoided? Of course, states are not unitary actors. Governments cannot be understood as one rational (or irrational) individual. Bureaucracies and organizational dynamics matter a great deal. This is less true in a communist dictatorship, but it still holds to a degree – and probably more than we might expect.

How will the future unfold? There are countless variables, but the realm of ideas may prove to be the most important. Ideas control actions. Understanding how a rival superpower thinks is indispensable. With such knowledge in hand, it becomes possible to better anticipate a rival's future actions and their most likely responses to various situations. Policy represents the thoughts government leaders entertain about their nation's rightful station in the world. Policy imparts logic and direction to grand strategy, which is the coordinated application of power in all its forms to the service of policy.[78]

Reading PRC government planning documents and listening to leadership speeches should tell us a lot about how China will compete against the United States and its allies in the years ahead.[79] Authoritative sources that describe Xi Jinping's vision might turn out to be a time machine into the future. At a minimum, they are windows into a mental universe we could otherwise never see. A trove of Chinese-language writings exist that can be exploited to analyze China's global strategy; many key sources, however, remain unexamined.[80]

As tensions rise, it becomes more probable that misunderstandings and mistakes could occur. Political violence, both physical and psychological, could take on a life of its own. Now more than ever before, Americans need to understand the CCP. Is there a coherent ideology driving their actions? What do official documents say about the Communist Party's worldview and aspirations for the future? We know from Xi Jinping's speeches that he wants to change the world.[81] What we have yet to fully learn is how he defines the objectives of China's plan, how the CCP is conducting its strategy, and what it means for the United States and other liberal democracies.

Tectonic Shift

The United States' strategy toward China is currently undergoing what appears to be nothing short of a tectonic shift. This is an earth-shaking event in the history of American foreign policy. The movement appears to have been triggered by Xi Jinping's monopolization of political power. At the nineteenth Congress of the Communist Party in October 2017, Xi removed China's semi-formal system of term limits. He enshrined his own personal ideology (Xi Jinping Thought) into the CCP constitution and refused to appoint a successor. Each of these moves was somewhat surprising. Taken together, they were astonishing.

Xi's power grab represented a sharp turn away from four decades of elite consensus-based rule. For the first time since the death of Mao Zedong in 1976, supreme power in China is being exercised by a charismatic and ambitious dictator whose legitimacy has been established through sweeping purges and a cult of personality.[82] Assertive Chinese military operations in the East China Sea, the Taiwan Strait, and the South China Sea, in addition to disruptive actions in space and cyberspace, have further led American leaders to conclude that China has become a strategic competitor.[83]

The first tremors in Washington were captured in the government's December 2017 *National Security Strategy*, which stated: "China ... wants to shape a world antithetical to U.S. values and interests. China seeks to displace the United States in the Indo-Pacific region, expand the reaches of its state-driven economic model, and reorder the region in its favor."[84] This assessment represented a fundamental break from decades of past policy. For the previous forty years, Washington had opted to work with Beijing in the hope that the Communist Party could be liberalized and ultimately replaced through a political reform process that would advance American interests. The prevailing assumption had been that a more prosperous and powerful China would be more peaceful and willing to accept the American-led, liberal international order. The National Security Strategy somberly concluded that such premise, "turned out to be false."[85]

It is still too early to know whether the U.S. government is prepared to sustain an open-ended strategic competition. According to China expert Peter Mattis, "The strategic shift in U.S. policy toward China has not been locked in either bureaucratically or politically."[86] Mattis argues that while it would be premature to discuss an overarching strategy and set of objectives until a new China policy takes hold, much can be done to build American capacity to compete with China in the near term.[87] He concludes, "The conversation has moved to the point where concrete ideas of how to better understand the Chinese Communist Party and China, and how to be more competitive, must be fleshed out and debated."[88]

As Washington studies the national challenges posed by China and develops a consensus around its new strategy to compete, a critical question American leaders will grapple with is how the CCP plans to achieve its own objectives. How do Xi Jinping and his top advisors view strategic competition? What are they doing to achieve their goals for the future?

Evolution of the Field

During the Cold War, the China studies community produced a small number of leading authorities whose work had a lasting influence on the field.[89] Then, starting in the late 1990s, a growing interest in the rapid emergence of Chinese power led a few American analysts to focus on Chinese strategy.[90] They believed that the main objective of China's government was to work on sustaining its impressive economic growth, and this necessitated the avoidance of arms races, strategic competition, and any potential confrontation that could negatively impact trade.

Most Western scholars then argued that Chinese and American national interests overlapped or were mostly complimentary. To the extent that China's rising power challenged U.S. influence, many believed that collaboration would result in the building of trust and the exchange of mutual goodwill.[91] One influential American scholar posited that, "The task of managing the security dimensions of the U.S.-China relationship is twofold: (1) to identify and develop areas of cooperation ... and (2) to manage the Taiwan problem."[92]

Two American specialists wrote, "It may be too much to hope for an equally cooperative relationship with China. Yet it is entirely plausible that the competition can be limited.... Given the potential benefits of such cooperation ... there are powerful reasons to work toward this outcome."[93] At the time, the vast power disparity between the two sides

and the seemingly positive nature of U.S.-China relations made it difficult for most Americans to imagine that achieving global ambitions, if
they existed at all, was even possible for Beijing.[94] Still, a few Americans
held a different view. They foresaw that the United States and China
were bound to compete with each other across the broad ecosystem of
international affairs. In their opinion, China's authoritarian rulers were
more ambitious and resilient than generally understood. And Beijing
would act to pursue its interests to the extent that its power allowed,
often in a zero-sum manner.

In 1999, a United States Air Force major, Mark Stokes, shocked the
analytic community when he published a book that argued China was
about to engage in a rapid military buildup that would challenge the
United States military. "The Chinese defense-industrial complex has
initiated a focused strategic modernization program to meet the needs
of 21st century warfare," he wrote, pointing to Chinese military research
into areas like ballistic and cruise missiles, space and cyberspace warfare,
unmanned systems, and nuclear strikes.[95] Stokes, who had received the
CIA's "spook of the year" award for performing special attaché missions
in China, wrote, "Most within the U.S.-based PLA watching community
are skeptical of China's ability to modernize its military. One helpful
measure would be to shift away from concentration on the PLA's many
shortcomings to a careful, sober examination of what the PLA could do
now and in the future."[96]

Michael Pillsbury, a China expert who worked for the Pentagon, also
asserted that the Chinese government was more strategically competitive
than most believed.[97] His research showed that China's rulers were obsessed with great power status and hierarchy, and constantly measured
the strength of potential rivals and partners to forecast their ability to
fight and win wars.[98] In 2005, Robert Kaplan made waves when he argued
that, "The Chinese navy is poised to push out into the Pacific – and when
it does, it will very quickly encounter a U.S. Navy and Air Force unwilling to budge from the coastal shelf of the Asian mainland. It's not hard
to imagine the result: a replay of the decades-long Cold War.... Pulsing

with consumer and martial energy, ... China constitutes the principal conventional threat to America's liberal imperium."[99]

James Mann's 2007 book, *The China Fantasy: Why Capitalism Will Not Bring Democracy to China*, made a prescient argument that the foundation of Washington's China policy was weak; Beijing was not reforming politically or moving in a positive direction as the result of cooperation and trade, nor was the Communist Party fragile and about to come unglued. He wrote, "If China's political system stays a permanently regressive one-party state, that will mean the U.S. policy toward China since 1989 has been sold to the American people on the basis of a fraud – that is, on the false premise that trade and 'engagement' with China would change China's political system."[100] Mann correctly predicted that China was likely to become fully integrated into the global economy and remain undemocratic. To stay in power, the regime could simply use increasing levels of repression.[101]

Aaron Friedberg's 2011 book, *Contest for Supremacy*, found that China's ability to grow richer and stronger while remaining a one-party state meant that it posed a mounting strategic challenge, and also an intellectual challenge to Americans, whom had long assumed events would play out differently. Friedberg wrote, "Since the days of Richard Nixon and Henry Kissinger, American political leaders, diplomats, and China specialists have been strongly inclined to 'accentuate the positive' ... generally understating or ignoring deeply rooted problems and enduring differences."[102] Friedberg went on to conclude that "China is not an ally, nor is it a trusted friend; it is an increasingly powerful and important country ... that, under its present leadership, has interests and objectives that are at times in direct opposition to America's own."[103]

While more recent events have validated the arguments made by Stokes, Pillsbury, Kaplan, Mann, and Friedberg, their writings were controversial, even scandalous, when they first came out. It was difficult for most observers of U.S.-PRC relations to imagine that China's rulers would be able to increase their nation's power and remain internationally competitive without making structural political reforms. And, of course, it seemed unthinkable that Beijing would engage in militant and geno-cidal behavior, including the construction of concentration camps and the destruction of minority ethnic group families, cultures, and religions.

If history teaches us anything, it is that China will continue to surprise American leaders and the American people. Mitigating the dangerous impacts of surprises, and seizing opportunities to advance American interests when they appear, will require the continuous development of deep insights into Chinese Communist policy making, especially in areas where our knowledge is currently embryonic, shallow, or simply nonexistent.

New Sources of Illumination

There has been a proliferation of scholarly writings about Chinese strategy in recent years; these have done a great deal to advance the quality of our understanding regarding U.S.-PRC strategic competition.[104] Analysts have submitted congressional testimonies and published re-ports on China's approach to integrated economic, technological, and military competition.[105] Some scholars have examined Beijing's political warfare and foreign influence operations.[106] Others have advanced public education on Xi Jinping's signature foreign policy effort, the "One Belt, One Road" strategy (OBOR, also known as Belt and Road Initiative).[107] Still others have contributed technical studies on China's development of advanced cyberspace, aerospace, and artificial intelligence.[108] China's extraordinary military buildup and the factors driving it have been topics of great interest to American researchers, who have produced works on the Chinese approach to military strategy and the possible nature of future conflict.[109]

Does the PRC have a secret strategy to overtake America by 2049, as Michael Pillsbury famously asserted in his best-selling book *The Hundred-Year Marathon*?[110] Or is China primarily focused on sustaining development and stability at home while increasing its ability to manage events around its periphery?[111] The question of whether the Communist Party had a plan to surpass the United States was not fully detailed until 2021, when Rush Doshi published *The Long Game: China's Grand Strategy to Displace American Order*. Doshi's detailed research makes clear that China's rulers developed an explicit strategy to compete with the United States in the race for global power. Moreover, the CCP has long made policy decisions with an eye to improving China's competitive position across a broad range of domains.[112]

Going forward, questions remain regarding how Xi Jinping and his advisors think about the world and how to change it. A cloak of uncertainty surrounds what the men who walk the corridors of power in Beijing are actually thinking, saying, and doing. While few publicly available sources exist that might help us understand the CCP's internal plans, a trove of Chinese-language materials are available that can be exploited to create a mosaic of China's official mindset.

The *People's Daily*, the official newspaper of the Communist Party, has constructed a searchable database dedicated to Xi Jinping.[113] This database lists hundreds of his speeches, writings, and quotations.[114] Many of Xi Jinping's works include references to international competition.[115] While Xi's top-level statements are often vague and amorphous, they nonetheless provide important points of knowledge and highlight major policies, which are then fleshed out by the bureaucracy. The State Council, the main governing arm of the CCP, regularly releases long-term plans and strategy documents.[116] These are implemented by China's national, provincial, municipal and local-level people's governments.[117] Communist Party organizations such as the Central Organization Department and Central Propaganda Department release their own respective planning documents.[118] Once released, these documents are analyzed and explained by government officials and state-backed scholars writing in approved publications. Insights abound across all of these sources, especially once the jargon is decoded.

What really matters the most, of course, is the CCP's overarching intentions and how they impact us. But how can we possibly know what goes on in Beijing's ultra-secretive conference centers? To begin, we might listen to the CCP's narrative and take China's rulers at their word. So, what are Chinese officials writing, what are they saying, and what do they mean?

The most easily available sources we get are from China's propaganda services. Such materials are notorious for the weak illumination they provide on the overall scene. Fortunately, the CCP's many departments and agencies write a lot, and they publish numerous detailed reports online. With enough patience, these can be pieced together. Xi Jinping himself writes and talks a lot too, sometimes quite frankly. A number of his never-before-translated speeches and writings inform this book.

Even better, new source materials have become available, including internal Chinese military documents on the CCP's global strategy. These can now be unveiled for the first time – along with previously untold stories that show how Beijing is spreading its ideas and putting them into action.

Artistic Rendering of Xi Jinping Portal in
the People's Daily, *by Grace Young*

3

BAD INTENTIONS

Xi Jinping Thought must be studied and implemented.
That is the most important political mission of the
entire Party and the entire nation.[119]

—CCP Propaganda Department

THERE are watershed moments in the life of a country that say something crucial about why it exists, what it wants, and where it is going. May 4, 2018, was such a moment for China. It was a day of immense pomp and circumstance across the entire nation, and especially in Beijing. It was a turning point after which, by design, nothing would be quite the same ever again.

The Great Hall of the People had been specially decorated to mark the occasion. Red banners with gold tasseled trim hung across the paneled walls. Blocks of Chinese characters announced the theme of the event, each character occupying over a dozen square meters of banner space. Three thousand members of China's high society filled the aisles. The room rippled and hummed with anticipation.

It was an eclectic crowd. Phalanxes of military officers occupied squared-off sections of the theater, each with the sharp look of a platoon poised to stomp out onto the parade grounds. Stony-faced, they seemed practically naked without their machine guns. They waited in an impatient yet disciplined fashion, brimming with undercurrents of pent-up aggression, their guttural barks briefly muzzled, their institutional malice for soft society tamped down for the sake of ceremony.

Not far away, ancient heroes of the communist revolution slumped in padded chairs, eyes watery and tired, their wrinkled suits undoubtedly smelling of mothballs and medicinal balm. For them, this was a proud but taxing break from their fussy nurses and retirement routines of television, tea, and table games. They had seen and overcome horrible things in their earlier days, things that would make those arrogant soldier-boys sob. They knew better than anyone that all life is a struggle. Now they dug in, each man preparing to engage in a battle to protect his dignity against the approaching fog of sleep and the mounting weight of bladder pressure.

Next to the revolutionaries were representatives of a different generation: aging but still relatively young and active officials, men driven by neurotic energy. They were ministers, department chiefs, and committee chairs: the overseers of China's rank-and-file, rack-and-stack bureaucracy. As was the custom, they had red pencils laid out on polished desks in front of them, ready for a marathon of ritualistic note-taking. These were supremely busy people. The wheel of the one-party dictatorship could never stop turning, and it was up to them to do the pushing. There were budgets to sort, personnel to manage, reports to coordinate, projects to implement, phone calls to make, inboxes to clear, meetings to attend, banquet toasts to give – a river of words feeding and sustaining the system.

The system's loyal guard dogs were there too, conducting overwatch. Hard men in black ties stood in the corners of the hall, scanning the room, alertly watching all points of entry. Everyone gathered knew that just out of sight, other agents would be pouring over surveillance camera feeds inside a command center, and a heavily armed tactical team would be milling about, relaxed but ready to come out shooting if saboteurs attempted to threaten any of the leaders present.

Power pulsed through the hall. It manifested itself in the polish of the well-heeled diplomats who signed treaties that could break nations on the far corners of the map. It whispered in the eloquence of the politicos who guided the regime through factional infighting and social turmoil. It gleamed on the wrists of the billionaire tycoons who bent vast energy sectors, industrial holdings, and telecommunications networks to Beijing's will. It loomed in the stern looks of the prosecutors and judges who investigated, sentenced, and sealed forever the fates of the state's many enemies.

A special section of the room housed the state's brainpower reserve. In it were tweedy professors, airy theorists, and wizened authors. Intellectuals. They were despised by some but respected – even feared – by the leadership for their mental prowess. They alone could capture and articulate the essence of the CCP's big ideas about the future. They alone had the ability to turn Beijing's intractable ideological contradictions over in their minds and find innovative ways to explain them away. They alone could pen those glossy books in English and give those TED Talks that made the global jet set melt at the mere thought of China.

Another section was filled by youngsters, representatives of the next generation: students blinking excitedly behind thick-rimmed glasses, each looking like she had just been yanked out of a musty library alcove at Peking University – or perhaps from one of the refrigerated data farms at Tsinghua University. They were nothing today. But one day they would be everything. All the assembled leaders hoped that eventually one of those whiz kids would bury them and carry on their legacies, making their lives and their work immortal. Without them little else mattered. They were the future, a link to eternity.

Last and certainly least (although still necessary) was a small delegation of foreign dignitaries. Old white men. Sitting in the middle, they basked in the limelight, their egos visibly fortified by the Propaganda Department's lavish attention. The CCP knew exactly how to manage and seduce their type. The imperial venues, the practiced showmanship, the obsequious handlers, the sheer drama of the moment – it never failed to intoxicate. Even the most toughminded and worldly visitor was always overcome by the VIP treatment. They would go home entranced, a simpering shadow of their former selves, bursting with admiration and praise for China.[120] Some would snap out of it after a short time back in the real world. Others would never be the same again.

Finally, with every piece of the set in its place, the grand ceremony began. The orchestra began an upbeat revolutionary number. The crowd rose to its feet. All eyes and cameras panned forward, homing in on the reason they were gathered.[121]

The Dictator

Xi Jinping strode onto the stage, hot waves of applause washing over him. His plain attire – a navy-blue suit, white shirt, and checked necktie – made him blend in with all the other officials present. But a massive chasm separated him from them. He was China's paramount leader, the general secretary of the CCP, the chairman of the PRC, and the chairman of the Central Military Commission. And those titles didn't even begin to capture the mammoth totality of his power. Xi was 64, and he had already secured more official authority than any Chinese leader before him. He was like the emperors of old, only more so.

Xi was the core leader, the commander-in-chief, and the chairman of multiple new super committees he had conjured out of thin air. Those bodies now allowed him to decide China's policies on state security, the economy, the Internet, and anything else that actually mattered. Xi had become an absolute dictator, the first China had known since Mao Zedong's death four decades earlier. Like Mao, Xi knew how to be ruthless, how to purge rivals, and how to wage mass campaigns that rocketed his strength to new heights.

In recent years Xi had developed a cult of personality around himself and overseen a series of brutal crackdowns on enemies both real and imagined, campaigns that seemed likely to go on indefinitely. A political egomaniac, Xi had appointed no successor and, so far, had destroyed all those that looked capable of replacing him during his lifetime. The hallmarks of his rule had become tightening the CCP's iron grip on all aspects of Chinese society while at the same time expanding all aspects of China's global influence.

He dressed plainly to show his oneness with the Party and the people. Yet that was merely an illusion. He stood alone, towering above all the rest.

At Xi's heels marched an entourage of sycophants, courtiers, and would-be rivals: the turbo-powered members of the Politburo. The room stood at attention as the national anthem blared through the speaker system. As he often did during ceremonies like this, Xi mouthed the words, emitting no sound. A heavy smoker, he was not one to spend his voice needlessly. He saved his energy for the long and fiery speech he was about to give.[122]

For Xi, this moment was the crowning achievement of a lifetime of misery, suffering, and grinding hard work. After paying his dues and making others pay theirs (many with their lives), he had now accumulated more power than any man in Chinese history. He had been constantly humiliated – as a child, as a young man, and even as a senior official – but had never broken. His resilience and determination to win at all costs had paid off handsomely. As his eyes scanned the beaming faces of a multitude desperate to please him, he might have marveled at the twists and turns of fortune. He hadn't always been welcomed with such acclaim.

The Bitter Life

If any of his biographies are to be believed, Xi Jinping is a man who bears many deep and ugly scars. Only no one can see them, not even his spouse or his doctor. No one can see them because they are on the inside, tears across his mind and his soul. Life had not been kind to Chairman Xi. Oftentimes, it had been downright cruel and unusual.

Born on June 15, 1953, Xi was raised by his father, Xi Zhongxun. Once a war hero and senior official in the fledgling PRC, the elder Xi had been disgraced by Mao's psychotic intelligence czar, Kang Sheng, and forced to take on the role of house husband – woman's work in a man's world. Xi was still a child when his dad was cast out of high office.[123] In a way, Xi Jinping was emasculated too. Growing up, he had to wear the used clothes and shoes from two of his older sisters, Qi Qiaoqiao and Qi An'an, hand-me-downs from girls – girls who carried his mother's surname and not his own.[124]

Xi's mother, Qi Xin, was a former revolutionary and loyal CCP member with a full-time job at the Marxism-Leninism Institute. She was gone a lot during Xi's early years. Her job helped secure young Xi a life of privilege, which included a spot at the elite Beihai Kindergarten in central Beijing and then the Ba-yi (August 1) Elementary School, named after the day the People's Liberation Army was founded. His classmates were from the most powerful families in China, including that of the state chairman, Liu Shaoqi.[125]

Xi's cloistered surroundings turned out to be more curse than blessing. His politically stigmatized family made him a weak and vulnerable student, an eyesore inside an institution built to groom small boys into Communist China's future leaders. We cannot say for sure just how much abuse he suffered in school, but at least one of his gym teachers bullied him. It seems likely the other boys in class followed their sports instructor's lead.[126]

When Xi was twelve, another round of political purges came, and trumped-up charges were brought against his father. The elder Xi was expelled from Beijing in the dead of winter, disappearing out of his son's life and into a labor camp in rural China, where he would undertake "thought reform" the hard way.[127] A shadow was cast over Xi's family. Along with his mother, sisters, and little brother, Xi Jinping was unceremoniously tossed out of the leadership compound where he had grown up. Rootless, his mother moved him and his siblings from place to place around Beijing.[128]

Xi had lost his primary caregiver and role model. He also lost all vestiges of the pampered life his parents' special status had once provided: the nannies, the Soviet-made car with driver, the cook, and, most important of all, an earmarked supply of foodstuffs – something that had been an immense luxury during his childhood when tens of millions were starving to death across China.[129] What happened next, however, would wrench apart young Xi's life completely.

During the chaos and terror of Mao's "Cultural Revolution," radical militants broke into the house Xi was living in and violently ransacked it. In the process, his elder half sister Xi Heping (born though his father's first marriage) was "persecuted to death" – Party jargon that might mean she was raped and murdered by thugs, or that she committed suicide to escape such a cruel fate.[130] It is unclear where Xi Jinping was when this all happened, and whether he tried to save his sister and failed.

Xi's mother reportedly took him and his surviving siblings to her institute at the Central Party School, the high church of New China, and they found shelter on campus. Soon, however, Qi Xin would turn her back on her firstborn son to save her own skin. Family ties were one of the cardinal sins of humanity according to Mao's communist ideology, and they had to be expunged. At a rally, Xi Jinping was rounded up and paraded across a stage so that a rabid crowd – which included his mother – could excoriate him. He watched from the stage as his mom publicly disowned him, her fist raised as she chanted along with his persecutors, "Down with Xi Jinping!"[131] He was fifteen.

Not long after, Xi Jinping was forcibly removed from the capital and sent to a live a life of abject poverty and brutal labor in the arid hills of rural Yan'an, outside the town where the CCP had built its revolutionary base in the 1930s and 1940s. Made to shovel and carry feces, coal, and other filth in the blistering sun, Xi slept in fetid "yellow earth" caves. A bucket served as his toilet.[132] At night he would toss and turn violently in the dirt, his skin crawling with fleas and other biting insects[133] He decided to escape, and he made it all the way back to Beijing before he was rounded up and sent to a work camp. For a time, he was forced to dig ditches, backbreaking punishment even for a stout teenager.[134] Then he was sent back to Yan'an, forced to continue his life as a manual laborer and a sleepless cave-dweller.

Xi's official biography sums up the long nightmare of his formative years in the following words: "During the Cultural Revolution he suffered public humiliation and hunger, experienced homelessness and was even held in custody on one occasion."[135] As the years dragged by, Xi had something of a political-religious transformation. He read and re-read the writings of Mao Zedong and doggedly sought Communist Party membership. His application was rejected by the authorities multiple times. Xi reportedly suffered more than ten rejections.[136] Finally, Xi plied the local Party boss with a fried egg and steamed bun, rare delicacies at a time when meals typically consisted of millet porridge and raw grain.[137] His food bribe worked. In spite of Xi's bad family name, the official allowed him to join the CCP, something that subsequently put Xi on the fast track for a reprieve from exile. After seven years, he could return to Beijing and attend Tsinghua University.[138] Yet his suffering was far from over.

After graduating with a degree in chemical engineering, a field chosen for him by the Communist Party, Xi joined the army as an officer. Things began looking up. Mao was dead, and Xi's dad had been fully pardoned by the new supreme leader, Deng Xiaoping. Xi Zhongxun was back in the upper reaches of power. Soon, Xi Jinping's family connections helped secure him a well-to-do wife, a spacious apartment, and a plum position in the PLA headquarters.[139] His first boss was a big name: General Geng Biao, then minister of defense. But after serving as Geng's personal secretary for three years, disaster struck. Xi was told to quit the uniform and get out of Beijing. The old general had evidently gotten on the wrong side of Deng Xiaoping, and further association with him could be dangerous.[140] Exile awaited Xi, again.

Making matters worse, Xi's marriage fell apart. In 1982, his elegant bride, Ke Lingling, abandoned him, a massive ego-punch in any country, but especially in hyper-conservative China.[141] Ms Ke was on her way to the glamor of London, where her dad was ambassador at the PRC embassy. Awaiting her was an ambitious and coveted life in the developed world. If she loved Xi, it wasn't that all-consuming kind of emotion that steered many young women off the pragmatic path. Xi was just a lowly official from a turbulent family. It seemed inevitable that he would toil his career away collecting unpopular taxes and enforcing the "One-Child Policy" (the largest campaign of forced abortion, sterilization, and infanticide in human history). The unseemly divorce piled more shame on his already heavy load.[142]

Xi's second boss, Gao Yang, then the Communist Party boss of Hebei Province, disliked him and roadblocked his every move.[143] Xi ended up working in harsh conditions in a cold, penniless village hundreds of miles south of Beijing, sleeping in his office and eating at a communal kitchen.[144] From there his career wound its way into China's deep south, to the backwater of Fujian Province, with its super typhoons, corruptions scandals, and gangsters. It was undoubtedly another wrenching culture shock for a sophisticated northerner like Xi.[145]

Five years after his first marriage ended in disaster, his luck with romance took a remarkable turn. Xi tied the knot again, this time to Peng Liyuan, a modelesque PLA soldier turned singer, a bright star with an amazing voice. Yet even this lucky break had its downsides. For the next two decades, Xi would live in the shadow cast by his second wife's immense fame. She was a national sensation, a television superstar whose songs were on everyone's lips. He was an unknown bureaucrat with uncertain prospects. Compared to her, Xi looked downright pitiful.[146]

Xi was left alone in the backward south for long stretches of time while his wife was on tour. His official biography says he would make long-distance phone calls to her, checking up on her at bedtime, "no matter how late it was."[147] Night after night he would call: after she had performed shows in Beijing aired on China Central Television, after she had sung for troops fresh from the Tiananmen Square massacre, after she appeared at glittering art festivals abroad as a cultural ambassador for China.[148] For twenty years they lived apart, separated at times by forty-eight-hour-long train rides between his posts in the south and her apartment in Beijing.[149] We can only guess how he felt and whether he worried about their future together. His biography refrains from any details that personal. It does, however, mention that he likes to stay up late watching sports and sometimes enjoys drinking.[150] Perhaps that's how he coped.

In 1997, Xi stood for CCP Central Committee membership, but failed to get the needed votes.[151] He had to work grueling hours and wait patiently for luck to manifest itself. It was years before he got another shot at the big time. In 2009, he was expected to be appointed Vice Chairman of the Central Military Commission. But then, mysteriously, he wasn't.[152] It was yet another rejection in a long series of rejections.

Finally, in 2012, after being painstakingly groomed as Hu Jintao's successor, an eleventh-hour power struggle before the eighteenth National CCP Congress nearly cost him the mantle of national leadership. A vicious inner-Party battle ensued. Prominent Chinese politicians, top-ranking PLA generals, and even China's intelligence czar opposed Xi, seeking to install one of their own in his place. Months of intrigue followed, which ended only after Xi asserted himself in a ruthless fashion. A tidal wave of arrests washed across the country.[153]

Xi had finally come out on top, but he still didn't feel safe. One of those he imprisoned was an official in charge of the Central Security Bureau, the shadowy bodyguard unit responsible for the security of the CCP's top leadership, including Xi and his family. Xi replaced the suspected traitor and all those linked to him, sparking rumors that Xi feared one of his rivals would put poison in his tea.[154] If Xi was paranoid, he had every right to be.

Xi's long years had given him a harsh schooling in what it meant to be powerless, what it meant to be under another man's jackboot, how it felt to have his face stomped on. He had learned better than anyone why obtaining power mattered. He had hardened, the innocence and idealism in his outlook turning to cold rage. Having clawed his way to the zenith of power, it seemed only natural he would fight to stay there.

The Communist Party was the source of his strength, the wellspring that fed and sustained him. The Party's power now flowed to him and through him like electricity bursting through a rail. He was inextricably tied to it. Knowing full well that it owned him and could kill him, he squeezed all the harder. Power was everything. He would never relinquish a single ounce. Never.

Artistic Rendering of Xi's Wife in
Tiananmen Square, by Grace Young

At Fever Pitch

The day's ceremony at the Great Hall of the People was not about Xi himself. It was about another man, a man he respected and revered above all others, a man he worshipped. Xi had gotten his doctorate degree studying this man's ideas and had dedicated his entire professional life to writing about, practicing, and spreading those ideas. This man was the reason Xi was now the most powerful leader in all of Chinese history. Xi believed that he owed this man everything and so did everyone else.

According to Xi, this man was the light and hope of the entire world. The grand event was the capstone of an all-out national education campaign to celebrate his legacy. And while the man's ideas were already widespread in China, Xi felt they needed far more hammering in. To this end, he had ordered the entire country, and especially the members of the Communist Party ruling class, to pour over the man's writings, gushing that the man was "the greatest thinker in human history."[155]

In a not-so-subtle reminder of what was considered politically correct, Xi's much feared loyalty enforcement unit, the Central Discipline Inspection Committee, circulated an article that opined, "In the entire history of human society and human thought, no one has contributed more." The article went on to order all Communist Party members and government officials to "deeply grasp the far-reaching influence" of the man's teachings, and "more correctly grasp" how important his ideas were for guiding the future of human society.[156]

Xi put China's vast resources behind the campaign. His largesse ensured that a historic series of commemorative events were organized across the nation and by Chinese embassies around the world. The week before, state media had begun airing a five-part prime time documentary, simply titled *He is Right.*"[157] This was followed by a two-part documentary about the great man's writings. Part one of the documentary had been shown on China Central Television the night before. Part two would be shown that evening after Xi's speech in the Great Hall of the People.[158]

The next day was a Saturday, the great man's birthday, and the weekend crowd was expected to pack into a museum event planned in Shanghai's affluent Xintiandi district, where the government would be unveiling a rare copy of the man's most famous book.[159] Dozens of similar museum exhibitions and commemorative events had been set up around China to mark the occasion.[160]

Propaganda outlets in Guangdong, one of China's most influential provinces, had gone so far as to produce audio programs in which government officials could be heard reading the man's works out loud in endless recording sessions. This and other related audio content were made available on mobile apps, so that anyone with a cheap smartphone could listen and learn.[161]

Xi had recently visited Peking University, the "Harvard of China," and given a speech in which he ordered China's educators to further promote the man's ideas "in campuses, classrooms, and among students."[162] In honor of China's paramount leader, Peking University had just opened a new research institute on Xi Jinping Thought. But, when he visited, Xi himself seemed far more interested in their programs on the thinking of his intellectual hero.[163] "Inspired" by his passion for the great man's ideas, the university was now hosting a world forum for international researchers from thirty countries who, like Xi, had decided to dedicate their graduate studies to him.[164]

In 2015, Peking University had hosted a world forum on the same theme, which had reportedly drawn more than five hundred participants.[165] But this time around the event would have an even greater reach and connect to a broader global audience. The Propaganda Department had been brought in to give the world forum muscle mass. The university would now be launching a dedicated website for the event in Chinese, English, German, and Russian.[166]

Meanwhile, a towering statue of Xi's savior had been commissioned and erected in the man's hometown, with hundreds of flag-waving fans cheering as the two-ton bronze monolith was officially unveiled.[167] Printing presses manufactured stacks of the man's books. Factories churned out a mountain of plastic memorabilia, including gnome-like renditions of the man's bust and baby bath toys made of rubber.[168] A special wine label was released in his honor.[169] Digital stoplights were programmed to show him directing traffic. Commemorative cash was even printed with his portrait.[170]

Hundreds of academic papers were published. An avalanche of editorials in the *People's Daily*, Xinhua, and other CCP mouthpieces lauded his ideas as the everlasting key to China's stability and development.[171] The man's hand-written notes had been obtained from a foreign institution and were now being displayed at the PRC National Museum in the way in which the Vatican might be expected to display the fabled Holy Grail should it ever turn up.[172] All of China was at a fever pitch.

China's Godhead

The moment had finally come. Xi Jinping strode up to the podium, bowed to the audience, and began to deliver his address. Directly behind him, a colossal portrait of the godlike figure dominated the wall. The painting was so large that anyone standing next to it would have appeared smaller than the man's billowing white beard, which flowed down over his chest. The man was depicted in a black bowtie, with his head turned all the way left, his fierce gaze piercing into the distance. Under the portrait were the numbers 1818–2018.

Xi began his sermon in signature fashion, his smoker's voice deep, flecked with grit and tar. He spoke methodically, weaving together the man's life story and the story of modern China, peppering the narrative with worshipful quotes from the man's friends and disciples. After a protracted warm-up, Xi finally came to the point, exclaiming:

> Comrades! Today, we are here to remember and celebrate Karl Marx. We are here to show our respects to the greatest thinker in human history. And we are also here to demonstrate our unshakable belief in the scientific truth of Marxism.[173]

Karl Marx was the father of *The Communist Manifesto*, a document that opposed the institutions of family, religion, democracy, free markets, and even countries – a document that urged followers to violently overturn their governments and establish a new system where all money, property, armaments, and political power were centralized in the hands of the despotic state.[174] Marx's manifesto was published in 1848 as the platform for a secret society in England, the Communist League. It was translated and disseminated, ultimately catalyzing radical movements that established communist governments around the world.

In his speech, Xi made clear that when he talked about socialism, he was not talking about the liberal democratic socialism practiced in northern Europe. He was talking about the communist type, the ideology practiced by regimes in North Korea, Cuba, and the former Soviet Union. He was talking about a form of government that had killed staggering numbers of its own people. In 1999, it was conservatively estimated that Marx-inspired communist regimes caused one hundred million deaths in the twentieth century, more than half of them in China itself.[175] One communist revolutionary in Cambodia, Pol Pot, is believed to have killed off at least 20 percent of the country's population, with many of his victims suffering fiendish tortures before death. And today, without a hint of irony, Xi was leading all of China in a celebration of the two hundredth anniversary of Marx's birth.[176] Yet, while that was the stated theme of the day's event, the actual purpose Xi had in mind was far bolder. It was downright revolutionary.

Xi proclaimed, "Karl Marx dedicated his entire life to overthrowing the old world and establishing a new world. He fought for that relentlessly his whole life." He went on: "Marxism is a practical theory, which guides the people in their actions to change the world.... Marxism is not to be kept hidden in books. It was created in order to change the destiny of human history."[177]

Xi told the audience that Marx's lifework had not been in vain. His long-term dream of creating a stateless collective, a global communist civilization and utopia, was still on track and would one day be realized. World socialism was coming. Thanks to China, the international communist movement was still alive, and, in fact, had never been stronger.

> Even though world socialism has had twists and turns
> in its path as its developed, the overall trend of human
> social development has not changed. And it will not
> change.... Today, Marxism is massively improving the
> progress of human civilization.... Comrades! Marxism
> has not only profoundly changed the world; it has pro-
> foundly changed China.[178]

Xi described the teachings of Marx as foundational, saying: "Marxism
is the ultimate guiding thought of our Party and our state. It is a powerful
thought weapon for understanding how the world works, for grasping
fundamental laws, for seeking truth, and for changing the world."[179]

He again emphasized that China would change the world. China would
use its power and influence to lead the global community toward the
long-term goal of international communism. The following words filled
the Great Hall of the People:

> We must deeply understand that realizing communism
> is an objective that happens in a historical process. It
> occurs in stages, one step at a time. It happens by us
> unifying the far-reaching ideals of communism together
> with socialism with Chinese characteristics, and then
> unifying them with everything we are doing right now.
> It happens by us confidently believing in our path of
> socialism with Chinese characteristics, with confidence
> in our theories, confidence in our system, confidence in
> our culture. We must firmly believe in the ideals of the
> communist man. Just like Marx, we must struggle for
> communism our entire lives.[180]

Then, in a thinly veiled threat to anyone in the audience who might
harbor other sympathies, Xi declared that the man who rejected Marxism
would make himself an enemy of the increasingly assimilated world. It

would be far better, he said, for everyone to help "Construct a Community of Common Destiny for All Mankind" (also commonly translated as Creating a Community of Shared Future for Mankind) – a slogan he equated to a beautiful collectivized world, something he promised was not far off.

> A collectivized world is just there, over [the horizon]. Whoever rejects that world will be rejected by the world.... Together with all the world's people on one path, we must work hard to construct the Community of Common Destiny for All Mankind. We must build a more beautiful world.[181]

And, with quasi-religious zeal, Xi reminded all the gathered CCP members that their souls belonged to Marxism. "Comrades! The Chinese Communist Party is a political party that has armed itself with Marxism. For the Chinese Communist Party member, Marxism is the soul of our ideals and our beliefs."[182] Xi Jinping's speech culminated in the following lines:

> It is the sacred responsibility of the Chinese Communist Party member to continually push forward the development of Marxism. We will resolutely use Marxism to observe this age, understand this age, and lead this age. We will use modern China's vitality and rich experience to push forward the progress of Marxism.... We will unceasingly spread modern Chinese Marxism and Marxism in the twenty-first century![183]

He capped the speech off with a quote from Marx's best friend and coauthor, Friedrich Engels. The ceremony ended with a rendition of "The Internationale" – a song inspired by *The Communist Manifesto*, which had served as the anthem of the Bolsheviks and early Soviet Union. This song had once been the national anthem of the Chinese Soviet Republic, the CCP's base in the early years of the Chinese Civil War. It was now the closing number for all major Chinese political events.[184]

As the curtains fell on Xi's grand ceremony, the following words of the Chinese version of the anthem rang out: "We will be masters of the world! This is the final struggle. Unite together. Soon international communism must be realized."[185]

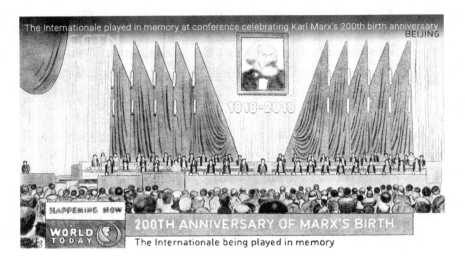

The Internationale played in memory at conference celebrating Karl Marx's 200th birth anniversary
BEIJING

HAPPENING NOW
WORLD TODAY
200TH ANNIVERSARY OF MARX'S BIRTH
The Internationale being played in memory

Artistic Rendering of CGTN Broadcast, by Grace Young

4

THE HALLOWEEN DOCUMENT

The Communists disdain to conceal their views and
aims. They openly declare that their ends can be
attained only by the forcible overthrow of all existing
social conditions.[186]

—*The Communist Manifesto*

O N October 31, 2019, in a scene remarkable for its timing, China's
dictator and his top lieutenants gathered again, as they regularly did,
in the Great Hall of the People, this time on Halloween to officially seal
a document with dark portents. Hours later, with the evening twilight
spreading over Beijing, the propaganda services issued a bland missive
reporting that the annual conference of the Chinese Communist Party's
Central Committee had concluded, and a new policy on governance had
been authorized. Glowing on digital screens across China, newscasters
were seen reading ponderous sections of the twenty-page document,
visibly trying to make their delivery buoyant, or at least less than robotic, but failing. The policy seemed exactly like so many others before
it: perfunctory, dreary, unimportant.

Foreign diplomats listening to the news in Beijing that evening would
have noted that buried in the document's strange prose about the superiority of the CCP's collective leadership path, and its control over

all aspects of life in China, was a peculiar paragraph on foreign affairs addressed to Chinese officials and Party members. "Actively participate in reforming and constructing the global governance system." Another line followed, exhorting them to "Raise the flag of our construction of a Community of Common Destiny for All Mankind." And finally, "Push forward the construction of a more just and rational international governance system."[187]

What did these puzzling formulations mean? What was the CCP Central Committee talking about? Did these lines of text actually signal anything substantive, or were they simply filler material used by faceless bureaucrats in the bowels of Zhongnanhai central leadership complex or the foreign ministry? Were these words being employed to prop up and give shape to a report that, in reality, was yet another chain of empty slogans? Or was there more to the story?

In fact, internal training manuals on CCP doctrine had been manufactured and distributed to explain what these and other strange-sounding concepts meant. The intended audience knew what the document was telling them even if no one else did. Perhaps that was Central Committee's aim: to covertly communicate with millions of undercover officers and agents around the world by hiding explosive messages in plain sight under the camouflage of dull prose. Any foreign diplomat paying attention had actually heard these same terms many times before. Had any broken the code?

The mind-numbing title assigned to the document offered the first clue: "The Decision of the Chinese Communist Party Central Committee on Several Major Issues Regarding Insisting on and Improving the System of Socialism with Chinese Characteristics and Advancing the Modernization of the State Governance System and Its Governance Capabilities." This was the kind of Orwellian title only a totalitarian regime built on a foundation of secrecy could appreciate. It was the kind of title used in China to convey officiality and power to insiders, while at the same time boring outsiders to death. It indicated that some important debate had been settled, but no one on the inside wanted anyone outside to know the details.

Another clue turned up two months later, this one making it clear beyond any doubt that the regime viewed the document as truly important. On January 1, 2020, Xi Jinping dedicated his entire ten-page new year's message to extolling and explaining the decisions laid out in the policy. His message was published in China's top political journal, *Qiushi* (*Seeking Truth*). In it, he framed the issues elaborated in the document in terms of a battle between China and the West, using language that made it almost seem as if Beijing had finally unlocked the mystery of some new knock-out weapon that would give the PRC lasting strategic superiority.

He wrote, "A superior [governance] system is the biggest advantage the state can have. The competition in systems is the most fundamental competition that exists between countries."[188] Rather than bury the document, Xi was shining a proud spotlight on it, albeit while still employing jargon that could be easily overlooked outside the small circle of *Qiushi* readers.

In his message, Xi suggested something that, properly understood, could have been expected to ignite a media firestorm in capital cities the world over: China was going to export its unique communist system around the world in direct confrontation with the liberal, American-led order. As part of this effort, Xi called on the Propaganda Department to ensure they embellished the advantages of Chinese Communism and promoted Beijing's superior Marxist path. With almost evangelical overtones, he directed them as follows: "Tell the good story about China's system at home and overseas. Constantly strengthen the persuasiveness and appeal of China's state system and state governance system."[189]

No longer content to hide behind the fiction that Marxism and Communism were dead and China had embraced its own version of free market capitalism, Xi stated that China's government was "fundamentally based on Marxist principles." To underscore his point, Xi described China's government as Marxist a total of ten times, for an average of once per page. He talked about the CCP's omnipresence in every domain of life in China and referenced the Communist Party an average of six times per page. According to him, it was imperative that all Chinese society boldly advanced the ideas he elucidated. Indeed, this was a "long-term strategic mission" and one that would be a powerful help to "the China Dream of realizing the great Chinese resurgence [also translated as the great rejuvenation of the Chinese nation]."[190]

After Xi's message came out, a tsunami of propaganda speeches and commentaries spilled across China's airwaves and digital networks. The supreme leader had spoken. Xi Jinping's ideas, his grand vision for the planet and all who lived under its skies, were repeated again and again like a broken record that wouldn't stop skipping. At that moment, a mysterious new virus was moving from host to host in Wuhan and preparing to escape into the international community. So too was a remarkable set of ideas, which everyone in the service of the one-party dictatorship was told to spread. The time had come for China to make the world anew.

Going Viral

It was April 15, tax day in the United States, the most dreaded day on the federal calendar. But this year, things had been wrenched 180 degrees away from normal. In a *Twilight Zone*-like scene that would have made Alfred Hitchcock smile, offices all over America sat eerily quiet. No frantic phone calls came into cubicle farms. No panicked emails lit up lines of computer terminals. There had been no all-nighters, or eleventh-hour scrambles to tabulate and report earnings and losses, what was owed to Uncle Sam and what he would surrender back. All the nation's commercial districts were deserted.

Post offices across the country found themselves in a state of vacancy. This year hardly a solitary soul could be seen anywhere. This year there was, in fact, not even going to be a tax day. For all intents and purposes, the Internal Revenue Service was closed for business and would not be opening its doors again until further notice. The entire nation was going to receive a penalty-free extension.

This was an extraordinary year. This was 2020. And, in view of the mounting toll of human misery and economic devastation exacted by the COVID-19 pandemic, taxes could wait. Like the rest of the nation, the U.S. government was hunkered down in emergency survival mode. A mass killer was at large, and the only thing that anyone could do was to hole up and wait it out.

On the opposite side of the globe, China was anything but paralyzed. To the contrary, the machinery of the Communist Party was running full out, the dials of command turned all the way up. That same day, April 15, Xi Jinping and his foreign minister, Wang Yi, each published major policy statements declaring that rather than bunker down, China's government would exploit the pandemic as an opportunity to play the key leadership role on the world stage.[191]

Having weathered the opening blows of the disaster in Wuhan, the men who walked the corridors of power in Beijing were determined to pull a propaganda victory out of the jaws of the public relations disaster. More than that, they intended to use the world crisis to advance the long march of Chinese power and prestige. Chairman Xi, sealed safely in the isolation of an antiseptic, if ornately appointed, leadership compound, monitored and participated in all the action. His daily schedule was reportedly filled to the brim with high-stakes meetings and phone calls aimed at asserting Chinese greatness.[192]

In March, during the peak of the emergency, he had donned his signature black nylon Mao-jacket to visit an undisclosed military base in Hebei Province, somewhere outside the capital. Army officers wearing soft-blue surgical masks, caramel-and-sand-colored fatigues, and polished black boots had stood at attention, flanking him as he monitored close-circuit camera feeds coming from Huoshenshan Hospital, ground zero of the pandemic.

State-run media showed Xi and his small entourage of military brass and Communist Party stalwarts standing in front of a giant screen in a seemingly vast and otherwise empty room. On the other side of the video call, harried hospital officials and afflicted patients some six hundred miles away in Wuhan could be seen crammed together and struggling to put on brave smiles. Undoubtedly many of them at that moment wondered if their breaths were numbered. The propaganda services, as ever, trumpeted Xi's wise and benevolent leadership. He was a man of the people. He was also a man of science. The same report showed images of him as he toured medical labs at his alma mater, Tsinghua University, and an unnamed PLA biodefense base involved in vaccine research. The report stressed Xi's leadership, emphasizing all the senior committee meetings he had chaired and all the phone calls he had made to other world leaders.[193]

There had indeed been many phone calls. Xi called Donald Trump at the White House. He called the German chancellor Angela Merkel, the French president Emmanuel Macron, the British prime minister Boris Johnson, and dozens of others. He used jargon-rich phrases that seemed to have no real meaning even in his native Chinese, and less so after being translated into German, French, and English. While we cannot be certain, his counterparts probably left their conversations feeling vaguely disappointed and very confused about what the Chinese were up to. We can only imagine the head scratching at 10 Downing Street in London. *What in the bloody hell is he doing going on about a "Community of Common Destiny for All Mankind"? What on earth does that have to do with stopping a killer virus outbreak?*

Had they compared notes, each of the leaders would have discovered Xi read some variation of the same script to all of them, repeating the following line in every communication he had: "We are promoting the concept of a Community of Common Destiny for All Mankind."[194] Xi gave the same pitch to the dignitaries assembled at an emergency session of the G20 summit in late March.[195] Then, on May 17, 2020, he gave it again, this time at a place few expected him to appear: the head table of the seventy-third World Health Assembly of the World Health Organization (WHO), an event held online due to the catastrophe which the organization had failed to prevent.

In his opening address to the WHO's annual assembly, Xi appeared relaxed and completely unfazed by the angry discourse surrounding China's heavy-handed cover-up and mismanagement of the initial outbreak, which had cost the international community months of precious time to prepare and resulted in the deaths of several heroic doctors. Ignoring the topic of his regime's perceived culpability for the disaster, Xi instead used his time on camera to encourage nations around the world to "construct a Community of Common Destiny for All Mankind (构建人类命运共同体)."[196] There was that strange term again.

By June 7, 2020, Xi had called or met in person with almost fifty world leaders, the men and women in charge of the governments and international organizations shouldering the burden of responding to the global pandemic that was by now killing hundreds of thousands of people with a frightening efficiency. According to the official PRC government report on China's response to the COVID-19 pandemic, Xi had a message of supreme importance that he shared with everyone during this time of peril. "He urged each of them to establish a belief in the Community of Common Destiny for All Mankind."[197] Again and again, he spoke of this idea with zeal.

Beijing's white paper on China's response to the COVID-19 pandemic underscored the extreme seriousness with which the CCP regarded the term by stating: "China maintains that all countries should make the correct choice for the future destiny of all mankind and the well-being of future generations of children and grandchildren by embracing the Community of Common Destiny for All Mankind."[198]

In the considered opinion of the Communist Party and the Chinese government, then, there was only one correct path into the future, and everyone on Earth was going to have to take it. To do otherwise would be to seal the doom of their progeny. This was a matter of life and death, and so it was imperative that all the world's people join together and support China's plan, not just during the current moment of crisis but for decades to come. Nothing less than the future of humanity was at stake.

The COVID-19 pandemic was hardly the first time Xi Jinping had attempted to persuade others to join his grandiose vision for mankind's future. In fact, he had been talking about it unceasingly since 2012, the year he rose to paramount power.[199] By 2020, the phrase had proliferated across Chinese officialdom to the point that it was omnipresent and firmly affixed to everything the PRC said and did in the world. It had become the cornerstone of every major foreign policy speech, international program, and strategic-planning document. Xi talked about it during U.N. speeches, business summits, and state visits overseas.[200] And so did all of his top lieutenants in the ruling elite. His foreign minister talked about what it meant for Chinese diplomacy.[201] His health minister talked about what it meant for global health.[202] His information technology administrator talked about what it meant for the future of the Internet.[203] The entire brain trust of the Chinese government seemed captivated by this concept and obsessed with promulgating it.

While many foreign observers had come to believe that the "One Belt, One Road" mega-project (OBOR, also translated as the Belt and Road Initiative) was Xi Jinping's signature foreign policy strategy, Xi wanted to make it clear that OBOR was merely a means to a much greater end he had in mind. Notwithstanding OBOR's vast scope and seemingly impressive funding levels, it was just one of many distinct lines of effort intended to support the CCP's long-term strategic objective.

In January 2020, just days after Xi's new year's message, the PRC foreign ministry emphasized this point. In a choreographed interview with state media, the deputy foreign minister said that, "One Belt, One Road is a way we put into practice our policy of advancing the Community of Common Destiny for All Mankind."[204] In other words, OBOR was not China's grand strategy. It was one of the supporting pillars.

Documents on Xi Jinping Thought are even more direct. "The answer to the question of what China advocates for, what kind of international relations it wants to construct, is a new type of international relations. For its part, a Community of Common Destiny for All Mankind helps answer the question of what kind of world China seeks to make."[205]

The same source describes the concept as a strategy aimed at making China a world superpower that is so large and influential that Beijing can define what the future of human progress looks like and enforce its will globally.

> Constructing a Community of Common Destiny for All Mankind ... is a macro-level plan for mankind's social development based on a deep investigation of major world trends.... It is an important part of Xi Jinping Thought and fulsome manifestation of the role played by the Chinese Communist Party, as a Marxist Party concerned with humanity's progress and destiny. It's a manifestation of our leader's wise and compassionate focus on protecting mankind's long-term interests. It is a manifestation of China, as a world power, playing its role as protector of all humankind's shared values.[206]

The Collective

If the CCP's strategic intention is to create something Xi refers to as a Community of Common Destiny for All Mankind, what do these peculiar words really mean?[207] According to authoritative sources, the CCP's anodyne-sounding goal is a modern-day version of Karl Marx's concept of a unified international proletariat, also known as international communism.[208]

Great Power Diplomacy with Chinese Characteristics is part of a series of internal documents produced to explain Xi Jinping Thought to Chinese military officers. It describes the CCP's objective as building a singular human collective. The book explains that the term "constructing a Community of Common Destiny for All Mankind" is jargon used to describe this quest.[209]

The idea of a Community of Common Destiny for All
Mankind inherits the Marxist idea of a "unified community of freely associated individuals." It is also based on
"collective" ideas found in many civilizations.... Marx's
community of free association saw communism as the
true collective.... He believed that the true collective was
the highest level of humankind's social development and
communism. The idea of a Community of Common Destiny for All Mankind examines the relationship between
nation-states and the Community of Common Destiny
from the point of view of all humanity.[210]

According to this official interpretation of Xi Jinping Thought, the
aim of the Communist Party is to create and dominate an integrated
and homogenized world order, in which all nations and individuals are
assimilated into the collective and unable to escape and survive outside
it.[211] The text goes on.

Xi Jinping points out the reality that nations are individual parts of a greater whole, which already cannot
escape from the Community of Common Destiny that
human society is currently forming. They cannot exist
alone.... A Community of Common Destiny for All
Mankind is going in the same direction as the unified community of freely associated individuals that
Marx emphasized.... Xi Jinping states that the idea of
a Community of Common Destiny for All Mankind
is a reflection of Marxist theory of the collective with
a modern spirit. Although Marx said that a communist society is a beautiful long distant vista, today the
world is already realizing mutual interdependence and
heading toward the objective of that "unified collective
of freely associated individuals."[212]

Since the late 1970s, China's government has gone to great lengths to encourage a foreign perception that China's rulers would gradually assimilate their nation into the post–World War II international order, and China would become a "responsible stakeholder." According to this narrative, the story of post-Mao China was one of economic and social reforms, an opening process whose endpoint would inevitably involve political reforms that, one day, might make China a free market capitalist democracy and a "normal" country.

Yet, internally, Xi Jinping was saying something very different. He was saying what many Communist Party faithful had known all along: China was not going to be absorbed. It was going to do the absorbing. The CCP's true mission was to gain access to the international system without being changed by it, to gain enough leverage to subvert it, and then to remake that system in the model of its own form of government. To this end, Chinese rulers since Deng Xiaoping had been conducting a campaign of global infiltration, betting everything on not a single Trojan horse, but rather a vast horde of them.

This was the final struggle. The CCP was executing a strategy to replicate on a global level what it saw as its own superior system. The textbook on Xi Jinping Thought says this clearly. "The Community of Common Destiny for All Mankind will mold the interests of the Chinese people and those of the world's people together so they are one and the same."[213] Readers of this and other official works were assured that their efforts were all for the greater good. The fruits of their labor would be world peace and equality. They were helping all mankind by being part of the long-term project to increase China's global power and influence. By doing their part to erode American leadership in the international community, they were part of something far greater than themselves. They were playing a role in the most epic story of all time: the battle against all odds to create a perfect society and paradise on earth.

In the words of *Great Power Diplomacy with Chinese Characteristics*, China's aims are wholly altruistic in nature. And if they seem nationalistic and self-reverential, that is only because the West is inferior and has so much to learn from China. The key challenge would be getting America and other democracies to understand how wrong they were, and help them change how they thought about themselves and their place in the world.

> The Community of Common Destiny for All Mankind aims to contribute Chinese wisdom and the China Model for the cause of international peace.... It acknowledges the world has differences and variety, but seeks a world unified.... Xi Jinping points out that transforming the global governance system is impossible without guiding the way people think. The Community of Common Destiny for All Mankind is an innovative way forward for global governance, which surpasses the West's thinking and international organizations.[214]

China's foreign policy and all its strategic actions abroad – everything the CCP seeks to do and have in the world – is guided by this vision. The ultimate objective of China's strategy is to use its influence to spread communism globally under the moniker of a Community of Common Destiny for all Mankind.[215] And the clock is reportedly ticking. The CCP aims to have accomplished its seemingly impossible mission by the hundred-year anniversary of the founding of the People's Republic of China.

Emphasizing the importance of this objective, the internal text goes on to claim: "To achieve the China Dream, we must also establish the Community of Common Destiny for all Mankind at the same time."[216] According to this source, the CCP's goals are interlocking, and it intends to achieve both by the year 2049. This is an aim with monumental implications for the United States and other democracies. If the CCP were to succeed, America would no longer exist as free and sovereign nation by the midpoint of the twenty-first century, and the world would be run by an integrated network of one-party dictatorships. China would rule the world.

In his 2020 new year's message, Xi Jinping said that it was China's task to ensure justice and equality for the world. What this actually meant was that he intended to overthrow the current free and open order, replacing it with its antithesis. Of course, similar documents had been saying the same thing for years. Xi Jinping and every other Chinese official had publicly used these same terms over and over again in countless settings. This time the message was perhaps a shade or two darker, and the lines slightly bolder, but it wasn't new. It was just more confident.[217]

Marx Is in the Warehouse

A notable manifestation of the CCP's global ambitions can be seen in its promotion of Xi Jinping's writings in bookstores around the world and, most notably, on Amazon, the planet's largest digital bookselling platform. The campaign began with one innocuous title, Xi Jinping's *The Governance of China*, a collection of his blandest public speeches, peppered with high-resolution pictures and wholesome anecdotes of his life and family.[218]

A second and third volume followed, capturing his more recent speeches and political achievements. Inside the books are glossy pictures of him leading China on the world stage. When pictured alongside other international leaders, he is in the center, smiling, pointing, teaching, benevolently dominating the group. All others are shown to be listening to him, or briefing him obsequiously. His close friend Vladimir Putin, the KGB spymaster turned authoritarian leader of the Russian Federation, features prominently in Xi's books, their bromance on proud display. The president of the United States is often absent, always silent. When they are included, President Obama and President Trump are each pictured listening respectfully as Xi talks.[219]

Other books on Xi Jinping Thought have come out more recently, their message closer to what had previously been seen only within internal CCP publications. In 2020, the Central Party School published a new text, which was not translated into English but was particularly candid in the original Chinese. After ordering on Amazon, customers in America received regular updates from the seller on the book's journey as it made its way from its point of origin (the CCP Central Committee Central Party School Press) to their homes.

Arriving in layer upon layer of protective bubble wrap, the book is remarkably heavy. Under the white dustjacket the hardcover is velvet with gold lettering. The interior is lovingly crafted with tight binding, thick pages, and a golden streamer for the reader to mark their progress without dogearing pages. It has the look and feel of a sacred document, the kind of book that is produced with an expectation that the reader will treat it like a devout preacher in Texas treats the Holy Bible.

In many ways, the Central Party School is the high church of Communist China. The CCP oversees a vast network of nearly three thousand training centers spread across China, schools where students are indoctrinated and prepared for leadership positions in local government, society, and business.[220] The Central Party School is the most exclusive. It is a finishing school where the superelite are groomed for the most important powerplays. Located near the Summer Palace in Beijing, the Central Party School campus is where the CCP molds the minds of future national leaders.

As an indication of the institution's importance, both Mao Zedong and Hu Jintao served as the school's president before ascending to their positions as paramount leader.[221] Xi Jinping followed the same path. In 2007, a full forty years after Xi's mother took him and his siblings to shelter on campus to escape marauding bands of radical militants, he became the school's president. He held that position until 2012, when he became general secretary of the CCP and chairman of the PRC.[222]

As of 2018, the Central Party School reportedly had some ten thousand students, who were learning to understand and interpret the fundamental truths, the high doctrine of their faith, what it truly meant to be in the service of the Chinese Communist Party. [223] In their classrooms, they receive what the regime terms thought armaments – the special weapons and tactics of the world's most successful secret political organization: the powers of mental manipulation, propaganda, and psychological warfare – the entire intellectual combat kit needed to increase Beijing's power and influence around the world.

The untranslated 2020 Central Party School textbook that's sold on Amazon like a sacred document is called *The Fundamentals of Xi Jinping Thought on Chinese Socialism in a New Era*. Its wastes no time getting right down to business. The book opens as follows.

> Marxism is the fundamental guiding thought of the Chinese Communist Party. It was the basis for the CCP's establishment as a political party, and, in turn, the basis for the CCP's establishment of the (PRC) state. Marxism seeks to evolve and to make progress over time. That is its moral character. The nineteenth century had nineteenth-century Marxism. The twentieth century had twentieth-century Marxism. The twenty-first century, of course, will have its own twenty-first-century Marxism. Xi Jinping Thought on Chinese Socialism in a New Era is just that: modern Chinese Marxism and twenty-first-century Marxism.[224]

Deeper into the book, the reader comes to a chapter titled, "Constructing a Community of Common Destiny for All Mankind." The text asks the following rhetorical questions: "What's wrong with the world? What are we to do? Cooperate or confront? Open up or isolate? Seek mutual benefit and shared wins or play zero-sum games?"[225] The reader is then assured that Xi Jinping and the CCP have the right answer to these questions, and an airtight strategy to get what they want.

The Chinese Communist Party is struggling for both the happiness of the Chinese people and the great enterprise of human progress. It has its own unique answer to these questions regarding humanity's future destiny: Focus everything on a singular point. That is exactly what Comrade Xi Jinping has proposed with his major strategic thought: "Construct a Community of Common Destiny for All Mankind" .... Its purpose is to make perfect world governance and point the world in the correct direction. It is a bright flag for China to hold up as it leads the world forward and advances human civilization.[226]

The Fundamentals of Xi Jinping Thought declares that the global economy and global markets should be controlled by the state.[227] In true Marxist fashion, the text reveals that achieving China's mission will mean the destruction of free market capitalism. Beijing will spread its socialist economic model and "the market and the state will be organically unified."[228] Also gone will be liberal democracy and the concept of universal values. The book argues against even the existence of universal values.[229] And it asserts that all cultures and ethnicities should be "fused together" and assimilated into a homogenized collective.[230]

The textbook states in no uncertain terms that "revolution is an ideal higher than the sky."[231] It bluntly says that the CCP aims to export communism to every country in the world.

The fundamental mission and aspiration of a Marxist political party is achieving [international] communism. Achieving this sacred mission and aspiration will be the grandest and most magnificent enterprise in the history of human society. It will also be the most difficult and complex mission ever.[232]

After decades of denial and deception, the CCP was no longer hiding its revolutionary global ambitions. The year 2020 marked an inflection point after which China would no longer even pretend to defer to the United States on the world stage. For Xi, it was time to go on the offensive and push the world toward his vision of a hivemind, a single integrated collective whose rules would be decided by a one-party dictatorship. In its way, the COVID-19 pandemic became an opportunity for China to do just that.

According to the Central Party School textbook, Xi Jinping Thought is modern-day Marxism. And the goal of modern-day Marxism is for China to spread communism and reshape the future of the world. But if this is the singular point on which all of China is focused, what exactly does the road leading there look like? And what will the advancement of human civilization entail?

Artistic Rendering of a book on Xi Jinping Thought,
by Grace Young

5

TRANSFORMATION

Building a Community of Common Destiny for Mankind, to me, is the only future for humanity on this planet.[233]

—U.N. General Assembly president Peter Thomson

BELIEVERS in conspiracy theories like those popularized by movies and television shows such as *The X-Files* think that a group of powerful men are plotting in secret to take over the planet and create a totalitarian global government. One of the premises of the New World Order conspiracy theory is that a Fourth Reich could be sprung upon an unsuspecting American public, leaving in its wake a regime with all the hallmarks of Adolf Hitler's Third Reich: racist programs, jack-booted militarism, and Orwellian mass surveillance of private citizens' personal lives.[234] As paranoid and outlandish as this conspiracy theory seems to most people, it touches on something very real.

Something remarkably similar to what American conspiracy thinkers imagine is going on in Washington, DC, is actually going on inside the halls of power in Beijing. According to official sources, China's government does aspire to create a totalitarian, one world government, and internal military documents on Xi Jinping Thought refer to this as the "new world order."[235]

Xi Jinping, by his own admission a devout follower of revolutionary Marxism, refrains from talking about a global revolution in his public speeches and writings. Instead, the term of art he often employs to describe the process of creating a new world order is "transformation." Whereas *revolution* generally refers to a violent movement to overthrow the old political order and fundamentally change society, a *transformation* allows for a radical metamorphosis to occur in a less dramatic fashion, albeit with no less dramatic results. If revolution is an orgy of popular violence and terror unleashed upon the current order to usher in its downfall, transformation is a covert action to place it on an inexorable glidepath into the waiting darkness. It's death by a thousand slices so expertly delivered the victims feel progressively weaker but cannot locate the source of their failing.

Internal teaching materials state that the CCP plans to create a new world order by exporting its ideology and exploiting its global influence to create a unified, Beijing-led collective. The PLA textbook *Great Power Diplomacy with Chinese Characteristics* tells its readers that the American-led international order – the body of norms and behaviors in the international system that seek to resolve confrontations without violence – is deeply flawed and must be rebuilt according to a superior Chinese blueprint. It asserts that American values, norms, and practices must be replaced by the CCP-engineered "China Model," and the Chinese government has the perfect plan to do it. Ideally re-construction can take place in an extended process, keeping the rotting outer structure stable even as it is being completely reengineered from the inside out. It is implied that peace depends on whether the West submits.[236]

In China's official view, transformation was bound to happen sooner or later. "Dissatisfaction with order is part of the human condition.... The current international order has already been around for over seventy years. It now faces so many new situations and new problems. The call for transforming it is growing louder by the day."[237] This Chinese military source argues that, thanks to Xi Jinping's visionary leadership, the replacement project is well underway, and the world is moving in the right direction. More and more countries are following China's directives, adopting policies and plans that will lead them into the collective. The promised land of an international utopia has never looked closer.

> The transformation of the global governance system and international order is now accelerating and moving forward.... Today, the world is not peaceful. How to construct a new international political system and realize lasting peace? Xi Jinping Thought on the Community of Common Destiny for All Mankind has given us the answer.[238]

Another internal textbook issued to military officers in China is called *Strategic Support for Achieving the Great Chinese Resurgence*. According to this document, Beijing's plan envisions sweeping changes to the international order, the likes of which have not been seen in four hundred years. For the betterment of humanity, the book claims, the CCP is building a new order to replace the old. This is a historic process – and one that according to the book has already gone too far for America and its democratic allies to turn back.

> Currently, the shape of international power is undergoing a profound change. A historic transformation is underway.... Today the world is undergoing a change larger than anything ever seen, certainly anything seen since the Treaties of Westphalia established the foundation for the current international system.... The Westphalian System was founded on the notion of a balance of power. But it has proven unable to achieve a stable world order. All mankind needs a new order that surpasses and supplants the balance of power. Today, the age in which a few strong Western powers could work together to decide world affairs is already gone and will not come

back. A new world order is now under construction that
will surpass and supplant the Westphalian System.[239]

The CCP's focus on subverting the world order has a long history, dat-
ing back to the Russian Revolution and the early days of the international
communist movement. Xi Jinping is hardly the first ambitious dictator
to read Marx and then try to overthrow all existing social conditions.
But before we discuss that and how the Chinese government is trying
to make it happen, let's take a quick look at the campaign to bring down
the Westphalian system. Where did it come from and why does it matter?

A History of Violence

The world as we know it was created in two unassuming cities in northwestern Germany: Münster, today known for its bicycle enthusiasts, and
the nearby factory town of Osnabrück. These two ancient population
centers played host to a series of diplomatic talks that culminated in the
Treaties of Westphalia. Inked in 1648, the treaties ended the Thirty Years'
War (1618–1648), one of the worst conflicts ever fought in Europe. More
importantly, the treaties laid the foundation for the modern system of nation-states by making the principle of state sovereignty the main feature of
the international system. The result was a dramatic reduction in the geopolitical influence of the Catholic and Lutheran churches and the establishment of the idea that empires (and eventually modern countries) had fixed
borders, within which their residents were subject to the laws decreed by
their own leaders, rather than those of outside religions or ideologies.

Over time the Westphalian system spread around the world. Although
widely accepted among the great powers by the turn of the twentieth
century, the system was far from sacrosanct. The trauma of World War
I, in particular, triggered a widespread crisis of confidence. A number of
revolutionary socialist movements sprung up seeking to overthrow the

notion of state sovereignty. The first to succeed was Vladimir Lenin's October 1917 Revolution in Russia, which resulted in the establishment of the Soviet Union. On March 2, 1919, several competing Communist parties united together in Moscow to establish the Communist International (Comintern), a centralized organization under Lenin's personal dictatorship. The Comintern sought to ignite a world revolution and taught its members to believe that a cataclysmic event was fast approaching that would result in the destruction of governments everywhere and the collective liberation of humanity.[240]

Whatever initial optimism may have been felt by the Communist International's members, it proved short-lived. In the early 1920s, socialist revolutions in Germany and elsewhere outside Russia fizzled out. The Soviet-led organization switched gears and proclaimed that the forces of international communism would inevitably rise up, but only when the time was ripe. Rather than usher in a global spasm of bloodletting, the Comintern now aimed to wash away the boundaries between nations in a long-extended process, dissolving borders and eroding the old ideas of sovereignty until one day they ceased to exist altogether. The mechanism for this was still militant in nature. In 1927, for example, the general secretary of the Comintern anticipated a potential mega conflict with the imperialist powers and boasted that in such a war, the capitalist states "would be shattered into a thousand fragments."[241]

This turned out to be little more than bluster, and over the next decade another totalitarian ideology emerged in the form of Nazism, which came to eclipse the Communist International menace feared in Europe's halls of power.[242] For the guardians of the Westphalian order, the rise of Adolf Hitler and National Socialism represented something even worse than that of the Soviet Union and the Comintern.[243]

On August 12, 1941, Winston Churchill and Franklin D. Roosevelt released the Atlantic Charter, a rebuke of Nazism and other expansionist movements. Their joint statement called for a future order in which countries refrained from territorial aggrandizement and instead respected the principles of self-determination and state sovereignty.[244] Four years later, the Allies won World War II, and the Westphalian system fell under the protection of the United States, the new dominant power and leader of the postwar order. Washington worked with its allies to quickly establish the United Nations and a raft of associated international institutions to protect the world from the spread of fascism and communism (and other militant ideologies that might emerge in the future).

Meanwhile, the Soviet Union took advantage of its wartime gains in Eastern Europe to create a bloc of communist countries opposing the United States and its allies. As it had before the war, Moscow actively supported revolutionary movements around the globe. But while the USSR was able to spread communism to China, North Korea, Cuba, Vietnam, and a handful of other states, Moscow ultimately failed to realize its larger goals.[245] The Soviet Union was isolated by the United States and its allies during the early decades of the Cold War, and it fell into a long period of stagnation and decline.

China's Forever Revolution

October 1, 1949, was one of the most consequential days in modern history, especially for those who believed in the cause of world revolution. This date marked the long-anticipated birth of the People's Republic of China, an event that transformed the most populous nation on Earth into a communist dictatorship. It had taken Mao Zedong and his army of revolutionaries twenty-two years of horrendous fighting to gain control of the Chinese mainland (they had still not captured Taiwan and its outer islands). Yet in spite of the millions killed and widespread food shortages, they were not about to turn inward and rest.

China had been devastated by the long civil war, but Mao's zeal for international communism was alive and well. If anything, his appetite for revolution had grown with the eating. Once in power, Mao began putting the ideas of Marx, Lenin, and Stalin into practice on a massive scale. Like the Soviet Union, the PRC would dedicate itself to the cause of upending the established order. For the next three decades, Mao made war and revolution the principal themes of Chinese diplomacy. China's overarching goal was to "export revolution," which it did by igniting and fueling civil wars in countries from Indonesia to Nepal and from Zimbabwe to Peru.[246]

In the 1950s, Mao worked hand in hand with his Soviet benefactors, believing the USSR-led communist world was rising and the U.S.-led free world was in terminal decline. Within a decade, however, Mao became convinced that Moscow had lost its stomach for revolution, and he began to oppose the USSR's leadership. The erstwhile allies soon became mortal enemies. From the Sino-Soviet split of 1962 onward, Mao struggled against his Soviet enemies for leadership of the international communist movement.[247]

By the end of the 1960s, the two communist blocs were locked in a series of armed skirmishes along their border, which threatened to escalate and push them over the brink of a nuclear abyss. It was at this moment that Mao reached out to Washington and initiated a warming in U.S.-PRC relations. President Nixon welcomed the opportunity, seeing it as useful for isolating America's most dangerous adversary, the USSR, which then appeared ascendant on the global stage.

In the early 1970s, the People's Republic of China joined the United Nations with tacit American support. Countries around the world turned their backs on Taiwan (officially known as the Republic of China, ROC), one of the founding members of the U.N., which until then had been a permanent member of the U.N. Security Council, to recognize Beijing's government instead. At the outset of the 1970s, only 45 countries had diplomatic ties with Beijing. By the closing days of the decade, 115 countries had established new embassies in the PRC, including the United States.[248] The Americans believed they had scored a major geostrategic win against their principal Cold War enemy. In return, Chinese Communist revolutionaries ended up getting the keys to the capitalist castle they had long dreamed of demolishing.

Inside Man

After Mao's death in 1976, the Communist Party began a long recovery period during which it officially toned down its rhetoric about revolution and a new world order.[249] The new paramount leader, Deng Xiaoping, sought to strengthen China against the Soviet Union by acquiring capital, technology, and managerial knowhow from the United States and the West. To win the support of capitalist governments, Deng made a historic trip to America, bringing with him the promise that China would stop exporting revolutions and embrace a more moderate foreign policy.[250] To convince Washington of his sincerity, Deng donned a cowboy hat at a Texas rodeo and toured factories making Coca Cola, Ford sedans, and Boeing jumbo jets.

If American elites believed that Deng's friendly gestures meant he actually intended to integrate China into the U.S.-led international system, they were mistaken. On March 30, 1979, just weeks after his visit to the United States, Deng announced the "Four Cardinal Principles," his hardline doctrine that spelled out what was (and was not) going to happen in China's post-Mao era:

- We must keep to the socialist road.
- We must uphold the dictatorship of the proletariat.
- We must uphold the leadership of the Communist Party.
- We must uphold Marxism-Leninism and Mao Zedong Thought.[251]

What these slogans meant was that China would forever remain a dictatorship, run by the Communist Party and dedicated to the cause of international communism. Foreign cooperation, exchanges, and business investments were all welcome, and, in fact, desperately needed. Yet economic reforms and market changes would be allowed only to the extent that they strengthened the regime's power. From the perspective

of Deng, revolutionary change was something to embrace, and it was good to turn society upside down and grow material power. But nothing could ever be allowed to change in China politically or ideologically. It was the United States and its democratic allies that were going to have to change in that regard.

Deng's reported intention was to infiltrate the West so that China could benefit from it, weaken it, and eventually replace it. According to official Chinese government sources, Deng never wanted the CCP to stop trying to transform the world so that it conformed to Mao's vision. Rather, he sought to use different tactics than Mao to accomplish the same end goal.[252] In the last days of the Cold War, Deng reportedly made his intentions plain by proposing the establishment of a socialist international political and economic order through the use of non-military means. On September 21, 1988, Deng told a visiting Sri Lankan leadership delegation that "China wants to establish both a new international economic order and a new international political order."[253] Deng told his visitors that doing so required a "good international environment without war, but rather peaceful coexistence."[254]

On December 2, 1988, Deng repeated his message, telling a visiting Japanese trade delegation, "Now is the period to establish a new international political order." In Deng's view, the prevailing conditions at the end of the Cold War between the United States and the Soviet Union meant that China needed to develop a unique path, avoiding Moscow's mistakes while working toward a new communist order.[255] In practice, this meant manipulating capitalism and free market economics to China's benefit, while purposely keeping all domestic Chinese reforms inside Beijing's political and ideological cage.[256]

If contemporary Chinese government sources are to be believed, Deng remained committed to the idea of spreading communism and sought to do so by accepting the theory that China had to thrive and gain pre-eminent global status for that to happen. Given China's weakened state, the CCP could fulfill its original mission only if it acted cautiously and pragmatically on the world stage. Internal military texts state that Deng set in motion a Chinese foreign policy strategy that remains basically intact to the present day.

> From that point onward, our nation always saw es-
> tablishing a new order as an important mission and
> constantly called for transformation. From the start of
> the twenty-first century to today, our nation has made
> real progress in speeding up the transformation of the
> international system, with a focus on participating in and
> playing the main driving force in the historic process. We
> have been able to make major policy changes at the global
> level, including in areas such as international finance,
> world trade, regional security, and climate change.[257]

This narrative holds that China's overall objective of creating a new world order has never changed, and the Communist Party was always revolutionary and has always known what winning looks like. What changed in the 1980s was the paramount leader's assessment regarding the methods to be used and how best to prevail.

The Iron Curtain finally fell in 1989, and, two years later, the Soviet Union came unglued and collapsed. This ushered in a period of globalization during which American political, economic, and social values reigned supreme.[258] Yet while the international communist movement may have gone dark in Russia and Eastern Europe, the desire for world revolution hadn't disappeared in China – far from it. And small pockets of radical leftists survived elsewhere, biding time in anticipation for the day when their movement could awaken from its long slumber.[259]

The Undead Ideology

poetic

Where did all the communists go in the 1990s and 2000s?[260] It turns out that many of them stayed in power. China was a communist country with growing global importance, and its frenzied industrialization, downsizing of state-owned enterprises, and experiments with market economics served as the perfect distraction. Westerners were too busy scrambling for access to China's mythical "one billion customers" to notice that, politically and ideologically, the country remained an oppressive Marxist-Leninist dictatorship. Little was said about the fact that the portrait of the worst mass murderer in recorded history, Mao Zedong, continued to dominate both Tiananmen Square and China's currency, the *renminbi.*

Foreign criticism was muted, and the savage tyranny of Beijing's one-child policy, the brutal *laogai* (labor camp) system, and the dehumanizing working conditions of ordinary Chinese people were all ignored. Almost nothing was said by anyone abroad about the horrors inflicted on the indigenous believers of the massively popular Falun Gong faith, who began suffering systemic persecution and fiendish tortures in the late 1990s. Hollywood superstar Richard Gere talked passionately about the plight of the Tibetans and worked with the Dalai Lama to keep Tibet alive in the public consciousness. Yet, by the early 2000s, Gere and his followers were regarded as eccentrics and increasingly given the cold shoulder in both Washington and Hollywood.[261]

International business and government elites failed to promote in China the ethical and moral standards they espoused and expected at home. Intellectual and political discourse in the PRC was cracked open. Once dissidents, scholars, and lawyers crossed the regime's vaguely defined "red lines," however, they were arrested or sometimes simply disappeared without a trace. China's propaganda and censorship machine grew more sophisticated and powerful with the introduction of Western technology, talent, and managerial knowhow. Local village elections were held with great fanfare and then quietly emasculated. The same treatment was meted out to interest groups of employers, trade unions, and independent media.

Vanishingly few journalists and academics from the West bothered to pry into the gruesome corners of Chinese society. The CCP's carnage-strewn past was downplayed or forgotten altogether. There were too many "happy" stories to tell. The global markets were suddenly teeming with made in China products. Chinese tour groups poured money into the luxury stores of every city Beijing allowed them to visit. Chinese students flooded into foreign universities, bringing with them generous tuition payments and a river of grant monies. Cash-strapped American universities warmly welcomed and even catered to Chinese students and scholars at the expense of academic ethics. Many schools went so far as to institute censorship on their campuses in order to keep the Chinese government content.[262] Seemingly hopeful ties of commerce and goodwill drew attention away from China's despotic actions at home and its support for like-minded dictators abroad.

Tibet, Xinjiang (East Turkestan), Inner Mongolia, and the Ningxia Hui Muslim "autonomous" region felt the jackboot. Communist indoctrination remained a staple of the centrally mandated school curriculum. From the bustling metropolitan centers to the rural countryside, CCP membership continued to be a basic requirement for any serious public, private, or military career. China's armaments industries boomed, and its military power skyrocketed.

Foreigners observed that, for the vast majority of the Chinese people, Marxism-Leninism and Mao Zedong Thought were often honored in ritual but ignored in practice. People in China would automatically parrot the nonsense they had to and then do whatever seemed pragmatic. The new system brought a profound sense of liberation to businessmen, who set up thriving companies reaching hundreds of millions of consumers, who could now enjoy better products and a higher standard of living.

Less trumpeted was that the gains acquired by the "workshop of the world" were offset by its new hordes of beggars, thieves, con artists, and opportunists. Beijing's amoral, top-down obsession with industrial power and urban growth-at-all-costs soon meant the air across China was choked by smog, the rivers poisoned by chemical runoff, and the soil laced with heavy metals. By the early 2010s, China suffered from the world's worst pollution levels and high suicide rates, blights that continue to the present.

After the Cold War ended and the Soviet Union fell, triumphant reports in the West of the mass extinction of communism were greatly exaggerated. North Korea, Cuba, Cambodia, Nicaragua, Ethiopia, Zimbabwe, Kazakhstan, Turkmenistan, and a raft of other former Soviet and Maoist proxies remained in the hands of communist (or "ex-communist") dictators. When convenient, regimes would wrap themselves in the flag of nationalism or religious piety. As it always had, communism continued to feed on human misery and a widespread sense of social and economic despair.

Bloody communist insurgencies continued in Asia, Africa, and Latin America. Examples of communist groups included the Revolutionary Armed Forces of Colombia (FARC), the Shining Path in Peru, the Zapatista Army of National Liberation in Mexico, and the Maoists in Nepal and India. The extreme left wing of the world shared an international agenda that varied little across countless groups. They opposed American world power, liberal democracy, open markets, and globalization. They promised social justice for the poor and downtrodden, while maintaining a Marxist hunger for political revolution and social transformation – all to be exercised through a suffocating system of dictatorship, state terror, mass mobilization, and civil war.

The red-stained atlases and globes of the world all changed in a reassuring fashion after the Soviet Union collapsed. Some communist parties suffered from a profound loss in morale and membership. Many drifted away from the writings of Marx, Engels, Lenin, Stalin, and Mao. Many changed their basic doctrine whenever it was believed to be politically expedient. Many embraced patriotism, nationalism, and liberal capitalist practices. Some joined moderate leftist coalitions and participated in elections. Russian communists ran casinos. Colombian communists ran cocaine. Chinese communists were different. They ran everything.

The CCP turned China into an industrial behemoth, making it the largest manufacturer, commodity consumer, and trading nation in world. The Party cut deals with tycoons in Wall Street and Silicon Valley. It wooed, captured, and censored Hollywood, along with universities and media outlets across the United States that had once been politically independent. The PRC hosted the Olympics and sent space rovers to Mars and the far side of the moon.

The diversity of post-Soviet communism hid a fundamental truth: communism was remarkably resilient. It hadn't lost its appeal. Wherever people suffered, there were openings available for a militant and internationalist ideology that had the potential to fundamentally transform societies and, perhaps, the whole world.

One Supreme Civilization

Under Xi Jinping's rule, the CCP has cast off Deng's policy of hiding its true nature while building China into a superpower. Authoritative PLA texts explain that China has become more "active" (assertive and aggressive) since Xi Jinping rose to power. China is no longer cautiously camouflaging its ambitions, because that is what the situation demands, and, according to Xi's reading of global opinion, that is what the people of the world ultimately want.

> Since the eighteenth CCP Congress [November 2012, when Xi gained supreme power], our nation has used every important platform available to actively propagate the call for constructing a Community of Common Destiny for All Mankind.... By real world action we have constantly pushed this high objective: the formation of a

Community of Common Destiny for All Mankind. And we have won support and praise from the international community for it. While the future road to realizing this objective may be arduous, our nation will still carry out this glorious and singular mission over the long-term. In the end, we will play the important leadership role.[263]

Among other things, the CCP-led future will supposedly see a process of mental liquefaction whereby individual cultures will be assimilated or "fused" into the collective. Xi Jinping and the ruling elite express a belief that this process is natural and overwhelmingly positive. In their view, human progress requires different cultures to come together and become one. "The plurality of human civilization has given this world so many beautiful colors. Plurality brings with it [cultural] exchanges. Exchanges then give birth to fusion. Fusion produces advancement."[264]

Internal military documents portray the assimilation of all the world's cultures into a single unified whole as the mega-trend of our times, a mass blending event that is inevitable, even the choice of history itself.[265] "Constructing a Community of Common Destiny for all Mankind is the inevitable outcome of the development of world civilization. It is also the model and objective of all human development."[266] The final result that Beijing seems to envision is a unitary human culture in which the essence of all past world cultures is maintained, giving the collective unmatched vitality and power.[267] And while all former civilizations would be nominally represented in an "inclusive manner and on the basis of equality," in reality, the text expresses unbridled optimism that China's culture will dominate all others.

"Today, there are over seven billion people in the world, divided into 200 countries and regions, with 2,500 ethnic groups speaking over 5,000 different languages."[268] The solution? To make them all into one harmonized collective that China can benefit from and control. "Today, the Chinese people still follow the Confucian tradition of 'the supreme leader serves all under heaven as his mission.' ... Deep down, we know that China's development is like a river, which needs to be constantly fed by other streams that it absorbs as it flows until, finally, it reaches the big sea of human civilization."[269]

Official textbooks describe a utopian vision of oneness and connection, an ocean of culture and knowledge. They portray a world in which China is deeply integrated into every aspect of the international system. "China is the world stage. The world is China's stage."[270] They state, "Today, China is doing its utmost to push the establishment of a Community of Common Destiny for all Mankind, fully demonstrating its welcoming of others and openness to others in order to fuse together all of the civilizations in all the countries of the world."[271]

On the surface, it would appear that such an internationalist vision might mean the end of Chinese nationalism. In practice, however, the new reality would mean just the opposite. Beijing's narrative holds that the coming world order will be dominated by Chinese culture, and CCP-defined cultural norms will be enforced through coercion whenever necessary. China's superior socialist ideas and material power will stand over the rest, and the planet will be governed and ruled according to the centralized, top-down methods the Communist Party uses to rule China. The following passage captures guidance given to Chinese military personnel.

> China's new view on the development of [a collectivized world civilization] is built on the foundation of China's own unique civilization. As we push for the fusion of the world's civilizations on the basis of our nation's unique civilizational developments, there are several things that must be done.... We must work hard to develop a prosperous socialist culture, building ourselves into a socialist cultural superpower.... We must insist on taking the road of development with Chinese cultural characteristics. And we must insist on our principles and our bottom line as we actively engage with others.[272]

According to CCP teachings, China's system is so superior that it must be reproduced, replicated, and foisted on every other country on Earth. Beijing alone deserves to chart humanity's future. And only the Communist Party's interpretation of Chinese civilization is legitimate; it alone represents the summit of human achievement and progress. All other national cultures are inferior subsidiaries, thin streams of water to be absorbed by the great Chinese river. For this to actually happen, China must become far more powerful and influential than any other nation on Earth.

"By realizing the China Dream of a great resurgence of the Chinese nation, we will put the two wings of material civilization and spiritual civilization into motion.... We will provide the correct spiritual guidance and a strong motivating force for all humanity."[273] Doing so, of course, will require spreading the tentacles of the CCP to all points of the compass, allowing them to seize all the levers of global power, including at the United Nations.

In January 2017, the president of the U.N. General Assembly, Peter Thomson, said on camera to a Xinhua News Agency reporter that, "Building a Community of Common Destiny for Mankind, to me, is the only future for humanity on this planet."[274] It seems likely that Thomson had been deceived and didn't understand what those words meant. He had nonetheless joined a growing chorus of elite voices calling for what the CCP interpreted to be a cry for international communism and China's domination over world affairs.

6

GLOBAL GOVERNMENT

The intelligence is clear: Beijing intends to dominate
the U.S. and the rest of the planet economically, mili-
tarily and technologically.[275]
   —U.S. Director of National Intelligence John Ratcliffe

D URING the darkest hours of the COVID-19 pandemic, when the
climate of world opinion seemed to be turning against China, an
astonishing number of international luminaries emerged to defend and
support the Chinese Communist Party's actions. Some accentuated the
positive and refused to comment on the things Beijing was doing to
harm global health. Others did more. On April 2, 2020, at a virtual event
hosted by Tsinghua University, the director-general of the World Health
Organization, Dr. Tedros Adhanom Ghebreyesus, thanked Xi Jinping for
"his leadership" on global health. Tedros also thanked CCP health officials
and a Chinese government employee, Dr. Margaret Chan (his immediate
predecessor at the WHO), for "responding to Xi Jinping's call."[276]

    We can only speculate how much Tedros knew about what Xi had done
to undermine global health. If Tedros was deceived or coerced, he was
not alone. On March 26, 2020, just days before the Tsinghua University
event, Xi Jinping had personally called the White House to mislead and
blackmail President Trump. According to insider accounts, Xi began the

conversation with a lie, telling President Trump that traditional Chinese medicine was highly effective against the virus. Trump was not inclined to trust him, but only because he'd been burned before.[277]

During a previous phone call in February, Xi had told Trump that warmer spring weather would stop the virus. Trump had believed the Chinese leader's reassuring claim and repeated it to the American people.[278] After discovering that he'd been duped, Trump began blaming China for covering up the origin of the virus and allowing it to spread around the world. This undermined Xi's goal, which was to bury any international discussion under an avalanche of propaganda and disassociate China from the virus's origin. Xi wanted to put the responsibility on others, not on himself or his regime. On March 12, 2020, the Chinese foreign ministry held a press conference where its spokesperson publicly suggested that the U.S. Army was to blame for the pandemic, and said that China was the first victim.[279] This served to further anger Trump.

Now it was spring. The killer virus was rampaging across America and Europe, and Xi was trying to see if he could get the U.S. president to help him spread disinformation again, this time about traditional Chinese medicine. But that was not his main purpose. Xi had called to warn Trump that he might have to extend his halt on the planes and ships carrying personal protective equipment from China.

The words Xi used were polite, the implications were not: Trump could either stop blaming China for its deceptive practices and unwillingness to share information sought by international medical authorities, or he could watch helplessly as America's hospital system collapsed. Chinese embassy officials in Washington repeated Xi's threat in less diplomatic terms, explicitly saying Beijing would continue to cut off America's access to critical supplies like hand sanitizer, surgical masks, and medical gowns (almost all of which were made in China and controlled by the Chinese government) if Trump didn't stay quiet.[280]

The president of the richest country on the planet and commander-in-chief of the most powerful military in human history was being blackmailed. And it worked. For the next few weeks, Trump and the entire

U.S. government decided to avoid saying anything they thought might antagonize China's ruler until they could stockpile needed supplies. It was only after Josh Rogin, an investigative reporter at the *Washington Post*, broke a story on State Department cables warning about safety hazards at the Wuhan Institute of Virology that American officials once again started openly discussing the pandemic's origin.[281]

This episode raised a disquieting question. If one of the most outspoken and brash presidents in U.S. history could be coerced into silence amid a national emergency when millions of American lives were at stake, what chance did Tedros have? What chance did anyone else have? When asked later that month if China should be held responsible for covering up the initial outbreak, super-philanthropist and pandemic thought leader Bill Gates told CNN viewers the following: "You know, China did a lot of things right at the beginning.... I think there's a lot of incorrect and unfair things said."[282] In the weeks that followed, Gates financially supported an online data repository operated by the Chinese technology company Alibaba, a move encouraging scientists around the world to pool their research on COVID-19 treatments and vaccines on a platform that could be monitored by the Chinese government.[283] For Beijing, it was another strategic victory.

Tedros, Trump, and Gates were incredibly important figures in the pandemic. But they were not outliers, people who thought differently and acted in ways outside the mainstream. When it came to China, their behavior was far from unique. They were just like everyone else, only more so. Indeed, their words and actions were indicative of a systemic change that had been taking place for years in the United Nations and nearly every other international organization. Political elites everywhere were operating along the same broad lines as these men, and they seemed unable to change course no matter how grave the situation became.

The Davos Man

On January 25, 2021, Dr. Klaus Schwab made a telling statement, especially coming from him. He was the founder and executive chairman of the World Economic Forum, an exclusive conference for the global superelite held every winter in Davos, Switzerland. Schwab was a visionary with tremendous reach and influence. When he spoke, presidents, celebrities, and CEOs listened and, more often than not, followed his advice.

That day, as Xi Jinping delivered his speech to the annual assembly, Schwab watched respectfully. He then took the virtual stage and declared, "There's only one planet Earth. And only one common future. Thank you, Mr. President [Xi] ... for reminding us that we are all part of a Community with a Shared Future for Humanity."[284]

As Schwab spoke, millions of families around the world were mourning recently lost loved ones, many of whom lay in fresh graves after strangely empty funeral proceedings. And more were coming. In America alone, hundreds of thousands of people were dying after the holiday super-spreader. Yet, while Xi was still energetically covering up the virus's origin and spreading disinformation that endangered global health, to Schwab, that didn't seem to matter. Whatever China's political faults might be (and those were never mentioned), its ruler still had what many elites believed was a laudable vision of the future.

By all appearances, the CCP's dreams were becoming reality. China had exploited the COVID-19 pandemic to great effect, elbowing America out of the limelight. Xi had positioned himself as the new "Davos Man," a world leader committed to multilateralism and strong global institutions (provided, of course, that everyone did what China's government wanted). Xi had publicly demonstrated China's influence. And he had pulled this off amid an unprecedented disaster – a disaster that his regime had failed to stop and continued to worsen by spreading disinformation.

The PRC's official white paper on the pandemic stated that China had successfully "coordinated with" a wide range of international actors to advance its interests amid the world crisis. In a section of the report titled, "Jointly Constructing a Community of Common Health for All Mankind," the Chinese government thanked the Group of Twenty (G20), the World Bank, the World Trade Organization, the Asian Development Bank, and, most especially, the World Health Organization.[285] Ironically, many of the institutions the Chinese government now trusted had been established to defend democracy. Their original reason for existence was to prevent the spread of authoritarian influence and totalitarian ideologies. Now they were doing something very different, working with a regime that sought to upend the current order and replace it with the antithesis of what the U.N.'s founders wanted. For Beijing, this was all part of the plan.

Rather than oppose or confront the U.N. and other affiliated international organizations, the CCP had targeted them for infiltration, and had done so precisely because they were foundational to the liberal world order. Like all large organized groups of people, these institutions were steeped in long years of history and tradition, often making them stubbornly resistant to minor reforms, to say nothing of radical change. Until now.

Internal writings indicate that the CCP sees established organizations with a global reach such as the U.N. as vulnerable, ready-made structures of control. Like healthy bodies awaiting the introduction of a zombie virus, the Chinese authorities view international organizations as latent hosts for transforming the world. The key is capturing and turning them into supranational governing bodies under China's control. To this end, Beijing's agents of influence have been instructed the following:

> Actively exploit the United Nations.... Today the United Nations is the world's most widespread, representative, and authoritative international organization. The "United Nations Charter" represents the cornerstone of the current international order, establishing the basic rules of international relations.... The United Nations is not

yet a "supranational entity" able to command all nations from above.... The superpower (U.S.) acts according to its own strategic interests, resolving international disputes using its "double standards," claiming "human rights are more important."[286]

During the pandemic, the U.N. and its affiliated organizations gave generously to China, providing many forms of help, including emergency streams of money, international legitimacy in the form of effusive praise, and global digital platforms to shape the narrative right when the regime needed them the most.[287] The white paper reveals that the CCP not only gained access to global vaccine experts and technologies, it also received billions of dollars in foreign capital – money which it used to maintain its industrial stranglehold on the global supply of personal protective equipment and other crucial medical supplies.[288] China was able to get back on its feet while the United States and other Western countries stumbled after being hit by wave after wave of a virus that they didn't understand, in part, because the Chinese government had the cooperation of the most influential people and organizations on the planet.

Most notable of the many organizations that supported Beijing's position was the WHO. The Chinese government repeatedly and publicly advocated for the WHO to lead international efforts to study what happened during this pandemic and how best to avoid the next one.[289] This campaign was remarkable – and illustrative – because Chinese officials worked overtime to re-write the history of the pandemic. The CCP carried out an effective effort to cover up the initial outbreak in Wuhan and censored information sought by the United States and other foreign governments. When the government of Australia asked for an open international investigation into the matter, China's official response was to lash out and hit the Australian economy with a series of punitive tariffs.[290]

Who Owns WHO?

If the CCP trusted the WHO to be the judge and jury of the pandemic's origins, it had every reason to do so. Throughout the pandemic, the world health body basically did whatever Beijing wanted. It ignored warnings from the Taiwanese government. It uncritically repeated contradictory and false PRC government talking points. It resisted medical reports that the virus was airborne. It encouraged cross-border travel based on politics instead of science. And it effusively praised the PRC government.[291]

"I will praise China again and again because its actions actually helped in reducing the spread of coronavirus to other countries," said Tedros.[292] The WHO leader refused to allow Taiwan to participate in the World Health Assembly, failed to disclose details of his contacts with Beijing, and ceded control over the investigation into the origins of the virus to the Chinese authorities.[293]

Chinese authoritarian influence over the WHO was already well established by the time COVID-19 burst onto the scene. On August 18, 2017, Tedros officially pledged support for the CCP's OBOR strategy. Traveling to Beijing for the signing ceremony was one of Tedros's first leadership acts after he assumed his new office.[294] His immediate predecessor, Margaret Chan, had paved the way. After stepping down in 2017, she revealed her true allegiance. Chan went from leading the WHO to working for the Chinese government and Communist Party-controlled organizations, including the Chinese People's Political Consultative Conference (CP-PCC), a United Front leadership organization engaged in operations to spread Beijing's influence and undermine global democracy.[295] As another indication of CCP influence over the WHO, Peng Liyuan, Xi Jinping's wife (and former PLA general), served as a WHO goodwill ambassador for almost ten years.[296]

It was not surprising, then, that during the pandemic the WHO decided to take Beijing's money to build a global health supply depot in China – a move guaranteed to increase the CCP's influence on the world stage and give it coercive leverage against vulnerable governments during times of disaster.[297] With the WHO's help, the Chinese government tightened its grip on critical supply chains. Countries that needed virus testing kits, surgical masks, hand sanitizer, face visors, gloves, and personal protection equipment of all kinds had to go through Chinese officials to get them.[298]

Unlike President Trump's White House in early 2020, the WHO had not been paralyzed. It was not watching helplessly as the Chinese government blamed others for the pandemic and openly pronounced its campaign to monopolize active ingredients needed to make anti-viral medicines and health supplies. Rather, it had actively helped advance the CCP's goals. With WHO support, Xi was turning China into the global hub for pandemic-fighting supply chains and the dominant player in the new biomedical economy. The global transformation, it seemed, was well underway. A new world order was coming.

One World, One Government

If the CCP was able to exploit the pandemic to move others toward its vision of a new world order, it was able to do so because it had a long-range objective in sight and a well-established plan for getting there. Chinese communist elites knew what they wanted the world to look like in thirty years and had been laying the groundwork. Meanwhile, the guardians of democracy were thinking only of their own small and immediate fortunes, making them desperate for China's help and vulnerable to deception.

According to Beijing's narrative, there were mega-challenges facing the world, all of which had been created directly or indirectly by the United States.[299] The solution was to establish a single world government under the control of the Chinese authorities.

"We need a world government." This has become the growing consensus of every country.... The plight of world governance is a reflection of problems old and new caused by the United States' withdrawal from related agreements and treaties, its strategy to organize new regional military alliances, the spread of international terrorism, and strict trade barriers between countries.[300]

According to the internal military document, *Great Power Diplomacy with Chinese Characteristics*, the CCP's ideas for global governance are superior and have a comparative advantage over their American rivals.[301] The book laments that under the current world system, "an overall structure and plan for the whole world is lacking."[302] But the text buoyantly notes that the current system could soon change. "Compared to other global governance concepts, our state's ideas for global governance ... represent the best solution for meeting the future needs of human society as it develops. It matches the interests of the majority of the world's countries."[303]

The book candidly informs its readers that the CCP has exploited China's growing economic clout to infiltrate international organizations, and, as a result, the Communist Party is now spreading "Chinese wisdom" and changing the old rules. Chinese government personnel are already running the day-to-day affairs of many U.N. bodies and affiliates. "As our nation quickened the pace of reform and opening," the text declares, "the speed with which we integrated into the global system, joined in the setting of governance rules, and carried out governance operations also accelerated."[304]

Even more important than asserting administrative control over the system's hardware – the brick-and-mortar buildings and the career trajectories of the people they housed – was switching out the software. New programing was needed. Xi Jinping Thought (twenty-first-century Marxism) was being introduced into the system. And the results were seen by the Chinese government as decisive.

> Once a thought is born, it inevitably leads to actions that are more powerful than the thought itself. This is exactly why our nation's ideas for global governance have such life force.... Chinese elements [a euphemism for the CCP] are pushing forward a deep transformation of the mechanisms of global governance.[305]

This document describes a future where all executive power will be collectivized under a Beijing-led, one world government. Its narrative holds that anything else is doomed to failure. In a description of the old software, *Great Power Diplomacy with Chinese Characteristics* claims: "A global governance concept focused on specific issues, with unofficial and official efforts running in parallel, and centered on small groups, can only lead to more fragmentation and more internal contradictions."[306]

Readers are told that foreigners will still retain a voice in the new world order. They would, however, have to be silenced whenever they went against the collective. Only China's centralized vision would count. "Our nation advocates for a concept of global governance based on joint consultations and joint projects. Our concepts should be anticipated to become the dominant thought regarding the future global governance ... such is consistent with the idea of a 'unified humanity' and 'lasting peace.'"[307]

A Centralized World

The all-encompassing nature of Beijing's plan means there is no sphere of human activity that the CCP can envision being outside its reach. By the century's midpoint, and perhaps sooner, everything will be turned upside down and inside out, if the strategy succeeds. The road to international Communism will be a rocky one for the United States and the West, as their governments lose power. But for Marxists, the journey through the decades ahead will see a magnificent series of wins that culminate in final utopian victory.

Great Power Diplomacy with Chinese Characteristics states, "As the transformation of global governance proceeds, the China element will play the major role. Mechanisms to target for this are numerous."[308] The text asserts that the Communist Party seeks domination over the following individual areas, which it aims to merge over time into a centralized world government.

- Global Manufacturing.
- Global Currencies.
- Global Finance.
- Global Trade.
- Global Security.
- Global Food.
- Global Environment.
- Global Resources.
- Global Developmental Assistance.
- Global Immigration.
- Global Human rights.
- Global Health.
- Global Internet.
- Outer Space.
- Transnational Crime.
- Global Terrorism.
- "And more."[309]

After listing each of the targeted domains to be captured, the text asserts: "Our nation has already fully intervened in the mechanisms governing all of the above areas to begin reforming them.... We will continually introduce major initiatives based on our own interests and those of the world."[310] The text goes on to list specific international institutions the CCP claims it has infiltrated.

China is enlarging its contributions to the United Nations, International Monetary Fund, World Bank, World Trade Organization, G20, Asia-Pacific Security Cooperation Organization, Shanghai Cooperation Organization, and is increasing its investments in the BRICS (Brazil, Russia, India, China, and South Africa) Development Bank [now known as the New Development Bank], Asia Infrastructure Investment Bank, Silk Road Foundation, and other organizations and foundations. As this goes forward, the role of the China element will become more obvious, and China's concepts and actions will also gain an even more powerful base of support. The China element will lead global governance actions and reforms.[311]

According to this document, the Communist Party has inserted itself into the inner workings of the global system by applying a holistic approach. "We have actively given the international community ideas, funds, technologies, personnel, security, opportunities, and other public goods." For Beijing, this indirect approach has paid off handsomely. "There is a new vista and new chapters being written in the book of global security and development."[312]

Another military document states that Beijing plans to expand the size of PLA peacekeeping units in countries around the world and increase the range of operations undertaken by them. If effective, the CCP could exploit the U.N. to increase its influence, protect its overseas economic interests, and repress groups it views as dangerous.[313]

Under the auspices of the United Nations framework, we will actively push forward and participate in key point peacekeeping missions around frontline "One Belt, One Road" areas. As appropriate, we will expand the scale of PLA participation in U.N. peacekeeping operations. We will expand the range of PLA participation in U.N.

peacekeeping operations. In this way, we will establish an image of our civilization as a teacher – and our image as an armed and powerful teacher. We shall thus win without fighting by effectively striking fear into terrorists and radicals, and thereby protecting our state's economic interests overseas and the safety of our personnel.[314]

Unlike the United States, which has historically taken a limited approach and tended to resolve international issues on a case-by-case basis, the Chinese government says it is prepared to fight for the progress of all mankind.

While America is spurning globalization, and, in some areas, even pulling out of integration, as the CCP nineteenth Party Congress Work Report clearly states "The Chinese Communist Party is the ruling party which seeks the happiness of the Chinese people, and it also is the ruling party struggling for the enterprise of human progress. The Chinese Communist Party takes it as its ultimate mission to make new and even greater contributions to mankind."[315]

The documents we have reviewed so far suggest that the CCP seeks to redefine the basic purpose of the U.N. system. The U.N. was previously understood to be limited in scope, an organization that would not override the sovereignty of nation-states except in extreme cases such as war or genocide. These constraints allowed the U.N. and its affiliates to serve as the stable foundation of the post–World War II order, an open structure that individual countries could build on, each according to their own sovereign choices. The main requirement to participate was that everyone respected the right to self-determination and agreed not to violate the borders of their neighbors. Even the smallest and weakest countries had an equal vote. And, whenever possible, the U.N. sought to spread freedom, democracy, good governance, and human rights, all of which empower individuals at the expense of their governments.

In contrast, the CCP plan calls for "consultations" with other nations through their leading elites, each of whom could be individually corrupted or coerced, allowing Beijing to decide for itself what is in those nations' best interest and speak for them in the global collective. In his 2016 new year's address, Xi Jinping declared, "The international community is looking forward to hearing China's voice and seeing the China Model. China cannot be absent."[316] But absent from what? Where would the China Model apply? The answer, it seems, is *everywhere*.

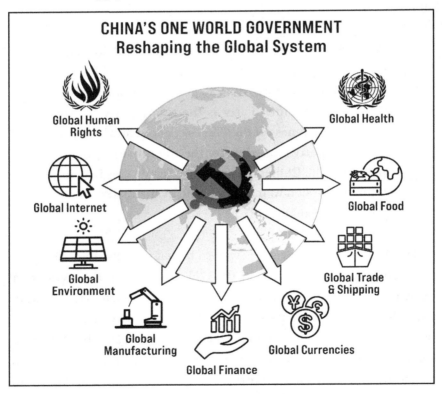

China's One World Government, by Louis Martin-Vézian

Chinese texts say the Communist Party plans to exercise power, in part, by dominating nuclear security and proliferation issues, the future

Internet, outer space, the deep seas, and polar caps.[317] According to official sources, the CCP will oppose what it views as American-led democratic movements in the Middle East, North Africa, and Eastern Europe. It will oppose the expansion of NATO and the encroachment on Russia's sphere of influence. It will support Russia and Iran.[318] China will seek to create a global "united front" against terrorism, which it will lead in accordance with its own particular definition of terrorism.[319] In the official Chinese view, the U.S.-led approach to terrorism will continue to fail because it is overly militarized and focuses on advancing a pro-democratic ideology and American values. A better way, according to Beijing's telling, would be to create a "fair and just" China-led world order, and to reject U.S. "hegemonism, power politics, and double standards."[320]

In effect, China's rulers intend to treat all the peoples of the world the same way they treat their own citizens. By casting China as the protector and champion of all human progress – something that the CCP says its model of one-party dictatorship best serves – the Communist Party is giving itself a broad license to interfere in the internal politics of every country in the world, all the way down to the unitary individual level. The internal guidance military officers in China receive reads as follows:

> Push the transformation of the global governance system forward.... Insist on the fundamental policy of opening up foreigners, using "One Belt, One Road" construction and other major international cooperation projects to create a more encompassing, deeper, and more multifaceted opening up.... Continue to push the current formation of a new world political and economic order and new type of international relations.[321]

The CCP is articulating a vision of a future world in which China's power and influence would be almost limitless. This would be a future where, under the aegis of Beijing's ever-expanding one world government, nation after nation would be ensnared and absorbed into the collective. It is unknowable what that might look like in practice. Nothing like it has ever happened before, and our sources don't describe the process in concrete terms.

While speculative, it seems reasonable to assume that, in many cases, this theoretical process would see democratic governments subverted and overturned in battles between groups driven by extreme-right and extreme-left political ideologies. In democracies, the collapse would probably be self-inflicted, with populist candidates elected by representative systems that they would later dismantle on the road to dictatorship. In other cases, revolutionary terrorists might upend society and drag them into bloody civil wars, and, when the smoke cleared, a CCP-linked strongman would be left standing who could force his nation to join the collective.

China Rising

In the considered view of Chinese strategists, the unceasing accrual of national power and strength is indispensable for China to serve as an engine driving the planet toward a new world order.[322] According to one official PRC reading of history, every great power has to pass through three phases as they rise up. First is a phase in which they build up their power and prepare to rise. Second is a phase in which they begin to rise up and push against the established powers. And third is a phase in which they overcome and absorb their rivals.[323]

Chinese writings observe that many countries in history failed to succeed during the second phase of their rise.[324] In most cases the friction these rising powers created as they grew and expanded into the domains occupied by established powers ignited debilitating wars. In others, their actions invited exhausting arms races or other forms of competition that ultimately proved crippling. PLA texts observe that as the result of forty years of economic growth, China has already successfully passed through the first phase of power, and is now well into the second.[325]

Given the mindboggling size of China's population and accomplishments to date, the CCP apparently believes it has the potential to obtain the kind of power which no single regime has wielded before in human history. Yet Communist Party theorists acknowledge that much will depend on how well Beijing can mitigate and neutralize the coming foreign backlash.

> Note that the peaceful rise of modern China is the peaceful rise of the most populated country in the world. It is also the peaceful rise of the largest developing country, one whose economic scale will ultimately surpass that of the United States. The implication is that it will make waves…. Such a large-scale development will inevitably produce a profound impact on the world situation and international affairs, inciting all kinds of reactions from the international community.[326]

China's continued rise will depend on how well the CCP can grasp and work the levers of power at the U.N. and other organizations. Beijing's plan calls for quietly conquering the world's most respected institutions, taking champions of freedom and democracy and transforming them into a hidden hand spreading the CCP's vision of international communism.[327]

China's official narrative claims that the plan is working: "The established and developed countries' grip on the international order is growing weaker and weaker."[328] The PLA textbook *Strategic Support for Achieving the Great Chinese Resurgence* includes the following lines from one of Xi Jinping's speeches:

> We have strengthened our foreign strategy and operations. We have energetically carried out great power diplomacy with Chinese characteristics. With each

passing day, our nation takes another step towards the center of the world stage. Our international influence, our power to move others, and our ability to shape events are all growing. The international community is paying attention to our nation and emphasizing us to a degree we've never seen before. We now maintain an advantageous position in the international system. We have the initiative.... Today, we sit at the head table on the stage of global governance. We are winning ever more narrative dominance and influence. We are better prepared than ever to lead the transformation of the global governance system.[329]

In 2021, the U.S. secretary of state, Antony Blinken, acknowledged the nature of the CCP's ambitions when he said: "This is one of the major, if not *the* major, challenge of our times.... The challenge is that the world order that China would prefer is a profoundly illiberal one."[330] He then stated, "When it comes to Chinese investment, there is no distinction between a so-called private enterprise and the state. If a private Chinese enterprise makes the investment, the state has access to whatever that enterprise has access to." He also stressed, however, that the United States' relationship with the PRC had cooperative aspects and said, "Our purpose is not to decouple."[331]

Perhaps Blinken's remarks show why the CCP felt confident in the success of its global strategy. American leaders knew their nation's power and prestige were being eroded and undermined. Yet they still couldn't imagine a future in which China wasn't a partner that helped solve international issues. Washington's best and brightest didn't even want to disentangle their nation from China's growing web of influence.

White Glove, Green Cash

In these pages we have seen how the CCP seeks to infiltrate international organizations to expand its global reach. That is one of Beijing's most important lines of effort because it provides Chinese agents of influence cover, a white glove of legitimacy in the form of trusted international name brands like the U.N. and the WHO. While it is not clear from the outside just how that process happens, we know that gaining dominance over these organizations seems to require spreading around money to sooth anxieties, something Chinese government officials euphemistically refer to as engaging in economic development, cooperation, and shared wins.[332]

If cash is king, where does the money come from, and why hasn't China's government run out by now? It has long been assumed in the United States that globalization and the advance of free market capitalism would force China to liberalize. We have all been taught to think that China's economic model is not sustainable because it is centralized, state-dominant, and Party-controlled. Sooner or later, China will stagnate and collapse unless the regime reforms itself out of business the way dictators in South Korea and Taiwan did.

This is an appealing and persuasive argument. After all, no country that has embraced any version of Marxism-Leninism has ever been able to become rich and prosperous over the long run. By their very nature, one-party dictatorships are irrational. They prize ideology and political loyalty over everything else, including the health and safety of their people. Such regimes tend to be intolerant and inflexible, traits that poison good economic decision-making. It's little wonder that they eventually all go bankrupt.

But what if our fundamental assumptions about the way the free market system currently works are flawed? What if there are holes and vulnerabilities in the system that the CCP has used to gain leverage over the world's most important economic actors? What if Beijing has changed the market to ensure the rules of the game don't apply to China the way they do to everyone else? What if, like the U.N. system, the open markets that were supposed to save us from totalitarianism are themselves being turned into mechanisms of tyranny and oppression? Could it be possible that it's not the socialist dictators, but rather the capitalist democracies that are reforming themselves out of business?

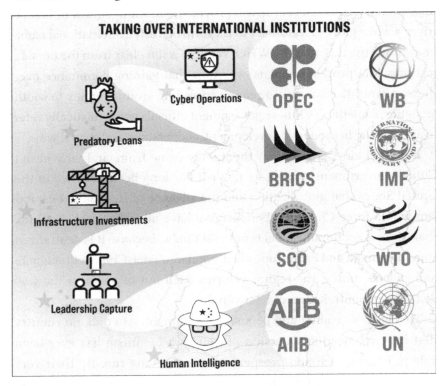

Taking Over International Institutions,
by Louis Martin-Vézian

7

ENSLAVEMENT

An authoritarian illiberal power is not going to want
the world to be liberal and free. It wants an order that
mirrors its own nature.... So what China wants for
itself it wants for the rest of the world.[333]

—Nadege Rolland

Monday, September 4, 2017, was a bright day in Xiamen. It had
rained overnight, and now the morning sun shined through wispy
clouds. A soft breeze gently pushed wavelets across the bay. Xiamen,
a major port city nestled in the hills of southeastern China, is located
directly across from Taiwan. And like Taiwan, it is known for its heat,
humidity, and violent storms. In the summer months it is common for
the atmosphere to press down on the city like a steaming wet blanket.
Then, just when it seems the air can't get any heavier, ferocious winds
rip up from the south, bursting the water-laden skies.

As Xi Jinping looked out his window that morning, he must have
smiled with satisfaction. The leaders of the BRICS countries (Brazil,
Russia, India, China, and South Africa) were all gathered in Xiamen for
a multi-day, supercharged summit that he was in charge of leading. Early
in his career he had served as the deputy mayor of this city. Afterward,
he had worked in Communist Party, government, and military positions

up and down Fujian Province for another fifteen years, jobs that took him in and out of Xiamen on a regular basis. Xi knew this part of China like the back of his hand. He knew that typhoons were a frequent and dangerous visitor this time of year.[334] When he had selected the time and place for his summit, he knew there was a chance it would have to be canceled or delayed. His gamble on the weather had paid off.

Xi's mood was visibly buoyant as he strode into the hall where the international delegates where gathered, the red carpet soft under foot. The weather was probably not the only reason he was happy. His glamourous wife Peng Liyuan had accompanied him on the trip. They had just celebrated their wedding anniversary together, an event they had marked on Friday, exactly thirty years to the day they had been married in this very same city. According to hints dropped in state media, Xi still enjoyed romancing his bride.[335] In 2014, a music video, "Big Daddy Xi Loves Mama Peng," went viral on China's tightly controlled Internet. "The chemistry between the couple has impressed many netizens and it inspired my partner and I to write this song," said singer-songwriter Yu Runze.[336]

Photos of Xi's public displays of affection for Peng were released by the government to coincide with their anniversary.[337] This made it seem like the couple might enjoy a romantic replay of their honeymoon over the weekend. If it was indeed a nostalgic love vacation, it was a short one, just like the one they had had back in 1987. One CCP media outlet noted that the couple was often separated by work, but emphasized that they were always on each other's mind.[338] Their union in Xiamen had been a humble affair, and she had left him to go on a two-month-long singing tour just four days later, leaving him to wait for her.[339] This time, however, Xi was the star of the show. This time she would wait for him.

Freshly printed copies of Xi's book, *The Governance of China*, sat piled high on tables at the nearby media center, translated into English, Russian, Portuguese, and other world languages. If Chinese government news outlets are to be believed, it was an instant hit with the three thousand reporters who gathered from the far corners of the map to cover the event. Their eagerness to learn what made China's paramount leader tick reportedly turned his book into a best seller over the weekend.[340] It wasn't long before the assembled masses would find out about what kind of win-win cooperation was, officially speaking, on his mind.

Sitting alongside Xi in the meetings was his good friend Vladimir Putin, who wore an outfit that mirrored Xi's own: navy-blue suit, purple tie, gold lapel pin. Brazil's president Michael Temer had on a matching suit and lapel pin, but wore a gold tie. South Africa's president Jacob Zuma was dressed the same, with a red tie. Indian Prime Minister Narendra Modi broke ranks completely and didn't even bother to wear a business suit and tie to the event. Instead, he wore a black Nehru suit with a white pocket square, making him stand out from the others.

That June, Chinese troops had violated the border with India's ally Bhutan, leading to a standoff between Chinese and Indian forces in the mountains. As the two sides jockeyed for tactical position along the contested border, clashes occurred and several soldiers from each camp were injured. At times the stalemate seemed likely to spill over into unchecked violence. Yet somehow discipline had prevailed, and armed conflict had been avoided. Just days before the BRICS Summit opened in Xiamen, China and India announced that they had each pulled their troops back from Doklam, the contested site. Border tensions remained, but passions were no longer so high that the national leaders couldn't meet each other and work on their statecraft.

This was the first time Xi had seen Modi since the crisis and he appeared eager to take a measure of the man, to gauge the depths of his resolve, to search for weak points in his policy position or his personal psyche. They would be holding bilateral side talks the next day. Having thrown him off balance, Xi would likely attempt to sooth his neighbor's nerves and then extract concessions from him. Later, after giving India a brief respite, he would ratchet up tensions again. And the virtuous cycle for China would spiral onward and upward. It was a diplomatic playbook that often seemed to serve the Communist Party well.

To build goodwill in the run-up to the leadership summit, China had hosted a film festival that included a feature-length movie produced by a team of five directors, one from each of the BRICS countries.[341] China hosted friendly sporting games, giving the five national teams a chance to face off in basketball and volleyball.[342] But as much as Xi enjoyed watching sports, his primary focus was always on the political game. He had gathered the BRICS leaders together in Xiamen so he could share his vision of the future. Underpinning his energetic pursuit of cooperation with these poor, troubled, and ambitious countries was something everyone in Beijing agreed was vital, to leverage economic interconnectivity to create a new world order. And that required looking for willing (or at least malleable) partners to help.

An internal PLA document later described the purpose of the Xiamen BRICS Summit just as Xi Jinping himself had in his keynote address. "China is doing its utmost to push forward a new round of globalization, one that will focus on the interests of all mankind, with new developments being led by new concepts and ideas."[343] The text parroted Xi's remarks at length, hinting that China and its partners would set the rules and create a global government. "To drive the transformation of the global economic order, we must respond to the macro-level realities of the world economy and create a more perfect set of rules governing new domains like the deep seas, the polar regions, outer space, and cyber space."[344]

The internal document revealed something, however, that Xi had omitted in his public remarks: "The reason China pushes international cooperation is that, ultimately, our objective is to play the role of the leading great power. Our objective is to do a good job leading the development of the world economy."[345] The document stated that Xi and the CCP elite envisioned the BRICS forming the core of an economically "rebalanced" world. These five countries were going to work together to establish new global supply chains and create market structures that gave them – and especially China – huge advantages over the capitalist West.[346]

According to *Great Power Diplomacy with Chinese Characteristics*, globalization was something useful that had been broken by the United States. It was something that, like so much else, needed to fundamentally change. The BRICS were an important part of that equation. Xi and his comrades planned to use this platform (along with many others) to create a collectivized future modeled on China's own system.[347] Left unsaid in Xiamen's glittering meeting rooms and on the floor of the press center was a hidden agenda. The CCP wanted its own interests to infiltrate global markets and become so entrenched that countries around the world could not be successful without Beijing's blessing, and all were dependent on it.

The document declared, "With each passing day, China is getting closer to the center of the world stage.... The world cannot do without China if it wants to prosper.... The China of today is integrated into the world. So, the world and China will either thrive together or they will suffer together."[348] The text repeatedly describes China's economic success as inextricably linked to the health and prosperity of the whole world. The benefits of China's growth, it asserts, will increasingly be felt by all mankind as people of each nation join together to construct the collective.[349]

The document portrayed globalization in its current form as fundamentally flawed, but also necessary and, with adaptation, something that could be used to reshape the world.[350] America played the leading role in the original process of globalization and allowed China to experience explosive growth. Yet Washington had never been inclined to let Beijing install its socialist software into the free market operating system of Globalization 1.0. Today, that no longer mattered. The United States was hardly in a good position to stop the relentless advance of Chinese interests. In 2008, America's red-hot housing market sparked a financial wildfire and a deep recession. Ever since, Chinese officials told themselves (and anyone else who would listen) that the Americans were in terminal decline, and the entire international system was ripe for usurpation.

> After the Cold War ended, the United States led a period of economic globalization. But it was afflicted with mistakes and it failed. The global economy sunk into

a long period of low growth. This shook the people of
the world's confidence in the global economy. Now we
need to rebuild confidence in globalization. We need to
improve the governance of the global economy, and to
begin a new round of economic globalization.[351]

China's rulers envisioned themselves leading a "new type of globalization." To this end, they were cultivating influence over the BRICS, United
Nations, WTO, and G20. They were pushing for a new economic order
that would be led by China instead of the United States. The document
said that China intended to serve its own national interests first, but
added the CCP would also keep an eye out for what it understood to be
the "long-term interests of the international community."[352]

Another internal document, *The Main Contradictions Facing Our Nation's Society in This New Era*, links China's campaign of global economic
integration to its broader strategy. "The relationship between China and
the world has entered into a new phase, with China steadily approaching
the center of the world stage. In this phase, China will go from integrating
into the world to participating in its governance and leading the world."[353]
This source goes on to state: "The globalized world needs a responsible
great power to lead it. A rising China needs to continue asserting itself
and taking the initiative to shape an international order that is just and
rational." Readers are told that China will soon have an opportunity to
leverage its global economic power to achieve supremacy. "When the
United States and Europe can no longer serve as the leader of the pack
and play the leadership role, the eyes of the world will inevitably turn
toward China."[354]

Strategic Support for Achieving the Great Chinese Resurgence predicts
a future where the power of the United States evaporates, allowing
China to build a Beijing-centric order and take over the mantle of world
leadership. "Today, the prospects for peace are undermined by instability,
complexity, and fragility in the world. The most fundamental reason for
this is that the United States is using its strategic power in an attempt

to maintain its old hegemonic system." This source argues that, unlike America, China is a force for good. "China is using its new strategic power to maintain peace and justice. But there's an imbalance between the two. Changing this imbalance in international strategic power is a process."[355] To accelerate that process, China's government was said to be mobilizing the power of "newly prosperous" countries around the world.[356]

This narrative points to a future of unparalleled Chinese dominance. "The world is now undergoing a transition so massive that nothing like it has ever been seen before. At its core, this transition is being driven by the following changes. The United States is becoming weak. China is becoming strong. Russia is becoming aggressive. And Europe is becoming chaotic."[357] The implications are clear. "The world has entered into a new age, one in which the world order will be remade.... China is at a critical moment. The Chinese nation is rising and the Chinese race is resurgent. This is a historic turning point."[358]

The document tells readers that, thanks to Beijing's economic policies, China has made tremendous gains and is now at the cusp of breakout growth. Meanwhile, America and its allies were in denial about how much ground they had lost. "Our nation's development has already brought changes to the world lay-out and the international order. In the future, we could truly shake the world. Western nations which currently dominate the international system don't want to acknowledge reality."[359]

New Market, New Master

At this point the reader might ask, what ever happened to the idea that trade ties between the United States and China would have a subversive effect, loosening Beijing's grip on Chinese society? Presidents from Ronald Reagan to Barack Obama justified their China policies by asserting that deeper bilateral integration and active U.S. support for Chinese economic growth would force the CCP to undertake a process of liberalization, leading to positive political changes that would benefit everyone. Even Donald Trump had been obsessed by gaining access to China's market. Why had their promises to the American people come up empty? Where had their intelligence estimates gone wrong?

As it turns out, the Communist Party had learned to stop worrying and love globalization and American capitalism. Or, more precisely, to love the opportunities economic integration afforded to absorb foreign capital, technology, and knowhow which it could exploit to gain influence, power, and prestige. The Chinese government discovered that institutions control people, and money controls institutions. If international organizations are the world's grey matter and conscience – those things that give expression to the fundamental values at the core of the world order and serve as inhibiting voices of reason – then the globalized economy is the wild, chemical charged bloodstream.

Beijing learned that free market capitalism can tempt almost anyone to indulge in some excess. Individual entrepreneurs, small family businesses, and major corporate boards are all vulnerable to the siren call of money. Because capitalism is built on an idea that says the unceasing accrual of profit is a good thing, greed is an ever-present and powerful motivating force, the engine of the economic machine. When finely tuned and maintained, the machine roars ahead and everyone benefits. But like any powerful force, it can be hard to control. Sometimes it crashes and people get hurt.

In recognition of humans' innate fallibility, the U.S. government had traditionally enacted laws and carried out audits to keep players honest. When properly run, America's version of globalization had a way of creating wealth without causing dependencies or debts that could put vulnerable governments and societies at risk of losing their sovereignty. The system, however, was far from perfect, and its openness gave the CCP wide avenues to exploit. Some of the system's American guardians were corruptible, while others simply grew complacent and allowed their vigilance to wane.

The COVID-19 pandemic was an illustrative case of how Chinese officials could manipulate poorly policed trading spaces to undermine the strength and sovereignty of their rivals. Prior to the global health crisis, the CCP had leveraged vulnerabilities in the American capitalist system to undersell international competitors and gain control over the market for critical medical supplies.[360] In early 2020, at least 90 percent of America's N95 face masks were supplied by the PRC.[361] This, in turn, allowed Beijing to create a dependency that it could use to advance its political goals.

When the outbreak occurred, government officials in Washington suddenly discovered that they were dangerously reliant on China's centralized, top-down supply system. Like addicts, they had lost control and could be held hostage and forced to submit to their supplier. As we have seen, President Trump felt unable to say "No" to Beijing even though he believed the Chinese government was the cause of the plague. What's worse, the CCP continued spreading disinformation throughout the pandemic that made the virus far deadlier for everyone. And the Communist Party exploited international institutions to deepen control over the market to ensure that, for its clients, the cycle of addiction and submission would never end.

How did that all play out in the United States? In the early days of the 2020 outbreak, the price of N95 masks spiked by a factor of five (or more) and stores almost immediately ran out.[362]

Rather than allow its "just-in-time" supply chains to function, the CCP halted exports of protective medical gear to America, effectively bringing Washington to its knees.[363] Then, months later, the Chinese government began exporting again, albeit only after it had serviced its own needs at home and abroad. According to the Department of Homeland Security, much of the PPE that came to America's shores later in the year from China was defective.[364] The lack of safe equipment led to devastating results: a high proportion of American medical workers were infected with COVID-19. In May 2021, the *New York Times* reported that more than 3,600 first responders had died on the frontlines of the battle against the virus.[365]

American manufacturers mobilized to domestically produce hundreds of millions of face masks and other critical health equipment amid conditions reminiscent of the defense-industrial surge of World War II. By early 2021, the nation was finally on track to break its dependency on CCP-controlled suppliers. Within just a few months, however, that changed. Beijing shifted gears again and, as it had before, used unfair trade practices to flood the market with below-cost safety items that had the effect of driving Americans out of business and making the United States more insecure.[366] The result was a stunning strategic reversal. At the time of this writing, America remains dependent on China for critical medical supplies and, as we will see, much more.

No government official in the United States should have been surprised this happened. For years, analysts had been warning that China's government was purposefully creating global dependencies and cultivating market conditions that would give it political leverage over other countries in times of crisis. By design, a new economic order was emerging, and at its core was China. CCP-controlled companies dominated global manufacturing and had immense influence over the logistics systems that delivered products from factory to buyer. Increasingly, this meant that the authorities in Beijing could decide who got how much of what product, and when. At the same time, China had become the world's largest marketplace for a large array of international products, from cars to planes and computers to movies. A single phone call from a PRC leader could make or break entire foreign business sectors, even governments.

Conquering the "Oxygen of Technology"

Perhaps the most notable case of Chinese economic warfare involved rare earth minerals.[367] Rare earths are soft heavy metal oxides found all over the world that have unique magnetic and electronic properties. Once extracted and processed, these minerals have amazing effects.

They interact with electrons in ways no other known material can, a power that makes them essential for the manufacturing of advanced technology products.

In 2010, China threated to impose a rare earths embargo on Japan amid a political spat over a boat collision in the East China Sea near the Senkaku Islands, uninhabited rocks that Tokyo owns and administers, but Beijing still claims. The Japanese government initially detained the crew of a Chinese fishing trawler for illegal fishing; but after it was reported that a Chinese rare earths embargo was coming, which would bring its already sluggish economy to a grinding halt, Tokyo backed down ignominiously. Under intense diplomatic pressure, Japan released the Chinese boat crew without charges, made an official apology, and paid money in compensation for the collision. China declared a diplomatic victory and changed regional perceptions. The CCP's ability to weaponize trade to successfully coerce Japan sent shockwaves throughout the international community. Everyone had assumed they had little to fear from trade with China. Suddenly that no longer seemed true.

For many in Washington, the incident raised unsettling questions: how strong were the supply chains that supported the American military? What would happen if China embargoed rare earths? Could the nation still produce the weapons systems it counted on to win future wars? Studies were commissioned and congressional testimonies were delivered. No one liked the answers they got. Everything from Virginia-class submarines and F-35 Lightening II fighter jets to Tomahawk cruise missiles and Predator drones all relied on specialized minerals sourced from China. There was simply no cost-effective alternative in sight.[368]

It turned out that the Chinese government had used an aggressive trade strategy to monopolize the international rare earths market and become the sole supplier for almost all of America's needs. China's dominance was so overwhelming that rare earths concentrate extracted from California's Mountain Pass Mine (the last operational rare earths mine in the United States) had to be shipped to China for processing before the elements could be used in American manufacturing. In spite of official concerns raised across multiple presidential administrations, nothing was actually done about the problem over the next ten years.[369] The market incentives for maintaining the status quo were simply too powerful to resist.

In the minds of China's strategists, cornering the market for critical materials is ultimately about which superpower will emerge victorious in the supreme contest of the twenty-first century. It is about whether the CCP will win the final struggle. Chinese political elites view rare earths as an important means to this end. Chinese propaganda outlets refer to these minerals as "strategic resources" for the "six new technology groups" – the cutting-edge competitive domains that Beijing sees as engines driving China's future growth. One of these competitive domains is biomedical technology: products such as medical testing kits, health sensors, and pharmaceuticals. Others include information technology, new materials, new energy sources, space technology, and advanced shipbuilding.[370] All require a preponderance of rare earths.

According to Chinese state media, a breakthrough in the application of rare earths is being made every five years, and one out of every six new inventions involves these minerals.[371]

Chinese military officers argue that rare earths are a domain of strategic competition. The PLA published an article declaring rare earths to be "strategic mining resources, especially important for protecting state security and winning modern warfare."[372] The article went on to call rare earths "the lifeblood of national defense" and darkly declared that: "Now the struggle between nations for these strategic resources is becoming increasingly fierce. So, we must ... strengthen our protection and control over these strategic mining resources."[373]

China's rulers saw the need to lock up the global rare earths market as a matter of life and death. Their sense of urgency translated into a series of centralized plans. Rare earths are part of "Made in China 2025," Beijing's ambitious plan to undermine America's high-tech industry and economic leadership by institutionalizing unfair trade practices as a matter of policy.[374] Rare earths are highlighted in Beijing's OBOR strategy and its five-year S&T plans, which envision using rare earths to develop futuristic technologies that will serve as a foundation for China's continued economic growth and rapid military buildup.[375]

On Xi Jinping's watch, the CCP has militarized large segments of China's economy. Here too, rare earths play an important role.[376] Rare earths are essential to the production of the electronics found in nearly all modern military systems that Chinese armaments factories produce. Stealth fighters, cruise missiles, submarines, supercomputers, and radars are all full of rare earths-powered components. These minerals are also a vital part of China's rapidly expanding nuclear weapons complex.

A year after the BRICS Summit in Xiamen, the prestigious Xiamen Institute of Rare Earth Minerals announced it was undertaking large-scale nuclear engineering projects for the Chinese military.[377] It was unclear what exactly the terse announcement meant. No further details were provided and little was said about China's nuclear enterprise for the next three years. Then, in 2021, American researchers publicly revealed satellite imagery showing that China was in the middle of a sweeping nuclear weapons buildup. New projects included hundreds of freshly dug silos for intercontinental ballistic missiles. China's armaments included super-sized truck launchers armed with missiles that could reach Washington, next-generation ballistic missile submarines, and stealthy strategic bombers, all for delivering sophisticated city-busting nuclear warheads.[378]

In the summer of 2021, the PLA tested a hypersonic missile capable of circling the Earth along a trajectory that had previously been considered only theoretically possible. The test reportedly shocked U.S. intelligence officers, who had never seen anything like it and had "no idea" how it worked.[379] A group of brilliant Chinese engineers had achieved something no one else ever had. Yet they hadn't done it on their own. They actually had American help.

8

HONEYPOTS & FOX HUNTS

Ever since the Chinese Communist Party was first established, realizing Communism has been the Party's
supreme ideal and ultimate objective.[380]

—Xi Jinping

FROM Beijing's perspective, the key to doing extraordinary things is
having extraordinary people, and the struggle between superpowers
is largely about a competition for human talent, without which "you
have a fountain with no water and a tree with no roots."[381] The logic is
as compelling as it is straightforward: whichever country has the best
and the brightest working for it will naturally be in a position to gain
more power in the long run. In 2018, the *Xinhua News Agency* published
a directive from Xi Jinping in which he said human talent would be the
deciding factor in international strategic competition. If China could
target, recruit, employ, and retain the top minds in the world, it would
be the nation that emerged victorious over all others.[382]

This was not an entirely original thought. The CCP had been prioritizing the education and cultivation of its own people for years. But on Xi's
watch, the aggressive recruitment of foreign experts has been taken to
another level.[383] Xi sees himself as a great man, a historic leader capable
of changing the fate of China, someone who can reshape the entire world

order. But he is under no illusion that he can do it all by himself. In his three-hour speech to the nineteenth Congress of the Chinese Communist Party, Xi declared: "Talent is a strategic resource for the resurgence of the Chinese nation and for winning the initiative in international competition."[384]

To acquire the global brainpower needed to gain and maintain primacy, the CCP has tapped into its "Thousand Talents Plan" a shadowy, multi-decade program run by the Central Organization Department to recruit the world's geniuses into the service of China. Targeted individuals are offered extraordinary paychecks and rock star-level perks to visit and lecture or, better yet, live and work, in China. There is little that Beijing won't do to ensure it has the best of the best on its side. As early as 2004, a renowned American scientist who had won the Nobel Prize in Physics and the Albert Einstein Medal, was enticed to move to China by a beautiful young graduate student. The woman, Weng Fan, had served as his translator when he visited Tsinghua University. She later sent him love letters after he returned home to Stony Brook University.[385]

The American scientist was Dr. Frank Chen-Ning Yang. He had been mentored by Enrico Fermi, inventor of the world's first nuclear reactor, and Edward Teller, the father of the hydrogen bomb.[386] Eventually, Fan convinced Yang to go China on a permanent basis, offering herself as an incentive. She was twenty-eight when they married. He was 82, a full fifty-four years her senior.[387] In a remarkable move, he officially gave up his U.S. citizenship and pledged loyalty to the People's Republic of China.[388] "She really makes me feel the energy of youth.... Now I am ten times more famous than before," Frank Yang was quoted as telling the *Xinhua News Agency*.[389] He was not exaggerating about his vitality or his fame. On September 22, 2021, he celebrated his one-hundredth birthday in Beijing. Xi Jinping sent him a flower basket and his personal best wishes.[390]

While the Chinese government has hidden the identities of most Americans who have been lured into its talent recruitment programs, it is known that one of the organizations that foreign recruits are assigned to is the national rare earths development zone in arid central China, a zone that is part of China's nuclear weapons program.[391] Internal PLA textbooks specifically call for using international scientific collaboration to advance the Communist Party's military space and nuclear weapons production goals.

> We will actively use "platforms [CCP jargon for front companies] to strengthen technical research and development for armaments. We will push forward international cooperation in the civil-use space domain and nuclear domain to strengthen the acquisition, digestion, and re-innovation of advanced technology for the defense domain. We will support the defense industry's work units as they establish international cooperation in areas like joint labs and joint technology centers.[392]

An official Politburo document issued in 2017 explicitly linked China's talent recruitment strategy to the CCP's military modernization plans.[393] Chinese planning documents show that gifted scientists and engineers who went to China ended up, by design, as employees of state-run weapons labs and plants. They ended up producing equipment for the PLA and the regime's security services, an arrangement they probably hadn't anticipated.[394] Winners of the Nobel Prize and other international awards are particularly sought after by China's government. Once in country, participants are pressured to contribute to projects the communist dictatorship has identified as strategic priorities.[395]

Dr. Andrew Chi-chih Yao, an American professor at Princeton, was one of their recruitment targets. In 2000, he won the A.M. Turing Award, a recognition with unparalleled significance in the computer science community.[396] The Turing Award is named after the British inventor of the world's first general-purpose computer and father of artificial intelligence: Alan Mathison Turing. While Turing's life was shrouded by official secrecy, it later emerged that he worked for British intelligence during World War II and played a pivotal role in cracking encrypted

Nazi communications, an accomplishment that shortened the war by months and possibly years.[397]

Like Turing, Andrew Yao was absolutely brilliant when it came to code-making and code-breaking. His award was given "in recognition of his fundamental contributions to the theory of computation, including the complexity-based theory of pseudorandom number generation, cryptography, and communication complexity."[398] Yao had been going to China on scientific exchange programs and lecture tours for years. In 2015, he joined Frank Yang in formally renouncing his loyalty to America so that he could become a PRC citizen. Both men went to work at Tsinghua University and joined the Chinese government-run Chinese Academy of Sciences.[399]

Another recruitment case ended differently. On December 1, 2018, at Vancouver International Airport, the Canadian police arrested Meng Wanzhou, the Chief Financial Officer of Chinese tech titan Huawei, on charges of violating U.S. sanctions on Iran. That same day, an American superstar professor who had been recruited into the CCP's Thousand Talents Plan died in mysterious circumstances in Silicon Valley.[400] Zhang Shoucheng was a gifted quantum scientist, rumored to be in the running for the Nobel Prize in Physics. His research had led to the discovery of a previously unknown state of matter, which was critical for producing cutting-edge microchips sought after by companies like Huawei.[401]

After a stint at Tsinghua University in 2008 courtesy of the Central Organization Department, Zhang returned home to Stanford and went on to establish a venture capital firm Digital Horizon Capital (DHVC, previously known as Danhua Capital).[402] His firm served a Chinese government-run entity in Beijing, the Zhongguancun Development Group (ZDG), helping it to develop an incubator in Silicon Valley that funded talented scientists, innovators, and engineers, and, whenever possible, recruited them to work in China.[403] The Chinese government wanted to gain influence over the next generation of megacompanies like Google and Facebook. And it wanted access to their disruptive technologies, which were being developed at Stanford and on nearby campuses.

By 2018, Zhang's firm listed 113 American companies in its portfolio, most of which were looking to commercialize technologies that had been targeted by Beijing as strategic priorities, such as biotechnology and artificial intelligence. Alibaba, Baidu, and other notable Chinese giants that had strong ties to the CCP had been spurred by ZDG to invest heavily into the firm. Professor Zhang raised $91 million in 2014, and another $250 million in 2016.[404] One of the recipients of his venture capital was a company that provided technology to Huawei.[405]

Just when it seemed like there was no limit to what Zhang might be able to achieve, everything came unraveled. His firm was highlighted in a U.S. government report on the Chinese Communist Party's infiltration of Silicon Valley. A week-and-a-half later his body was found, along with a short note, suggesting he committed suicide. His note said he was battling depression, but some posited that Chinese agents might have been involved.[406] His wife told police investigators that he had visited China three weeks before his death, and had suffered "lots of anxiety and near-nightly insomnia" ever since his return.[407]

In 2020, FBI Director Christopher Wray told reporters that the CCP had been carrying out a covert action it called "Operation Foxhunt" in the United States. The operation was part of a global campaign to locate, stalk, and eliminate ethnically Chinese individuals who Beijing perceived as threats to state security. Chinese agents used extralegal measures to force victims to return to China or, failing that, forced them to commit suicide. Wray said,

> Fox Hunt is a sweeping bid by General Secretary Xi and the Chinese Communist Party to target Chinese nationals here in the United States and across the world who are viewed as threats to the regime … when it couldn't locate a Fox Hunt target, the Chinese government sent an emissary to visit the victim's family here in the United States. And the message they said to pass on? The target had two options: Return to China promptly or commit

suicide. And what happens when Fox Hunt targets do refuse to return to China? Their family members, both here in the United States and in China, have been threatened and coerced; and those back in China have even been arrested for leverage. These are not the actions we would expect from a responsible nation state. Instead, it's more like something we'd expect from an organized criminal syndicate.[408]

A 2008 document issued by the Central Organization Department on the Thousand Talents Plan states that targeted individuals who were not interested in going to China (or were uncooperative) were to be captured via "special methods." In other words, Chinese agents were to force them to do their bidding.[409] Planners in Beijing had anticipated all manner of scenarios and left nothing to chance.

Professor Zhang's tragic case might seem extraordinary, but FBI statements and CCP documents show that his experience was probably normal in a system that relies on terror tactics to sustain itself. If he died alone, he was a victim among many, and in very good company. In 2018, shortly before the PRC's official Thousand Talents Plan website went off-line, Beijing announced that it had successfully netted over 8,000 experts from abroad, who had been assigned to 115 entities selected by the Chinese government and military.[410] A research paper published by the Hoover Institute, a think tank at Stanford University, reported that over 300 government and 600 corporate personnel from America had been among the recruits.[411]

Assimilation

The Thousand Talents recruitment program was just one of many programs. Acquiring the brainpower of overseas Chinese nationals and foreign experts was a top priority of China's ten-year talent development plan (2010–2020), which ordered the party-state to produce 3.8 million researchers, led by forty thousand elite S&T experts with deep international ties. The plan further issued quotas for forty-two million business professionals that were needed to compete for world markets. Most important, the plan called for the CCP to build a superelite of one hundred strategic executives. Centrally selected billionaires would be in charge of running China's mega-corporations and tasked with dominating the ranks of the global Fortune 500.[412]

To ensure absolute loyalty, the long-range talent plan called on Chinese government officials to hone "innovative methods" for deepening influence over its super-performers, thereby protecting state security.[413] When CEOs grew complacent, stepped out of line, or became embroiled in corruption scandals, Beijing had no compunction about arresting them, shuttering and restructuring companies, and destroying massive fortunes.[414] Maintaining top-down control was far more important to the regime than petty economic considerations. This was a matter of grand strategy. It was about ruling the world.

According to the textbook *Great Power Diplomacy with Chinese Characteristics*, pulling great minds into China's orbit goes hand in hand with the regime's broader aims.

> Innovation in science and technology and manufacturing requires access to technology, talent, capital, and markets.... China has long benefited from those countries in the world with open economies. It is necessary for us to maintain the initiative as we strengthen international cooperation and open others up and open ourselves up. Xi Jinping has said that we must both "recruit others in" and "send ours out," assimilating into global innovation networks for the purpose of raising the level of China's international cooperation in science and technology innovation. This will ensure that China can maintain and increase its ability to innovate.[415]

China's global strategy hinges on Beijing's ability to leverage predatory economic policies to exploit the American-led capitalist system. Here's how it works. On the one hand, Chinese state-backed companies take advantage of the openness of the system to attack American competitors, poaching their talent, stealing their proprietary technology, gaining their managerial knowhow, and finally underselling them to erode their competitiveness. On the other hand, the Chinese government uses a great wall of red tape and protectionism to keep foreign companies from gaining any defensible position within China's own market.

American executives who move their companies to China are forced to form joint ventures with local CCP-controlled entities. These partnerships are usually profitable at first, sometimes intoxicatingly so. Then, over time, the foreigners are systematically infiltrated, manipulated, and corrupted. In the end, they are either taken over by CCP-controlled companies or financially destroyed, paving the way for the titans of Chinese industry to take over the Americans once lucrative market shares. As FBI Director Wray put it: "China is violating laws and norms left and right, from sophisticated cyber attacks targeting our data and personal information, to economic espionage targeting our intellectual property and our trade secrets. And they're using that information to gain influence on the world stage, to gain economic and political power."[416]

One of the outcomes is that the rare earths products that used to be made by U.S. companies are now made by China's military-industrial complex. The results of Beijing's strategy have been jaw-dropping. China currently has the world's largest rare earths reserve stockpile and is the only country capable of producing every known rare earth mineral. It maintains a centrally managed stranglehold on the global market, leaving the United States and its allies dangerously dependent.[417] This is a remarkable development considering America was the world's largest producer of these minerals during the Cold War.[418] And while the PRC has replaced the United States as the world's leading exporter, it is also a gigantic consumer of what it makes at home.[419]

For American leaders and national security professionals, China's monopolization of medical safety equipment and rare earth minerals should be instructive. The same basic strategy is being leveraged across all the drivers of future technology and economic growth, from green energy to aviation and telecommunications to self-driving vehicles. Unlike their rivals, Chinese companies don't have to make a profit. They are arms of the CCP, subsidized by the state and the military in countless ways. Nor do they have to follow international law. What they must do is to obey Beijing's orders and overtake their foreign rivals. In the absence of a countervailing strategy, this will continue to be a winning formula for China.

With supply chains, the Chinese government and military found a soft underbelly to exploit. Medical equipment and rare earths products are vital to America's society and economy. Domestic production in the United States, however, has withered. China's adversarial approach to trade has pushed investment overseas notwithstanding the vast capabilities and capacities that lay dormant in the United States. The result has been an import reliance that has placed countless lives in danger. It is imperative for the continued security and prosperity of the United States that Washington wakes up to China's strategic successes (and its own policy shortcomings) and begin to act accordingly.

Yet such warnings often go unheeded. Little has been done, so far, to ensure America is able to supply its own needs from trustworthy suppliers.[420] This leaves the nation, and especially the military, in a precarious situation. The Chinese authorities have demonstrated that they will go to great lengths to undermine American interests.[421] Are our government leaders willing to take necessary measures and deny Beijing veto power over their access to essential materials? Prioritizing American manufacturing and encouraging domestic investment, production, and stockpiling is one option. Forming trade blocks with democratic allies and like-minded partners is another. It remains an open question if and when such reforms might actually happen.

Turning Wall Street Red

On December 8, 2020, the U.S. State Department published an extraordinary fact sheet. It was a Tuesday, that day of the week when government reports are believed to have the biggest media impact (when Foggy Bottom wants to bury something, it will publish on Friday afternoon, just ahead of the weekend). The fact sheet showed that a dizzying array of Chinese companies affiliated with China's government, military, and intelligence services were listed on the New York Stock Exchange. These companies had been labeled as "malign" by the U.S. Commerce Department and the Defense Department. But, as the fact sheet indicated, greater transparency alone did little to restrict their access to American money.[422]

Derek Scissors, an expert on China's economic statecraft, estimated that American investment in the PRC exceeded $1 trillion by late 2020.[423] Contrary to the popularly held belief that a trade war was driving the U.S. and China to "decouple," in reality, more than $500 billion in American capital flowed into Chinese government securities during the Trump administration.[424] By 2020, all of the largest publicly traded companies in American were heavily invested in China, and so were federal contractors, state pension systems, mutual fund providers, and university endowment funds.[425]

Beijing uses its influence on Wall Street to tie the future prosperity of U.S. companies, government employees, and individual investors to the stability and success of the Chinese regime. The State Department fact sheet observes: "The Chinese Communist Party (CCP) threat to American national security extends into our financial markets and impacts American investors."[426] As is the case elsewhere across the economy, Wall Street and other major American financial markets are being exploited in ways that threaten their own security. But they can't seem to stop the cycle of addiction and dependency.

For the U.S. government, the first step toward a solution seems obvious:

to shine a light on the problem and hope the private sector will take the threat into account and begin to divest their capital accordingly. Malign Chinese front companies are so deeply embedded in the open U.S. market, and Americans so heavily invested in China's state-managed economic system, that Washington worries actions taken against the CCP could harm all manner of vested American interests and undermine the health of the U.S. economy, itself a national security imperative. In the eyes of government leaders, it usually seems wiser to impower investors with information than to punish them for making bad bets.

Of course, if that doesn't work, harder measures are available. The federal government can conduct intrusive audits of Chinese companies with U.S.-traded stocks, and delist those with ties to CCP entities. The feds can enforce laws that ban American citizens from investing in hostile foreign organizations. They can restrict Chinese investments into sensitive industries such as technology, media, and transportation. There are many instruments of power that can be applied. Still, each measure will require elected officials to confront ugly dilemmas, make painful trade-offs, and overcome powerful lobbying campaigns.[427]

In the meantime, American investors are free to continue flowing their money into Chinese companies known to be supporting China's military buildup and its system of mass surveillance, repression, and genocide.[428] Firms on Wall Street increasingly understand the unfair advantage Chinese companies have and, in many cases, are betting on China's continued growth because of it. In 2021, when officials and lawmakers in Washington attempted to pass legislation closing regulatory gaps that allowed outbound investments into China (and the offshoring of critical supply chains and technology infrastructure), business groups lobbied against the bill. A spokesman for the U.S.-China Business Council said that current export controls were already good enough to ensure national security.[429]

White House National Security Council officials often disagree with the pro-China business community. But they seem to have little prospect of countering the generous tax breaks and subsidies offered by China's government, which financially incentivize American companies and investors to support the CCP's bid to dominate those critical technologies that it needs for future geopolitical primacy.[430] In America, corporate executives have a responsibility to maximize shareholder profit. This means that, as long as its legal, they must go wherever the money is. The genius of Beijing's approach is that it allows the Chinese government to ensnare the West's capitalists, turning them into unwitting agents of international communism. The same Chinese companies that are helping the Communist Party lay the groundwork for its future plans are also some of the hottest stocks on the New York market.[431]

As of this writing, Wall Street and its clients continue to invest avidly in China and, by way of extension, the eventual demise of capitalism and democracy. The attempts of American business leaders to profit off a repressive system are far from unique. Silicon Valley's largest companies are actively engaged in the business of techno-authoritarianism. For decades, they have been developing and selling the surveillance and censorship tools the CCP needs to maintain its one-party dictatorship in China.

Fortunately for those living in Silicon Valley, their technologies could never be applied the same way in the United States. Or could they? Is it possible that the amazing algorithms American programmers have sold to the Chinese government might be weaponized and turned against their own homes, their own families, their own freedoms and liberties? Is America sleep-walking into a surveillance state nightmare?

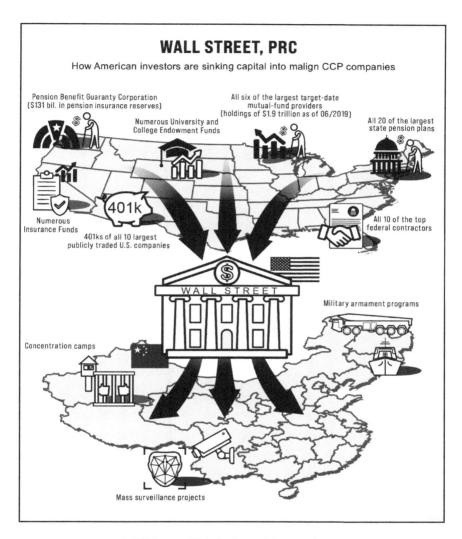

Wall Street, PRC, by Louis Martin-Vézian

9

REWIRING THE PLANET

With the technologies we have laid out in the last two or three years, I have come to recognize that communism can indeed be achieved in our generation.[432]

—Liu Qiangdong, CEO of JD.com

T HE Christmas shopping frenzy was just hitting its peak when the head of the Department of Homeland Security, Chad Wolf, made a stunning public revelation about an item that was on many Americans' wish lists. "DHS is reviewing entities such as the Chinese manufacturer TCL. This year it was discovered that TCL incorporated backdoors into all of its TV sets exposing users to cyber breaches and data exfiltration."[433] Delivered on December 21, 2020, Wolf's remarks received surprisingly little media attention, especially considering the broader context of his message.[434]

TCL is a global electronics titan thought to be worth $98 billion.[435] According to its website, it is one of the largest TV producers in the world and the fastest growing TV brand in America.[436] TCL products are a mainstay at Best Buy, Target, Walmart, Costco, and other big-box stores. The company even owns the naming rights to the iconic Chinese Theater in Hollywood, where film stars attend movie premieres and leave their handprints to the delight of visiting tourists (the theater is now called the TCL Chinese Theater).[437] TCL is an official corporate partner of trusted names across the entertainment industry, from *The Ellen Show* to the Rose Bowl and from *Call of Duty* to the Minnesota Timberwolves.[438] From 2016 to 2020, TCL owned the brand rights to Blackberry mobile devices, allowing it to manufacture handhelds used by corporations and governments around the world for sensitive communications.[439]

Just days before Christmas, a top U.S. lawman was describing a situation to the American public that seemed absurd: millions of families across the nation might have listening devices sitting in their living rooms, hacking their networks and collecting their personal and private information. As they watched Netflix, played video games, and worked online, their own smart TVs could be surveilling them, piping their images and conversations back to server farms in China.[440] It was almost too dystopian and dark to believe. It sounded suspiciously like some counterspy at DHS had read George Orwell's classic novel *1984* one too many times and had come to believe his screens were spying on him.

But the DHS security review had not been triggered by warnings from intelligence agents. The alarm had been sounded by a geeky team of independent security researchers who had discovered a strange technical glitch in their smart TVs and reported it to the company. The researchers made the issue public only after they were ignored by TCL representatives and then discovered the company had accessed their TVs without their knowledge and prior consent.[441] When pressed by a reporter, TCL said it had a security vulnerability that it fixed with a patch, a patch the researchers complained had been applied remotely, "without any notice from the company and no visible notification on the device itself."[442]

The remote "silent patch" indicated that the company had installed backdoors in its smart TVs. One of the researchers concluded, "This is a full on back door. If they want to they could switch the TV on or off, turn the camera and mic on or off. They have full access."[443] TCL denied any wrongdoing but admitted it had remote entry tools for "maintenance." These could give it, or others, control over the machines, including their cameras and microphones.[444] TCL's website belatedly released a security alert, and the company issued a statement that thanked the security researchers and said,

> Once TCL received notification, the company quickly took steps to investigate, thoroughly test, develop patches, and implement a plan to send updates to resolve the matter.... TCL takes privacy and security very seriously, and particularly appreciates the vital role that independent researchers play in the technology ecosystem. We wish to thank the security researchers for bringing this matter to our attention as we work to advance the user experience. We are committed to bringing consumers secure and robust products, and we're confident that we're putting in place effective solutions for these devices.[445]

Yet for all its assurances, best practices, and positive impact on American culture and society, TCL was a still Chinese company. And that meant, by PRC law, it had a legal obligation to cooperate with the Communist Party's military and intelligence services whenever asked.[446] The DHS chief said, "TCL ... receives CCP state support to compete in the global electronics market, which has propelled it to the third largest television manufacturer in the world."[447] Secretary Wolf pointed out that there were "numerous examples" of the Chinese government "leveraging PRC institutions like businesses, organizations, and citizens to covertly access and obtain the sensitive data of businesses to advance its economic and national security goals." As a result of this, "CCP-aligned firms rake in tremendous profits."[448]

No evidence was produced that showed TCL had broken American laws or shared user data with the Chinese government, and fears of a worst-case scenario were probably overwrought. Nonetheless, this was not the first time U.S. government officials had voiced concern. On Tuesday, November 26, 2019, just three days before the Black Friday shopping blitz, the FBI warned: "Your TV manufacturer and app developers may be listening and watching you.... A bad cyber actor may not be able to access your locked-down computer directly, but it is possible that your unsecured TV can give him or her an easy way in the backdoor through your router."[449]

A week later, the FBI issued a follow-on notice, saying that the risks didn't end with smart TVs. Thanks to the Internet of Things (IoT), the entire American home was vulnerable. "Basically, this means everything else in your home that connects to the world wide web.... Digital assistants, smart watches, fitness trackers, home security devices, thermostats, refrigerators, and even light bulbs are all on the list," wrote the FBI. Potential threats facing holiday shoppers even included "remote-controlled robots; games and gaming systems; interactive dolls; and talking stuffed animals."[450]

It seemed unlikely that the FBI and DHS could prove beyond a reasonable doubt that Chinese companies were dangerous without exposing classified information. Nonetheless, American national security leaders decided they had a professional duty to stop taking chances, and their actions spoke volumes. In 2020, it was reported that a growing list of Chinese technology products, including TCL's smart televisions, could no longer be used by the federal government.[451]

For some experts, the restrictions didn't go far enough. State and local governments were still spending taxpayer money on Chinese products that Washington had felt compelled to ban. The very same electronics that the White House and Pentagon kept off their own networks were still spread across the nation. A report published by Strand Consult, a technology consultancy firm, cautioned local government leaders that, "Once the products from these vendors are installed, they can access sensitive personal and financial information held by courts, police departments, elections departments, education departments, children and family services, and other social service providers and agencies."[452]

A *Forbes* article painted an even bleaker picture, suggesting that a hemorrhaging of vital personal and private information might be the least of the nation's worries. American prisons that had installed TCL sets within their facilities could have their networks hacked from the outside, according to one of the computer security researchers it quoted.[453] This was about much more than breaches of privacy and the exfiltration of commercial secrets. China's government might be poised to conduct devastating sabotage attacks against facilities that hold dangerous criminals, and Americans might not know what hit them until it was too late.

Security authorities suddenly questioned the wisdom of allowing Chinese technology companies access to the U.S. market. But while officials grappled with the problem of how and where to establish guardrails to protect the essential functions of government, it was increasingly clear that everyday Americans were exposed and would probably have to fend for themselves. The FBI notice urged concerned citizens to change their passwords, secure their networks, and regularly update their devices. "Your fridge and your laptop should not be on the same network. Keep your most private, sensitive data on a separate system from your other IoT devices."[454] But what if both the fridge and laptop were made by Chinese companies that had been ordered by the PLA or MSS to install back doors? The FBI didn't say.

In Washington, the Internet was increasingly being viewed through the prism of strategic competition. That made it a critical geopolitical domain, something that affected the entire country. Yet it still seemed far removed from the humdrum concerns of most of society. A large and growing body of evidence suggested Chinese machines that connected to the web could become a potential threat vector for Beijing to exploit.[455] What was going on behind the scenes, however, was never fully explained. Why should it matter to the average consumer if China's government could monitor his or her home, or purloin their state tax records from seven thousand miles away? What difference would that make?

Dan Tobin, a Mandarin-speaking intelligence analyst who taught at the National Intelligence University in the DC suburbs, sought to correct the oversight. He knew that the CCP's online ambitions went far beyond what most observers assumed. In testimony submitted before the

U.S.-China Economic and Security Review Commission, he wrote that the regime in China was exporting its authoritarian system. To this end, the Communist Party planned to use digital infrastructure to "rewire global connectivity through Beijing."[456]

Tobin made his case using open-source intelligence – publicly available documents and academic studies – and said the debate on China's strategic intentions should have ended years ago. Tactfully left unsaid by Tobin was that the debate obviously hadn't ended because Congress, like the entire China studies community, was still asking basic questions, rehashing old disputes, and achieving little consensus.[457] The future of American-style democracy and freedom was at stake, and no one agreed about what to do.

How had CCP-controlled electronics makers neutralized their opposition, infiltrated store shelves, and gained such a strong position in the American information ecosystem? Why was removing them a seemingly intractable problem? And if Big Brother actually existed and wore a Mao suit, what did he plan on doing with everyone's data?

A Curious Field Trip

One Monday morning, Xi Jinping decided to take the Politburo's regular study session outside the confines of the CCP's leadership complex in central Beijing.[458] There was a chill in the air, and the skies were the color of fresh concrete. It was a smoggy day, hardly ideal weather for a bunch of old timers to take a daytrip. Nonetheless, they set out, and after a relatively short drive the twenty-five members of China's top decision-making body arrived at their destination.[459]

Little is known by the Chinese people about the Politburo's operations. Prior to this moment, China's superelite officials had always gathered together behind closed doors. Nothing like this field trip had ever happened before.[460] So, it was a big deal when they rolled in, flanked by their bodyguards and a handful of generals. And it was an even bigger deal that they chose to grace one particular location with their power and presence.

Referred to by the CCP as "China's Silicon Valley," the Zhongguancun Science and Technology Park (or Z-Park for short) is located in northwestern Beijing near Tsinghua University, the Central Party School, and the government-run Chinese Academy of Sciences. A galaxy of China's most famous business stars calls the area home. It's the birthplace of computer giant Lenovo, search giant Baidu, entertainment giant Tencent, online shopping giant JD.com, consumer electronics giant Xiaomi, and social media giant ByteDance (the entity behind TikTok, Douyin, and Toutiao).[461]

The district plays host to countless Fortune 500 companies. Microsoft, Intel, IBM, and Google all have offices and R&D labs there.[462] Z-Park's linkages across the international tech ecosystem are proudly heralded by the Chinese government. But for all its seeming openness to the outside world, Z-Park has many secrets, and it shares little in common with California's original, free-spirited mecca of start-ups and misfits.

Apple's legendary founder, Steve Jobs, who told the world to "Think different," could never have made it big here. Z-Park is a government-planned science and technology base, controlled in a Marxist-Leninist fashion by the state. There is no civil society in China, and no organization or group is allowed to exist outside the control of the CCP. Like everything else in China, Zhongguancun's affairs are overseen by a Communist Party committee, whose members are charged with the development of long-term strategy documents and the fulfillment of a quota system.[463]

Z-Park is the kind of place where people put on nerdy airs and claim to seek authenticity and uniqueness. A sign outside a local café promises "You are just one garage away from entrepreneurship, one coffee away from innovation."[464] In reality, the electronics district is an extension of the regime, and independent political views and maverick dispositions are rigorously repressed. By design, it's a place full of mainstream, corporate yes-men hiding in hipster clothes. Aspiring unicorn founders have to submit to their political masters and conform to CCP dictates before they can do anything else. A star that wants to shine brightly in China's IT universe has to agree to serve the government and the military.

Hundreds of local technology companies have security clearances and are major players in China's military-industrial complex.[465] An authoritative report that was posted online (but later digitally scrubbed by the authorities) said that Z-Park's future "will be driven by the Chinese military's needs.... It will be about seizing the opportunities presented by the buildup of national defense and the PLA as they go from modernization to informationization."[466] The report said that Z-Park's companies manufacture encrypted communications, military robotics, and big-data products – everything the regime's watchmen need to keep the Politburo safely at the top of the obelisk that is China's rigid social hierarchy.[467]

The conformity expected of Chinese businessmen extends up to the summit of power. After the Politburo's visit to Zhongguancun, the government acknowledged that the senior leaders had been there and released photos of them. Those images showed China's great men all wearing the same facial expressions and matching outfits. Everything from their nylon jackets and white shirts to their badly tailored suit pants and scuffed-up black shoes appeared to have come from the exact same wardrobe. And the dazzling backdrop to the group portrait seemed more like a film set than a campus of learning.[468]

The Politburo's scripted visit to Z-Park was Chinese political theater at its finest. So much so that the overall scene presented by the Communist Party's propaganda services looked like something right out of a science fiction movie. We can imagine the script: two dozen humanoid robots made by a FBDM (Faceless Bureaucrat Duplication Machine) escape the lab and wander sleek exhibit halls with glowing digital wall screens, trying to find their creator. Adventure and drama ensue![469]

Yet, while they may have appeared somewhat robotic, these men were actually flesh and blood, and their time and attention had limits. According to media reports, they were given a quick introduction to Z-Park by

China's science and technology czar. They toured the spotless grounds and chatted with unnamed executives and scientists to hear about the latest research. They asked a thing or two along the way about big-data analytics and advanced chips.[470] They glanced at diagrams explaining what was being developed in areas such as cloud computing, additive manufacturing, and nanotechnology.[471] Then, they got on VIP buses and rolled out. Total time on the ground? One hour.[472]

Images of the officials seem to indicate that, for most of them, this was an unwelcome study session and probably very boring.[473] An official at the Central Party School claimed the leaders' outdoor study session was "a great innovation that shows that the [CCP] is a Marxist ruling party that is good at learning, knows how to learn, and loves to learn."[474] Nonetheless, had the Politburo taken a vote by secret ballot that day, it seems likely that they would have chosen to stay tucked behind the forbidding walls of their headquarters, where they could enjoy the private comforts of their warm conference center, their charming attendants, and their purified air.[475]

The Party elite are used to eating ingredients sourced from a network of "special farms" built for their safety.[476] And, as a general rule, they expect researchers to come to them with intellectual nourishment, not to have to go out and harvest it themselves.[477] Moreover, they prefer discussions on political theory to the hard sciences. "The communists have always attached significance to the basic tenets of Marxism," explained a *People's Daily* article on the Politburo's study habits. "During the course (of recent study sessions), Marxist Philosophy has been studied twice, and basic Principle and Methodology of Marxist Political Economics has also been studied.[478]

Chairman Xi has a different view than his comrades on certain issues, and the application of Marxism seems to be one of them. The power of advanced technology fascinates him and, unlike his predecessors, he has little interest in collective decision-making. He has made himself the one man in China empowered to "think different," and that's just what he intends to do. We have every reason to believe the day's trip to Z-Park engaged his imagination and invigorated him. A photographer captured him gesturing and talking excitedly as he led the dull, tired-looking cohort around the grounds.[479] At the conclusion of the visit, he declared to the group that the technology revolution they were witnessing presented the CCP with a rare strategic opportunity.[480] Sources would later emerge to explain what he meant.

Team China: World Thought Police

A leaked military document references the Politburo's historic tour of Zhongguancun. *Great Power Diplomacy with Chinese Characteristics* tells readers that the technology revolution Xi spoke about that day will affect all mankind.[481] And the new information age, based on the Internet, will affect every domain of human life: the way people work, shop, and live. Here, then, was the chance that the Communists had long been waiting for. "As innovations and breakthroughs in technology impact more and more areas, they have the power to advance forward the wholesale re-shaping of production and the economic structure of humanity," states the document.[482]

"Every nation is engaged in a fierce competition in the domain of science and technology. Every new breakthrough has the potential to bring unforeseen competitive advantages."[483] The text explains that the CCP aims to become the apex predator on the food chain of international production. It describes a race for global tech supremacy and says Beijing will win by infiltrating global innovation networks. China will siphon off international talent and technology, while investing outward to capture elites and shape foreign organizations. Its far-reaching influence campaign will put the Communist Party in a position to set new global standards, make new global rules, and enforce new global norms.[484]

"We will provide China's Thought Path and the China Model for governing the development of the entire global Internet," declares the document. "As a great power leader, China has responsibilities and burdens. This is a manifestation of that."[485] Another document, *Realizing the Deep Development of Military-Civil Fusion in Our Overall Setup*, confirms that the CCP plans to use the Internet to create a global collective.

> Network and information technology are integrating in every way into society and production. The interests of every country overlap and merge in cyberspace. One singular cyberspace domain that is safe, stable, and prosperous. This is increasingly important for the peaceful development of any country and indeed the whole world. "A Community of Common Destiny in Cyberspace" is China's proactive answer to the developments of this age.[486]

The document goes on to say that mankind's reliance on the Internet is continually getting deeper, and China's government will strive to intertwine humanity together, ensuring that all countries of the world become part of a Marxist collective. The CCP's technology web will be so all-pervasive that Internet users won't be able to escape, even when they are off-line. The prevailing relationship between individuals and Beijing's collective will thus become: "We either prosper together or suffer together."[487]

Information networks, the document asserts, are the "central nervous system" of modern societies. "They are infiltrating into every last space relevant to the life and survival of mankind." This system can be applied to accelerate the advent of a radically different global order. "Across society, virtual space and the real world are being woven together. Objectively speaking, the international community is becoming so interconnected because of the global Internet that, with each passing day, it comes closer to becoming a singular collective body."[488]

If the world of the future is going to be seamlessly integrated through tendrils of technology so vast that they make all mankind resemble one living organism, whichever government controls the brain will have unmatched power and reach. In 2001, China's then-paramount leader Jiang Zemin referred to the Internet as a "political, ideological, and cultural battlefield."[489] For him, the global battle started at home. On his watch, the Chinese government ordered technology companies, both domestic and foreign, to help it monitor and censor online content.

The Party constructed what became known as the "Great Firewall of China," a system of content filters that today prevents Internet users in China from accessing foreign social networking sites like Facebook and Twitter. News stories, academic reports, and blogs on subjects the CCP doesn't want people to see are blocked, and their authors in China hunted down. When the regime's secret police can't stop overseas Chinese dissidents or human rights groups, they hit them with malicious cyberattacks or arrest their relatives and friends in China, holding them hostage to gain leverage.[490] In many cases, the Chinese government sends agents abroad to find and intimidate their targets on foreign soil.[491]

In 2004, Yahoo! China was ordered by MSS to finger a Chinese reporter who had used his Yahoo! account to send an internal document to a human rights group in New York (the document was a list of censorship instructions for the June 4 anniversary of the Tiananmen Square massacre). Under pressure from Chinese intelligence, Yahoo! turned over the name behind the account. It also gave up the contents of the email and the locations where it was accessed. The journalist was subsequently arrested and, after a two-hour long trial, sentenced to ten years in prison for "leaking state secrets."[492]

In 2007, then CCP general secretary and PRC chairman Hu Jintao told his Politburo colleagues that their defensive approach – blanketing the Internet with government propaganda, while censoring regime critics and stopping the spread of unwanted foreign ideas – was necessary but insufficient. The Great Firewall's smart barricades and online human monitors needed an offensive army of thought police. Hu said the Communist Party must "assert supremacy over online public opinion."[493] This was an expansionist endeavor. To gain narrative dominance, China's government had to crush ideas that it deemed as hostile before they could spread. That meant attacking them at their point of origin, which could be anywhere on the planet.

By 2012, when Xi Jinping rose to power, web searches in China for the word "truth" had been blocked by regime censors. Evan Osnos reported that web users looking for the truth saw the following notice pop up on their screens: "In accordance with relevant laws, regulations, and policies, search results for 'the truth' have not been displayed."[494] By tightening its censorship regime, the CCP managed to maintain control over Chinese society even as the economy boomed. Pacifying the Chinese Internet was a remarkable achievement. Yet for Xi and his comrades, this was only the beginning. Beijing was in the process of building online thought weapons the likes of which no one had ever seen before.

The CCP has developed artificial intelligence technologies that could find and obliterate unwanted content and automatically write and spread its own messages globally. According to Kai-fu Lee, author of *AI Superpowers: China, Silicon Valley and the New World Order*, ByteDance was one of the first companies to master the relevant technologies and techniques. Its news and information platform, Jinri Toutiao "Today's Headlines" (more commonly known by the shorthand Toutiao), trained a special algorithm to hunt and destroy "fake news" online. The company then wrote another special algorithm to create and sow disinformation. When both these AI weapons were ready for battle, Toutiao launched them against each other. What followed was a digital contest of wits that made both programs stronger and helped the company become extremely valuable.[495]

In 2017, Toutiao bought a news aggregator in France and Musical.ly, a massively popular Chinese video app that's now known as TikTok.[496] In August 2019, the *Washington Post* reported that ByteDance was "working closely with the Communist Party to censor and surveil Uighur Muslims in China's western region of Xinjiang."[497] Shortly thereafter, the *Guardian* newspaper in London reported that TikTok censored users' videos and was "advancing Chinese foreign policy aims abroad through the app."[498]

In 2021, TikTok updated its privacy policy in America to say it "may collect biometric identifiers and biometric information as defined under U.S. laws, such as faceprints and voiceprints." The new policy said TikTok may "share all of the information we collect with a parent, subsidiary, or other affiliate of our corporate group."[499] Samantha Hoffman, an expert at the Australian Strategic Policy Institute, wrote:

> ByteDance's own privacy policy says it will share data without the subject's prior consent if "the data relates to national security, national defense, public security, or public health." ... The very definition of activities that allegedly harm national security is arbitrary at best in China. It effectively boils down to what the state wants, the state gets.[500]

If these revelations blemished the company's reputation, it didn't show. Users around the world continued to trust ByteDance's apps. By late 2021, TikTok reportedly had one billion monthly users around the world.[501] This included an estimated seventy-three million users in the United States, where the app had been downloaded 165 million times and was being used by approximately 18 percent of the nation's mobile Internet users every day.[502] A whopping 63 percent of Americans between the ages of 12 and 17 reportedly were active users.[503]

Other Chinese tech titans, including Tencent, Baidu, and Alibaba, have also made significant inroads into the American market. Tencent's WeChat super-app is believed to collect more data than any other commercial system in the world, making it attractive to American investors and researchers alike.[504] In 2017, Tencent opened an AI lab in Seattle and quickly began poaching Microsoft talent.[505] Not to be outdone, Baidu opened two labs in Silicon Valley, one for AI applications (like cloud computing and cyber security) and one for autonomous vehicles. It then opened another AI lab in Seattle.[506]

Alibaba announced a $15 billion plan to establish a global network of research centers, including in both Silicon Valley and Seattle.[507] According to Alibaba, these labs would have an advisory board with members recruited from MIT and other top American universities, and they would collaborate on research with the University of California, Berkeley. Alibaba's aim was to discover "new disruptive technologies" and be "at the forefront of developing next generation technology" in areas such as data intelligence, the Internet of Things, and quantum technologies.[508]

According to Kai-fu Lee, PRC technology leaders tell the following joke. Question: When it comes to AI research, how far does China lag behind Silicon Valley? Answer: 16 hours, the time zone difference between California and Beijing.[509] The dark humor behind the punchline, of course, is that the work of top researchers in America is instantly available to government-controlled research labs China. Some of the smartest professors, scientists, and engineers in the United States already work directly with and for Chinese companies. And almost everyone in the international tech world is willing to collaborate and share insights with their Chinese counterparts. The result is that, increasingly, the transfer of knowledge happens at the speed of broadband.[510]

After two decades of herculean effort, the CCP has gained what appears to be a virtually unassailable position at home. Its domestic Internet is a fortress so strong that few ever attempt to crack its firewalls. This allows Beijing to go on the offensive and export its products and its messages abroad. Perhaps, in retrospect, this was entirely predictable. Perhaps we should not be surprised that the Chinese government tries to convince foreign users to accept "China's Thought Path" and the "China Model." Perhaps we should not be surprised that Beijing attempts to entice foreigners into helping it achieve global digital domination. After all, every government aims to advance what it views as its own national interests. The surprise is that so many freedom-loving Americans agree to the arrangement.

10

DIGITAL DICTATORS

Xi has shown that the subversive promise of the Internet can be inverted ... from an instrument of democratization into a tool of omniscient control.[511]

—John Garnaut

As an experiment, the CCP organized and held its first inaugural World Internet Conference in 2014. A town in the Shanghai suburbs called Wuzhen, known for its historic waterways and canals, was selected to hold the gathering. The conference was a huge hit and has been held in the same place every year since, growing in scope, scale, and influence. Thanks to the conference, Wuzhen's fashionable hotels and coffee houses now routinely play host to Chinese government, military, and intelligence authorities – and foreign tech stars, including billionaire executives like Elon Musk (Tesla and SpaceX), Tim Cook (Apple), and Sundar Pichai (Alphabet and Google).[512]

Xi Jinping personally values the conference so much that he has made it a fixture on his annual calendar of public appearances. For business leaders hoping to catch some face time with the chairman, there's arguably no better venue. Xi gave the keynote speech at the founding conference and has either attended in person or sent remarks via a special representative ever since.[513] According to Xi, the aim of the forum is to promote his Marxist vision of the future. "A Community of Common Destiny in Cyberspace is the extension and development of the Community of Common Destiny into cyberspace. Cyberspace is becoming an important platform for putting the thinking behind the Community of Common Destiny into practice."[514]

In 2021, the theme of the Internet summit was "Towards a New Era of Digital Civilization – Building a Community with a Shared Future in Cyberspace." CCP-controlled media outlets reported that the event drew two thousand representatives from ninety-six "countries and regions" ("regions" likely means Taiwanese delegates were there). In addition, three hundred "renowned companies and institutions" joined the tech expo.[515] By way of comparison, only eighty-three heads of state joined the 2021 U.N. General Assembly, the world's largest annual gathering of world leaders, which was held in New York just a few weeks prior.[516]

Prominent CEOs from Tesla, Intel, Qualcomm, and Cisco Systems all delivered remarks at the event, which was organized by the CCP's Central Network Security and Informationization Committee (also known as the Cyberspace Administration of China), a new body formed by Xi Jinping to facilitate his personal control over the Internet and to promote his ideological influence.[517]

In a recorded video message to the conference, Elon Musk said that he believed next-generation IoT would transform the lives of people around the world. Intelligent and connected vehicles would be especially important, and China would be at the forefront of that transformation. "China spends a lot of resources and efforts applying the latest digital technologies in different industries, including the automobile industry, making China a global leader in digitalization," Musk observed.[518] In compliance with local laws, Musk said Tesla had built a data center in China to ensure that all personally identifiable information the company generated in the PRC could not be transferred abroad and would remain securely stored in China. He concluded, "Tesla will continue to expand investment and R&D efforts in China. Tesla hopes to contribute to building a digitized future of shared benefits, responsibilities, and governance."[519]

The CEO of Cisco, Chuck Robbins, made an appearance at the forum virtually and delivered a keynote speech online. "Cisco is honored to have been part of China's story of development for the last 30 years," he said. "With technologies such as Artificial Intelligence, big data, cloud computing, edge computing, and IoT rapidly developing over the past few decades, we live in a world that is deeply connected."[520] Robbins said that Cisco's work in the PRC was being awarded by the Chinese government "as the best practice of Building a Community with Shared Future in Cyberspace.... We thank you for that honor." He told viewers that Cisco was "well aligned with President Xi Jinping's concept of Building a Community with Shared Future in Cyberspace.... We truly are entering the New Era of Digital Civilization." Robbins said, "Cisco will continue to do all we can to be a model for constructive U.S.-China cooperation."[521] His remarks were welcomed by CCP-run propaganda platforms.[522]

Xi sent a letter to the World Internet Conference that was read aloud to the audience at the opening ceremony by his special representative: "China is willing to work with other countries in the world to jointly bear the historical responsibility for human progress ... [and] enhance the effectiveness of digital government." Xi's letter said China aimed to "let digital civilization benefit the people of all countries and foster a Community with a Shared Future for Mankind."[523]

Xi's remarks at the 2021 World Internet Conference closely echoed the speech he gave at the Zhongguancun Forum, held in Beijing's Z-Park just days prior.[524] At that event, Xi said, "I hope the forum participants will have in-depth exchanges and pool wisdoms to offer insights on how to advance global sci-tech innovation and ... build a Community of Shared Future for Mankind."[525]

According to Xi's speeches (and officially approved writings on Xi Jinping Thought), the Chinese government sees global tech forums, cooperative foreign companies, and international research projects as critical for advancing its global strategy. Speeches from seemingly pliant American CEOs were nice, but they meant little if they weren't translated into real-world actions that benefitted the Communist Party. In 2016, the Chinese government reportedly used extortion tactics to force Apple's CEO Tim Cook to sign a five-year $275 billion deal to continue its operations in the PRC. The coerced agreement was revealed on December 7, 2021. In it, Apple had to agree to support Chinese government research programs and invest billions in Chinese technology companies that directly competed with their American rivals. Apple further agreed to use more components and software from CCP-controlled suppliers in its own devices, a move making Apple more reliant on companies and logistics lines that Beijing controlled.[526]

China's government had drawn Tesla, Cisco, Apple, and other American businesses into the CCP's orbit. Xi's plan envisioned keeping them in place, digesting them, and feeding off their creativity as nourishment to change the political landscape of the world.

> The digital economy is an important component of the global economy.... As the largest foreign market for every internet company in the world, China has already developed a relationship with the world whereby they are assimilated into us, and us into them. We are becoming deeply fused together into a Community of Common Destiny."[527]

Realizing the Deep Development of Military-Civil Fusion in Our Overall Setup says that Chinese-controlled information technologies "are infiltrating into people's lives, into social governance, into economic development, into science and technology and innovation. The Internet is rapidly developing into a bright new point of light in China's economic expansion. It's a new force remaking the world economy."[528]

The document argues cyberspace is not a level playing field, and there is nothing egalitarian about the Internet. Whichever country dominates the core technologies and infrastructure of the Internet can decide how technology resources are allotted to users around the globe. The dominant nation will control the market with their own patented equipment and form monopolies or cartels. They will orchestrate rule-setting bodies and decide online norms. They will use the Internet to manipulate global narratives, influence the way people around the world think, and control what everyone believes to be true.[529]

While this document portrays the Internet as offering China tremendous opportunity, it also highlights what could happen to the regime if it does not gain the upper hand. If the CCP isn't on guard, hostile foreigners could hack into China to steal personal and private information, commit financial crimes, paralyze power grids, and even foment pro-democracy movements. "The American Central Intelligence Agency exploits all manner of gaps to monitor the globe's smart phones, laptop computers, desktop computers, even smart televisions and network-enabled cars," states the PLA textbook. "Incident after incident shows that our cyberspace security mission is heavy and the road is long."[530]

Great Power Diplomacy with Chinese Characteristics makes a similar argument. It foresees future technologies wrapping themselves around every moment of the human experience. It predicts that technology developments will trigger a chain reaction, and the resultant social explosion will cause radical changes across the world. Country after country, business after business, and person after person will be engulfed in China's technology revolution.[531] Reportedly, the CCP has no choice but to race toward a state of supremacy and absolute security. "In the majority of new technology domains, China must control the critical links and dominate."[532]

The document presents robotics as an illustrative case study. "Xi Jinping cares a great deal about China adapting to robotic technologies. He believes that China will become the largest market in the world for robots."[533] The text goes on to state, "We must not only elevate the quality of our Chinese robots, but also do our utmost to dominate the market. China will give robots and smart manufacturing priority in national S&T key point innovation areas."[534] But how to ensuring the robots are loyal followers of the regime's directives and ideology?

"We must control the critical infrastructure of the Internet, which is based on information technology, and control how it is used. That way we can realize a major restructuring and updating of each economic domain."[535] To this end, Beijing is tracking emerging global science and technology developments with an eye to achieving outright control. "We will work hard to catch up and surpass all others, strive to shrink any gaps in critical technology areas, and gain comparative advantages. Comparative advantages decide one's position in the value chain. They decide whether or not we will occupy the summit of the international value chain."[536]

China's electronics exports, digital infrastructure deals, and links to the other global centers of technology production are said to have been successful in changing the political landscape of the world. And the CCP plans to keep expanding.

> Innovation depends on international cooperation. The world has already become an integrated whole thanks to the advance of information technology and the formation of a global economy. Every country, every region, every domain of life have now reached the point where they cannot escape from the demands of the outside world. In order for China to collectivize and exploit the long-term benefits of this, we must cast a wider net and bolster international cooperation in every way.[537]

The Communist Party, then, is in the process of subjugating the Internet and assimilating once-competitive market actors into its centralized collective. "Beijing doesn't want an Apple, Facebook or Google. It wants a super integrated Apple-Facebook-Google that is part and parcel of the CCP," wrote Emily de La Bruyère and Nathan Picarsic in a report on the CCP's approach to technology.[538] China's government intends for its own companies to expand on an epic scale and absorb foreign challengers. It cooperates with American rivals precisely in order to conquer them.

Plugging In

Examining Chinese government and military documents gives us the ability to see right into the CCP, past its outer shell of structures and material power, and into its brains and guts. This gives us, at a minimum, a glance at what the Communist Party thinks and feels, a sense of what makes it tick. It seems clear that the PRC is harnessing the power of cutting-edge technology to spread its ideas and influence around the world. Rather than empower individual users, networked infrastructure can be used to form a dependent, submissive, assimilated world, especially in an age of super-fast and growing connectivity.

Beijing's written records should probably raise questions in our minds. Is every made in China microchip and Wi-Fi router bugged? Is every piece of software and hardware that is manufactured in CCP-controlled facilities a potential Trojan horse? Is every switching room in every Chinese telecommunications company the place of black boxes? Is every smartphone full of malware? Is China colonizing cyberspace and poisoning the digital well?

The answer to these questions matters a great deal. Everything flows through the Internet: diplomacy, ideas, money, weapons, secrets, and influence. The CCP is building the arteries of power in the twenty-first century, arteries allowing all Internet and mobile traffic, every videocall, every chunk of metadata, to flow into and out of China. And countries around the world, including the United States, are plugging in.

The average American doesn't know it, but they are surrounded by unsafe information technology products that are capable of vacuuming up their data and cyber stalking them.[539] Approximately one hundred Chinese companies have already been blacklisted by the federal government because of their links to the PLA. These same entities are nonetheless allowed to sell electronics products to everyday consumers in the United States.[540] Think you can avoid the long arm of the Communist Party by buying products made outside China? Think again. Hundreds of leading and trusted brands have incorporated Chinese IoT technology into their consumer products. This technology enables those products to be become "smart," but also makes them vulnerable to exploitation.[541] It is likely that CCP-controlled products are currently in your home and office, your bank and pharmacy, your local grocery store and police department. Unless you live off grid, they are all around you.

The following list highlights six Chinese companies that are either directly owned by the PRC government or are ostensibly private but have been named, restricted, or blacklisted for security reasons by the U.S. government. All have strong positions on America's commercial IoT market. As you read, remember that these are just illustrative cases, and non-Chinese brands are vulnerable to exploitation too.

GE Appliances (Owned by Haier): Smart refrigerators, smart ranges, smart wall ovens, smart microwaves, smart dishwashers, smart washers, smart dryers, smart ice makers, smart range hoods and vents, smart water heaters, smart water softeners, smart water filtration systems, smart air conditioners, smart dehumidifiers, smart air purifiers, smart coffee makers.[542]

Motorola Mobility and Motorola Home (Owned by Lenovo): Smartphones, cordless phones, corded phones, smartwatches, smart televisions, modems, routers, Wi-Fi range extenders, cable boxes, baby monitors, home surveillance cameras, home security systems, pet safety systems.[543]

TCL: Smart TVs, tablets, sound bars, video call cameras, smartphones, headsets, air purifiers, Wi-Fi routers.[544]

Lenovo: Computers, laptops, monitors, tablets, webcams, docking stations, graphic cards, headsets, speakers, soundbars, adapters, smart plugs, smart switches, smart bulbs, smart light switches, smart security keypads, surveillance cameras, motion detectors, temperature sensors, ambient light sensors, smart power strips, Wi-Fi smart door locks, wireless printers, Bluetooth tracking devices, intercom stations, big-data analytics, artificial intelligence solutions, cloud computing, data centers, edge computing, high performance computing, business applications, client virtualization and infrastructure.[545]

DJI: Commercial flamethrower drones, smartphone camera drones, crop dusting drones, multispectral drones, mapping drones, firefighting drones, law enforcement drones, rescue service drones, oil refinery inspection drones, pipeline monitoring drones, oil and gas exploration drones, construction management drones, power grid management drones, land surveying drones, urban planning drones, educational robots.[546]

Hikvision: Surveillance cameras, video recorders, web cameras, metal detectors, card readers, fingerprint readers, access keypads, identity authentication terminals, video access control terminals, network access controllers, body worn cameras, smart doorbell cameras, video/audio distributors, video intercom monitor tablets, security alarms, switches, encoders, decoders, monitors, digital signage boxes.[547]

As we've seen, Beijing is exporting tools of mass surveillance, automated censorship, and totalitarianism. To shed light on why this is happening and what it means for the future, it may be instructive to explore not only how the CCP does business, but also how it, as an organization, thinks and feels about the West and the United States in particular.

What hidden forces animate China's ruling elite? How do they see things, what do they want, and what does their strategic playbook mean for U.S. citizens? Could China's government use its growing leverage to curtail Americans' freedom to express themselves? What are the implications of its digital dominance for our jobs and livelihoods? Can democracy survive in a re-wired world?

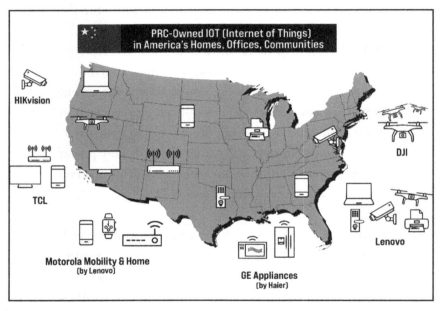

PRC-Owned IoT in America, by Louis Martin-Vézian

11

STRATEGIC SATURATION

> When it comes to combat in the ideology domain, we
> don't have any room for compromise or retreat. We
> must achieve total victory.[548]
>
> —Xi Jinping

I MAGINE you are a communist. Imagine you have gone through the
Chinese Communist Party's invasive vetting process and done all that it
requires. Imagine you have sworn your loyalty to the hammer and sickle.
You have made the right connections. You have read the right books,
written the right self-criticisms, said the right things at the right times.
You have enjoyed many lucky breaks along the way and succeeded at
navigating the secretive, alternative universe of Communist Party politics.
You have cultivated strong patrons, influential friends, and a veritable
legion of well-placed clients who want to do you favors. You've risen
up through the ranks all the way to the top and now occupy a critical
seat on the Politburo.

How have you been trained and indoctrinated to perceive the world?
What have you seen and learned in Beijing's halls of power? What perils
have you dodged? What cruel misfortunes have you overcome? Who
have you been forced to squelch to climb up – or maybe just to survive?
How has your lived experience as a Communist changed you over time?

What are the undisciplined desires, unhealthy appetites, or fearful visions that keep you awake at night?

Now look ahead. What's your next power move? What's after that? Where do you want to be in five years? In ten, in twenty? Where do you want China to be? What's your vision for the future of your nation, your culture, your race, your world? And what are you willing to do to breathe life into those dreams of yours?

There are many ways we can try to answer these elusive questions. Whatever we do will require a considerable dose of speculation and creativity. After all, these are extraordinarily complex issues, and some things are inherently unknowable. It seems likely that the best path for us to take is the route of "strategic empathy." In other words, we can try to place ourselves in the position of China's political elites. This doesn't require sympathizing with them. We don't have to agree with Xi Jinping and the CCP's ideology and actions. But we do need an open mind and capacity to explore their frame of reference. If we actually want to understand where they are coming from, we will need to listen to their narrative, take it seriously, and try to place it in the context of their own history.

Spies and Secrets

The CCP has a murky and rarely discussed past that helps explain, arguably more than anything else, its current view of the outside world and approach to foreign policy. Let's start our organizational mind mapping exercise, then, at the very beginning. From its birth in July 1921, the CCP was a secret organization whose members were constantly in the presence of death and the frequent victims and perpetrators of intense, traumatic experiences. The Party started out – and long remained – an illegal, underground revolutionary movement inspired by Marxist ideas.

While the CCP was still in its infancy, Communist International agents from the Soviet Union helped organize and school its fledgling leaders. By the mid-1920s, the Comintern was recruiting and sending hundreds of CCP members to the USSR for clandestine training.[549] Recruits learned that secrecy was always paramount. The right-wing dictatorship that ran the Republic of China (ROC) thought of communists as dangerous terrorists. The authorities would stop at nothing to hunt Party members down and kill them. Many would-be revolutionaries didn't learn their lessons quickly enough and vanished from the scene, often in hideous fashion. Many more would follow.

April 12, 1927, was the CCP's first "Pearl Harbor" moment. That day, Chiang Kai-shek, the dictator of the ROC, launched a massive surprise attack. Thousands of Communists were arrested and executed, many after being tortured for information, primarily the names of their undercover comrades. For a time, the CCP's entire network trembled at the brink of an abyss. By the end of the ROC government's "cleansing," the Party's ranks had plummeted from sixty thousand to ten thousand.[550]

Those who survived, stayed alive by running, changing their identities, and denying their true affiliations. Afterward, they rallied and counterattacked when they could, using their Soviet training to wage a campaign of insurgency and terrorism. Red terror squads organized and led by Zhou Enlai (who later became the PRC's premier) abducted and murdered government "collaborators" and their families, ignited car bombs, and assassinated officials. CCP intelligence intercepted government leaders' communications, infiltrated their offices, and rotted out their military ranks.[551] Nonetheless, the Communists were all hunted men and women, and most were living on borrowed time.

In April 1931, the CCP suffered its second "Pearl Harbor" moment. ROC counterspies arrested Gu Shunzhang, the thuggish director of the Special Services Section, the Party's secret intelligence wing (and predecessor of today's MSS and MPS). Facing torture and certain death, Gu defected and agreed to provide his detailed knowledge of his underground organizations, operations, and agents across China. The damage wrought by the betrayal of its spymaster shattered the communist movement and, once again, almost consigned the Communist Party to an early grave. Fortunately for the revolutionaries, they had an undercover spy ring inside Chiang's secret police force, which saved the CCP from suffering total annihilation.[552]

The spies alerted the CCP leadership to Gu's betrayal, giving them a twelve-hour head start to close safe houses, destroy documents, and flee into the countryside.[553] Nothing could be done to save the rank-and-file from their cruel fates. In the cities of China, the ROC's campaign was decisive and devastating. Thousands of Party members were rounded up and neutralized. Mao Zedong, Zhou Enlai, and their comrades were reduced to waging guerilla warfare in the Jiangxi Soviet, located in the rugged mountains of southeastern China.[554] Soon thereafter, it was estimated that 90 percent of the CCP's urban intelligence assets had been destroyed.[555]

In 1934, the Communists experienced their third brush with death. ROC forces launched a series of effective encirclement campaigns, which trapped the Red Army (the precursor to today's PLA) and then slowly, methodically tightened the noose. Once again, the CCP leadership was saved by spies. They had a secret agent: an ROC general who gained access to Chiang's detailed war plan and alerted Mao and Zhou that an enemy offensive was about to be launched to crush their forces.[556] Surrounded by eight hundred thousand ROC troops, vastly outnumbered, and at the cusp of defeat, the Red Army made a desperate attempt to break through Chiang's lines. Communist agents succeeded at identifying a weak point, a corrupt local strongman, who betrayed Chiang and allowed them safe passage into China's western wilderness.[557]

"The Long March," as the blood-soaked retreat was euphemistically called, was a traumatic episode that killed off most of the revolutionaries left in China. A force of eighty-six thousand Communists left the Jiangxi Soviet in October 1934. At the end of the year-long slog to the revolutionary base at Yan'an, only around five thousand were left.[558] The flame of Marxist-Leninist ideology flickered and smoked for a time but was never entirely extinguished. Mao and his comrades tended the fire for the next fifteen years, feeding it increasingly large quantities of fuel, purging rivals, and spreading communism until, ultimately, it engulfed all of China.

Every organized group of humans has its own collective memory, those stories passed down from generation to generation, words that transmit insider knowledge and share the group's formative experiences. Here was a lesson that would be forever seared into the deepest layers of the CCP's psyche. To stay alive, Chinese revolutionaries had to develop a culture of secrecy to protect themselves against capture, torture, and death. If they survived, they survived against all odds, and it was mostly because of intelligence, their unrivaled ability to know the enemy better than the enemy knew them.

Back in 1922, the Chinese Communists had adopted Lenin's united front concept, which called for using alliances of convenience with enemies to absorb them or, failing that, to kill them. "The Party sought to penetrate the enemy camp within which the CCP could plot against, weaken, subvert, and ultimately destroy its opponent. Akin to a biological virus, united front work attempted to infect the host and then eat away the host from the inside or hijack the host's major organs," wrote Toshi Yoshihara, an American expert on the Chinese military.[559]

Party members either learned to master the dark arts of united front work, or they suffered and died. Survival meant scheming, finding a way to get inside the enemy's head. It meant knowing how to disarm, preempt, and cooperate with the enemy until the moment of truth arrived, that instant when knives flashed and gruesome work began. Success also required fending off inner-Party plots while purging one's comrades. As it evolved, the CCP became supremely pragmatic, flexible, calculating, and ruthless. These were the traits demanded by the job. Coming to power on the road of insurrection, internecine red terrors, and civil war meant adapting to a life of jungle rules.

The Chinese Civil War lasted twenty-two years. During that time, the CCP made and remade itself, adapting to some of the most desperate circumstances imaginable. Mao and his comrades lived inside a nightmare, the kind of thing that people are always quick to hush up after it's over, or simply bury under a mound of glory and myth. Both happened when the CCP established the PRC, a party-state dedicated to radical social engineering, international communism, and world domination.

Rather than forsake the lessons they had learned at such terrible cost, the CCP elite continued acting as though the civil war had never ended. They continued to carry out mass campaigns and purges of those suspected of treasonous tendencies within their own ranks. They infiltrated and destroyed local cultures across the hinterlands: in Tibet, Xinjiang, Ningxia, and, eventually, Hong Kong. They waged an unceasing campaign of coercion and political warfare against the ROC government after it retreated to Taiwan, all while preparing for a possible future invasion.

The Chinese Communists continued recruiting spies and collecting intelligence on enemies near and far via foreign liaisons and united front operations.[560] They remained deeply suspicious, even paranoid, obsessed with monitoring insiders and outsiders alike. The revolution was all-consuming and could never end. There was always another enemy of the people to infiltrate and take down; and, if authoritative CCP sources are to be believed, there always will be until the "original mission" of achieving international communism – and, with it, an earthly paradise – is finally realized.

Mind Control

Today, Chinese textbooks and propaganda materials continue to portray the CCP as a revolutionary, militant party that is locked in a life-and-death struggle for the future of the world. According to its own narrative, the CCP must control ideas and engineer human thoughts and values to maintain control. With the Soviet Union destroyed and Taiwan weak and isolated, the Party now perceives the United States as its main enemy, especially the U.S. Central Intelligence Agency.

An internal PLA textbook, *The Basis for Building the People's Military: The Strong Military Spirit*, informs its readers that the CIA and other "Western Enemy Forces" are engaged in a long-term campaign to infiltrate and destroy them. The document says that China's enemies in the West attack Marxism, Socialism, and Communism. They lure Chinese people, including CCP members and PLA officers, to embrace Western values and individualistic lifestyles.[561]

To defend against CIA infiltration, Chinese military officers are taught to intensify their political indoctrination or "thought work," with a focus on Marxism, Socialism, and patriotic education.[562] To fight back, they are taught to use propaganda – and especially the Internet and social media – to infiltrate their own ideas into the enemy's camp and conquer hearts and minds.[563] The text quotes a speech by Xi Jinping, drawn from a PLA General Political Department document titled *Selection of Chairman Xi's Important Ideas Regarding Military Political Work*:

> The crumbling of a regime always starts in the realm of ideas. Political upheaval and the toppling of a regime could occur in a single night. But changing the way people think is a long-term process. Once the front lines of human thought have been broken through, other defensive lines also become hard to defend.[564]

The text goes on to declare, "The battle for 'mind control' happens on a smokeless battlefield. It happens inside the domain of ideology. Whoever controls this battlefield can win hearts. They will have the initiative throughout the competition and combat."[565] The document again quotes from one of Xi's secret speeches. "When it comes to combat in the ideology domain, we don't have any room for compromise or retreat. We must achieve total victory."[566]

The following pages of the textbook provide PLA officers with a series of directives and guidance on what the Party expects them to do in order to achieve total victory. It exhorts them as follows:

Unceasingly spread Marxism. Constantly make the quality of our propaganda better and better so that it becomes highly appealing and infectious. Make sure that, in the end, Marxism conquers the battlefield of thought and ultimately becomes mainstream across the broad swath of peoples and groups.[567]

The document continues, "Take over the Internet and new media [blogs, podcasts, social media, etc.].... Use positive propaganda to make online media serve our thought work." The text tells its readers that they must, "Strengthen our ability to guide public opinion online.... Strengthen our management of the Internet."[568] The human mind is portrayed as a battlefield, and words, images, and ideas as weapons to be wielded in mental combat.

Strategic Support for the Great Chinese Resurgence has a section that tells PLA officers why they fight. "In the face of China's rapid development and growth, some countries are unwilling to see any other country surpass them. They are especially unwilling to see Socialist China, which has a different ideology and way of social organization than they do, catch up and surpass them."[569] The document makes what could be seen as a thinly veiled reference to the CCP's traumatic experiences in the 1920s and 1930s. "They [the Americans] unceasingly increase their strategic containment and encirclement of China. They engage in political plots, economic containment, ideological infiltration, and, especially, military encirclement against China."[570]

This depiction makes the United States appear remarkably similar to the Republic of China government, which during the Civil War the CCP waged guerilla war against: a massive, domineering force, bent on asphyxiating them. According to this telling, America is a warmonger that weakens others to stay ahead. She wields her power in irresponsible ways to destabilize and debilitate countries around the globe. "From Kuwait to Iraq, from Afghanistan to Libya, and from Ukraine to Syria, the last twenty years have seen the United States leading other Western countries use armed force and sanctions as their main 'hard power' methods," warns *Great Power Diplomacy with Chinese Characteristics*.[571] "The result has been that they leave behind one disaster after the next. Not only have their confrontations caused the people in the affected countries to pay the cost in terrible suffering, the country provoking the trouble [the United States] also has to face the financial deficits caused by its own massive military spending."[572]

Chinese military textbooks interpret Washington's intentions as fundamentally hostile. Proof is offered in the form of White House and Pentagon documents, which are said to represent a clear and present danger to world peace. "On December 8, 2017, the United States published its 'National Security Strategy;' and, in January 2018, it published its 'National Defense Strategy.' It did this to fully exploit its advantages in relative strategic power, to contain its competitors and rivals." The text says, "In the past, terrorists were America's main strategic rivals. Now this has been changed so that China and Russia are its main strategic rivals. Such a change will directly lead to a deepening of global international strategic competition. It constitutes a direct threat to peace."[573]

Readers are told that China is a peace-loving nation, a resurgent nation, a nation with new strength that will be applied toward making the world a better, fairer, more just place for all people. China faces an uphill battle and is not yet strong enough to overcome the United States and its allies to achieve all its revolutionary aims. But it is growing. "China is a peaceful power, a force that restrains war. China's development means that its power to restrain war and promote peace have already greatly grown."[574]

Digital Tyranny

How is China to protect itself from an aggressive, external foe that first encircles and then erodes its enemies from within, leaving ruin in its wake? The CCP's answer is to stitch the Internet into the fabric of Chinese life, to deeply entwine the digital world with the physical world. The regime will make it impossible to buy or sell anything in the new cashless social order without using a smartphone loaded with apps like WeChat that allow the regime's political police to monitor and track each user's every move and control every aspect of their life.

This is akin to assigning each person in China and every Chinese traveler abroad their own mobile surveillance team. If the Gestapo, KGB, or Stasi spymasters of the twentieth century could see China's state security architecture today, it would undoubtedly make them feel infantile in comparison. With the click of a button, the Party can erase any user's bank accounts, lock them out of their own email and social media, and even freeze their digital wallets, making it difficult (if not impossible) for them to purchase a hot meal or use public transportation.[575]

This is Chinese Communism 2.0, a turbocharged social engineering complex designed to be so all-pervasive that no one can escape. By going online, the CCP, the leader of the collective, is ensuring that it can be literally everywhere at once. And by using artificial intelligence tools to automate much of its work sifting through an ocean of data, the regime is making itself so powerful that it might one day no longer even need labor camps. Each person will walk through life trapped inside their own digital prison, and each cell will be tailor-made to fit the occupant's individual eccentricities, flaws, and fears.

Each person in China will have their individuality and autonomy weaponized and turned against them, enslaving them. This is why China's government has invested massive sums and mobilized all its top technology companies to dominate the future information and communications technology battlefield. The CCP has created and is continually refining a thick latticework of digital tyranny at home, and is now in the process of exporting that system around the planet to ensnare governments and societies everywhere. In their textbooks, Chinese military officers receive the following guidance.

We must strengthen the buildup of our intelligence system's capabilities. On the foundation of a large and strong professional intelligence force, we must establish the concept of a large intelligence system. To this end, we must strengthen intelligence collection from Chinese companies overseas, think tanks, civic organizations, and critical people engaged across China's society. We will thereby bolster our intelligence analysis and decision-making capabilities. We must form an intelligence system comprised of both professionals and civilians, all deeply fused together for the purpose of information sharing.[576]

China's government is constructing an AI-powered universe of deception, a neon labyrinth aimed at convincing viewers that true information is false and false information is true. The end goal is to lure, bewilder, paralyze, weaken, and overcome the West.[577] The CCP seems to judge itself most effective when its victims help by investing their own time, money, and talent into the process of their downfall. An amateur will use force to get you into the gallows. A pro will sell you the rope with which to hang yourself. But a master will first convince you to pay him to make the rope, then talk you into recruiting others like you, and finally watch as you all eagerly hang yourselves. That is the kind of power the CCP seems to envision having over the guardians of the free and open world, and, as we've seen, probably already does in many respects.[578]

Smart Leverage

As an icebreaker, consider employing the following weird piece of trivia at your next dinner party. Question: What does the smart "Goliath" crane used to make England's two newest aircraft carriers (HMS *Prince of Wales* and HMS *Queen Elizabeth*) have in common with China's military bases in the South China Sea? Answer: They were built by the same engineering arm of the PRC government.

It may seem strange, but it's actually true. The super crane used by the Royal Navy to build its most important capital ships was supplied by Shanghai Zhenhua Heavy Industries Company (ZPMC), a state-owned enterprise and branch of China Communications Construction Corp. (CCCC).[579] In 2020, the U.S. Department of Defense blacklisted CCCC after the company constructed thousands of acres of artificial islands in the South China Sea and turned them into military outposts.[580]

The company's ties to the Chinese military establishment run deep. In fact, its equipment is routinely used in combat drills. Considered vital military-civil fusion assets, CCCC and ZPMC crane-delivery ships train with the PLA in preparation for future amphibious landing operations against Taiwan.[581] In spite of its known military links, CCCC and its sub-sidiaries continue to build, maintain, and operate critical infrastructure around the world. The state-owned company has such market dominance that, so far, being named and sanctioned has done little to slow it down. Indeed, the U.S. government continues to allow the company to supply critical infrastructure to the American market.[582]

In the United States, ZPMC has coast-to-coast operations. The company's automated gantry cranes are a fixture in nearly every American container port. As you read this, smart cranes supplied by the Chinese government are loading and offloading ships in Los Angles, Long Beach, Oakland, Tacoma, Seattle, Philadelphia, Wilmington, Charleston, Jacksonville, Gulfport, Tampa Bay, Miami, and, among others, Elizabeth (New Jersey).[583] ZPMC has major supply depots in Portsmouth (Virginia) and Los Angeles. This arrangement allows the employees of a Chinese government-run company to enter American port properties, conduct work, and supply cranes built by other manufactures with its own equipment.[584]

"ZPMC has seven known offices in the United States and exports gantry crane equipment to ports across the entire country ... creating ... possible disruption vulnerabilities at U.S. strategic locations," said a report by Pointe Bello, an American strategic intelligence firm.[585] According to Pointe Bello's Ceci Joy Perez, "The presence of ZPMC cranes in US ports presents surveillance risks at key logistical nodes. These cranes are increasingly tapped into ports' digital environment."[586]

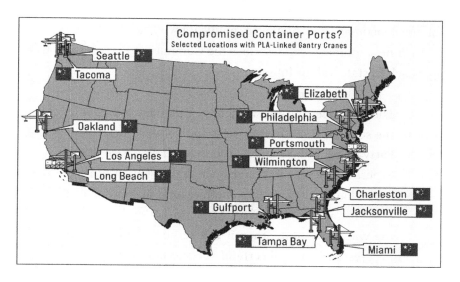

Compromised Container Ports? by Louis Martin-Vézian

In Australia, CCCC builds maximum-security prisons through its wholly owned subsidiary John Holland. These construction projects include the installation of alarms, security camera networks, access controls, and other automated "security solutions."[587] The same PRC state-owned company is involved in the construction of Australia's metro systems, train lines, power grids, data centers, port facilities, water pipelines, and other critical infrastructure.[588] In Mexico, CCCC has updated or expanded the nation's four main ports of Veracruz, Manzanillo, Ensenada, and Lazaro Cardenas, all of which are owned and operated by CK Hutchison, a PRC-based conglomerate that also controls the Panama Canal.[589]

PRC companies are extraordinary actors in the global economy. To outcompete rivals, they draw from China's vast reserves of capital and manpower and, importantly, their bids on international projects are backed by China's diplomats, government banks, and intelligence services. They have made considerable inroads into the Western Hemisphere. As of 2020, CCCC was involved in over fifty major projects in at least nineteen countries in Latin America and the Caribbean.[590] Critical infrastructure projects give Beijing access to huge volumes of data, influence over the health of foreign economies, and, of course, political leverage.[591]

A Chinese military text describes the Communist Party's collectivist approach to statecraft as follows:

> The CCP rules the government, the military, the people, the schools. From east to west and south to north, the Party is everywhere and it leads everything.... Real world experience proves time and again that, in China, as long as the Party cares about something and makes a major effort toward that endeavor, then it can certainly harness the will of the state, then it can certainly make broad progress, then it will certainly be successful.[592]

Chinese telecommunications companies such as Huawei and ZTE have a strong presence in the Americas (and indeed around the world) even though they have been restricted in the United States on national security grounds. In 2017, the Spanish telecoms giant Telefónica chose Huawei to build a its large-scale 4G LTE telecommunications networks in thirteen countries: Brazil, Argentina, Uruguay, Mexico, Colombia, Peru, Panama, Costa Rica, Nicaragua, El Salvador, Guatemala, Germany, and Spain.[593] Telefónica selected ZTE to construct its large-scale virtual network infrastructure in Latin America, covering Panama, Costa Rica, Nicaragua, El Salvador, Guatemala, Ecuador, and Uruguay.[594] While these business deals delivered low-cost digital communications services to customers, they also exposed sensitive government and business communications to CCP surveillance.[595] Countries from Norway to South Africa and Panama to India have all plugged in. Other ZTE partners include Vodafone, Airtel Africa Group, Deutsche Telekom, and Telenor.[596]

China's Grids

In November 2019, Risa Hontiveros, a senator in the Philippines, became concerned when she learned that China's government owned a 40 percent stake in her nation's power grid. It turned out the Philippines government had awarded their power infrastructure to a private corporation that, in turn, used Huawei equipment and employed PRC nationals from China State Grid, a state-owned enterprise. Chinese officials ran the monopoly and directed sensitive operations across the Philippines on a daily basis.[597] According to Senator Hontiveros's testimony, "China is in charge of the nuts and bolts of our country's power grid, with full control of operations and maintenance." She said, "The chairman is Chinese, almost all of the contractors are Chinese, the systems software is made in China and the training is done in China. Which part here is Filipino-run?"[598]

Senator Hontiveros led lawmakers in Manila to call for an urgent national security review. Documents soon emerged that revealed only PRC personnel had the ability to access critical elements of the Philippines' power system. This meant their electricity could in theory be turned off remotely on Beijing's orders. "With a single switch, no electricity would be transmitted to any of our homes, our businesses, (or) any of our military facilities," said the chair of the Senate Energy Committee.[599] But two years later, the situation remained unchanged. A December 2021 review of NGCP – the private corporation in charge of the Philippines power grid – showed its board of directors remained stacked with Chinese government employees.[600]

The Philippines is far from alone in its reliance on the CCP for electricity. China State Grid is the largest utility provider in the world. It builds critical infrastructure and runs utility operations in Brazil, Portugal, Australia, Italy, and at least twenty-one countries in Africa.[601] The state-owned monopoly has deep ties with the PLA. China State Grid has collaborated with the PLA on military research programs, military space projects, and arms deals.[602] Nonetheless, the company has apparently had little trouble convincing foreign leaders to give it the extraordinary responsibility of building and operating their power grids. China's control over critical infrastructure exposes its client nations to extreme levels of coercion. The Communist Party could credibly threaten to shut off their electricity at any time, in many cases along with their gas, water, phones, internet, and, of course, the smart cranes in their container ports.[603] In fact, it could do even more.

A report by Pointe Bello, a strategic intelligence firm, summed up some of the physical threats posed by Chinese infrastructure, warning, "With backdoors, for example, the CPC (Communist Party of China) now has the capability to attenuate systems that connect to a wide range of remote controllers."[604] The report lists the following scenarios:

- Through embedded interfaces a remote actor could stop a ship bridge from raising as ocean traffic approaches and cause a collision that catastrophically interrupts ocean to river or port traffic.
- Remote controllers could cause engines in power plants to over-speed, overheat, and damage their capability to generate electricity for hospitals, factories, storage facilities, server farms, offices, and neighborhoods.
- Potentially fatal catastrophes attach to systems that manage access to traffic lights, tunnels and bridges, airports, and dams.[605]

Global Proxies

The CCP portrays its construction and acquisition of critical infrastructure around the world as a way for China to share the benefits of its immense progress in industry and trade. More cynical observers in the West have come to view these altruistic claims as little more than a thin marketing veneer covering the fact that China is a shrewd player that acts in its own economic self-interest. For them, the idea that Chinese investments are being made out of charity is laughable. It certainly appears to be the case that the cynics are right. But what they often miss is that politics are more important than economics in the PRC, and the power gap between those spheres of human activity is not a narrow crack. It's a yawning chasm.

The ideological drivers for China's international behavior are the main ones to watch.[606] By controlling other countries' physical and digital infrastructure, the CCP seeks to reinforce global dependency on China's government. Are there economic profits to be made? Of course, but that is in many cases more of a long-term concern and in any case of secondary interest to the Party. Some of China's foreign projects are cash-absorbing sponges. Yet while they might do little to bolster the balance sheets of Chinese state corporations, these mega projects have the benefit of plunging their host nations into debt. Those debts must be paid to Chinese banks, which are financial wings of the Chinese government. When countries cannot pay back their infrastructure loans, political concessions are extracted (something which happens rather often since many Beijing-backed projects are high-risk undertakings).

To put it simply, the CCP is investing in the expansion of its influence. It is just as interested in exporting its ideology and political system as its labor pool and industrial capacity. If others will pay for the infiltration of their societies with their own money and political capital, for China, so much the better. As the rulers of the Soviet Union learned in the 1980s, it is unsustainable to prop up proxy governments in the outer empire if the cash flow goes only one way. Beijing does not intend to repeat Moscow's mistake.

The CCP's proxies are expected to pay for the privilege of surrendering their independence and sovereignty. How many countries will continue to do so in the coming years will hinge, in part, on the integrity of their elites and the resiliency of their governments in the face of hostile campaigns to corrupt and conquer them from within. Open societies with robust systems of checks and balances will have a distinct advantage. But any country with strong commercial ties to China is far from safe. The more integrated they are with China, the more data, capital, talent, and technology they risk hemorrhaging, and the farther their national security is likely to drift off course.[607]

Intelligence Failure

Back-to-back administrations in the United States and allied nations have failed to acquire the intelligence they need to obtain strategic empathy. Instead of acknowledging the CCP's political ideology, they simply pretend it doesn't exist. They deny the reality that the government in Beijing has its own unique history and the capacity to think and act independently of what others expect. They treat China like it has little or no agency, like it is just any other member of the international community.

"Politics isn't everything but there is no country on earth where it is more omnipresent, with the exception of North Korea. And there is no political system that is as tightly bound to ideology," observes John Garnaut, who led a Western intelligence effort to counter CCP operations.[608]

Lacking strategic empathy, the United States and its closest allies appear to have been led astray. They ignore voices of caution, ostracize dissenting opinions, and cast prudence aside. In a remarkable indication of how deeply penetrated Western governments have become, Garnaut warns that he and other policy advisors felt compelled to "normalize" the Chinese Communist regime and remove ideology from their intelligence briefings. Empirical evidence is too alien for time-strapped leaders to digest, and, tellingly, China is known to be an issue of extreme sensitivity. Any public servant who wants to be taken seriously in the rarified universe of intelligence and foreign policy has to avoid being seen as "anti-China."

Garnaut writes, "Taking the 'Communist Party' out of 'China' was a way of deactivating the autoimmune response that can otherwise kill productive conversation.... But by stripping out ideology we are giving up on building a framework which has explanatory and predictive value."[609] The result of this intelligence failure is that democratic governments have sleepwalked into a real-life nightmare, the dimensions and horror of which are only just becoming apparent and, if China's staggering military buildup is any indication, may no longer be escapable.

An internal textbook given to PLA officers observes the following: "Xi Jinping has emphasized that our state's ideology and social system are fundamentally incompatible with the West. Xi has said, 'This (incompatibility) decides it. Our struggle and contest of power with the West cannot be moderated. It will inevitably be long, complex, and at times extremely sharp.'"[610]

The same source shines light on what the future might look like. "To use war to protect our national interests is not in contradiction with peaceful development. Actually, such is a manifestation of Marxist strategy."[611]

We Surround You! by Louis Martin-Vézian

12

WORLD EMPIRE

The two aims of the Party are to conquer the whole
surface of the earth and to extinguish once and for all
the possibility of independent thought.[612]

—George Orwell

IT's not clear when the fateful decision was made by the Politburo to act.
Nor is it clear how it happened, what confluence of events pushed the
debate in that direction. And, let's be perfectly honest, we are assuming
the policy was actually debated, but who knows? Maybe it was one of
those ideas that had already grown so popular among Chinese Communist Party elites that, by the time it came to a vote, the consensus was
universal. Maybe it had long seemed like the obvious thing to do, and
the only question was when to begin and how fast to move. Maybe it
was inevitable, a simple matter of waiting for enough money to accrue
and for the right window of opportunity to open.

Or maybe there was no deliberation. Maybe Xi Jinping woke up one
morning, went into the Zhongnanhai conference center brandishing a
sawed-off shotgun, and his comrades immediately complied with what
he demanded. The latter possibility seems whisker close to zero, but
who can say? Given the opacity surrounding PRC policy making, if

something crazy happened, would we ever hear about it? Would we even know the difference?

While the particular circumstances of the decision are shrouded in mystery, it seems clear that sometime around 2013 Chinese officials agreed to launch a quiet, long-term campaign to do something they had never done before, something they had, in fact, sworn they would never do. What at first appeared to be a few halting, tentative steps, now appears to be a sprint. What seemed very modest and limited, almost meaningless, then escalated.

Beijing started, of all places, in the remote wilderness of Argentina's Patagonian Desert. In 2013, Chinese engineers broke ground on what was supposed to be an international science project. But by 2015, it had morphed into a PLA-run space base, off limits to all outsiders. It was ostensibly a compound for monitoring and tracking extraterrestrial objects in support of China's space program. Today, its true purpose can only be guessed at due to a remarkable lack of transparency. Argentina's government does not have any staff at the site and, for reasons that remain murky, has agreed to allow the Chinese military to operate on its soil without oversight. Official delegations from the local government can access the base only on pre-scheduled tours arranged by Chinese authorities.[613]

The PLA next went to the deserts of Djibouti. The African continent's smallest country by population, Djibouti occupies a strategic location astride one of the busiest shipping lanes in the world, making it an important refueling and transshipment hub. It links the Indian Ocean to the Red Sea and, by extension, the Mediterranean and all of Europe. Various foreign militaries have bases in Djibouti, including the United States, France, and Japan. Chinese navy ships were routine visitors to the area. They had been escorting ships and conducting anti-piracy missions off the Somali coast for years. So, it seemed only natural when, in 2017, China opened its first overseas naval base in the country.

Few seem to have anticipated just what the PLA had in mind and how its installation in Djibouti would be used. Satellite imagery showed that base construction included a large barracks complex for marines and special forces troops, extensive tunnels and other underground facilities, and a long tarmac for helicopters and drones.[614] In 2018, personnel at the base began firing military-grade lasers at U.S. Air Force planes flying into Djibouti, injuring American pilots and triggering a diplomatic incident.[615] The Chinese military expanded the base, which is next to a PRC-owned commercial port, so that it could dock aircraft carriers and nuclear-powered submarines.[616]

Over the next few years, the Chinese government made moves to acquire military airfields in Greenland and the Azores, but were rebuffed by U.S. diplomatic countermoves.[617] Beijing then attempted to set up naval bases in the Persian Gulf and on Africa's Atlantic coast. They were exposed by U.S. intelligence and delayed, albeit perhaps only temporarily.[618] Chinese military representatives suddenly seemed to be everywhere, eager to sign military basing deals at ports and airstrips at far-flung strategic locations.

American officials discovered to their chagrin that Chinese companies already managed a network of approximately one hundred ports around the world. These ports gave Beijing leverage because, once the local governments acquiesced, their civilian logistics nodes could be transformed into PLA bases with relatively little effort. New bases could allow the Chinese military to project power against the continental United States. Moreover, American forces are now being held at risk in places where the Pentagon long assumed it could operate with impunity, places like South America and Africa.[619]

In 2021, the Pentagon sent a report to Congress on China's growing military power that, by Defense Department standards, was extraordinarily candid about the darkening threat picture.

> Beyond its base in Djibouti, the PRC is pursuing additional military facilities to support naval, air, ground, cyber, and space power projection. The PRC has likely considered a number of countries, including Cambodia,

Myanmar, Thailand, Singapore, Indonesia, Pakistan, Sri Lanka, United Arab Emirates, Kenya, Seychelles, Tanzania, Angola, and Tajikistan, as locations for PLA facilities. A global PLA military logistics network and PLA military facilities could both interfere with U.S. military operations and support offensive operations against the United States as the PRC's global military objectives evolve.[620]

The unclassified report warned Congress that PLA bases might soon come online that could be used to launch attacks on the U.S. homeland. "In the unlikely scenario of a war with China, the first strikes will likely come from containerized missiles," one anonymous defense official said, pointing to the possibility that China's global network of commercial port facilities could hide long-range cruise missiles disguised as shipping containers.[621]

In 2019, the CCP Propaganda Department published a handbook on Xi Jinping Thought, a propaganda manual that officials were expected to internalize and quote from to explain China's policies to audiences both foreign and domestic. The manual (or "study doctrine" in Party speak) included the following line: "In the blood of all ethnically Chinese people, there is no gene for invading others and becoming a world hegemon."[622] The implication was that those in the service of the Chinese government were to downplay the CCP's global ambitions. Chinese state-run propaganda outlets followed suit, claiming that, unlike the United States, China "has never encroached on others in history and will not do this in the future."[623] Leaked PLA documents say something very different about Beijing's vision for the future.

Going Global

"If a state wants to strengthen its international strategy and operations, to create a good international environment for itself, the key can be found in strategic capabilities, and, especially, military power. We must be more clear-eyed about the strategic role that military power plays in influencing and shaping the international system," said the PLA's *Strategic Support for Achieving the Great Chinese Resurgence.*[624]

This Chinese military textbook teaches officers that the status of their country is about China's relative power compared to others. It argues that real power comes from a nation's war-making potential and capacity for violence. The text asserts, "The status and role of countries in the hierarchy of the international system, at a fundamental level, comes from their national power, whether they are big or small, strong or weak."[625] The next page of the document further underscores the perceived importance of military power for China's future.

> Countries pursue their national interests. That's their purpose. In their diplomacy, countries use political and military power as their primary means of resolving conflicts between themselves. That's how they obtain their national interests. Looking to history, when we talk about the international system changing shape, without exception, this comes about through the use of violence and war.... Every time the international situation changed in shape and form, military power was used in a major way.... During the most recent example, the Cold War contest between the United States and the Soviet Union, military power also played the critical role.[626]

The text says, "The use of military power in great power competition must not be underestimated.... Military power is always an important metric for measuring each side's strength. It is an important guarantee for both gaining victory in war and obtaining an advantageous international status."[627]

This document offers Chinese military officers an easy way to measure their national power and, in so doing, makes a remarkably jingoistic claim.

> From the perspective of China's military, any provocation from one of our opponents, no matter how large or small, should rightly be seen as evidence that our military power is not yet adequate to meet our state security requirements. It is an inevitable choice to use a strong military to effectively respond to those complex confrontations and severe challenges we will meet during the course of our development as we realize the China Dream of the Great Chinese Resurgence.[628]

In 2018, China's National Defense University published a textbook explaining military-civil fusion and how it fits into the CCP's grand strategy or "overall setup." *Realizing the Deep Development of Military-Civil Fusion in Our Overall Setup* is part of a series of internal PLA teaching materials on Xi Jinping Thought.[629] The textbook was written by a team of military researchers, who compiled and analyzed both open-source and restricted-access speeches and writing they attribute to Xi Jinping.[630] Given the document's purported access to otherwise secret materials, and its unique level of candor regarding CCP intentions and plans, it seems worth quoting at some length.

> Our military is "going out" into the world and integrating into the global economy systematically. As part of our overseas strategy, we are steadily forming an integrated military-civil collective, whereby civilian activities abroad provide camouflage for military activities abroad.

The military follows in the footsteps of civilian entities as they spread. The military then provides protection for civilian entities wherever they go. As the pace of "One Belt, One Road" construction and our military's march outward quicken, the trend is for our internal military-civil fusion strategy to extend out beyond our borders....[631]

[We will] integrate our foreign economic deployments with our strategic and defense deployments so they are one and the same. This includes at foreign ports, docks, and other basic infrastructure projects that are being planned and built. By employing tactics such as "camouflaging our military with our civilian" and "building civilian [infrastructure] for military use," we will stockpile or preposition military capabilities.

At whatever locations matter for China's interests, we will exploit Chinese entities abroad and companies involved in the international transportation business to support PLA joint military exercises, sea lane patrols, international peacekeeping, and other military operations overseas.

[We will] exploit every linkage and every project. We will use all manner of ways to steadily build an interlocking network of backbone military bases, widely spread supply bases, and fueling and logistics depots to support them. These will cover China's main resource supply areas and strategic passageways, radiating around the globe to form a system of support nodes wherever our nation's overseas interests are located.[632]

This text plainly states that the CCP is using commercial ventures to lay the groundwork for a string of military bases overseas. The Chinese government intends to blanket the world with PLA proxies, intelligence collectors, and warfighting assets. Brick by brick, China is establishing sites from which, one day, it could launch attacks and sustain combat operations against America. The Party is putting China on track to become a world hegemon. If Pentagon reports to Congress and internal PLA documents are any indication, China's overseas military bases will rapidly multiply in the years ahead. Beijing harbors global ambitions and plans to gain basing rights at all points of the compass.

Expansion

Realizing the Deep Development of Military-Civil Fusion in our Overall Setup includes several sections on how OBOR supports China's global military strategy. The textbook shows that the Chinese government intends to expand naval power projection around the world by exploiting civilian ships, personnel, ports, and other infrastructure.[633] It points out that China has over 2,000 cargo ships capable of global transport missions and 650,000 merchant marines. It states that China's massive shipping industry has over 1,000 subsidiary organizations spread around the world, and the CCP controls and operates over one hundred foreign ports.[634]

In the text, PLA officers are told to use business deals and local media proxies to gain control over foreign political leaders. The document states in no uncertain terms that Beijing plans to compete against the United States and its democratic allies to seize key territory around the world.

> [We will] engage the United States and other Western forces in contests to grab and buildup strategic points whenever it makes sense, whenever we have the advantage, and whenever the result will favor us. The basic thinking here is that we must protect the security of China's broad economic footprint. The method is to go

through our major enterprises, which are deeply embedded in those nations that matter for us strategically.

[We will] pay attention to "grabbing both heads to push into the middle." In other words, we must gain a grip on foreign government leaders and their business elites by encouraging our companies to invest in their local economies. We must also do a good job packaging and maintaining the images of our companies, and we must guide local public opinion with our propaganda. Finally, we must also "push into the middle" by doing a good job cultivating their middle classes so they like and understand China....[635]

When expanding outward, we must use a range of tactics, pushing straight ahead and around the flanks. [We will] concurrently use methods direct and indirect, hard and soft, to realize a comprehensive security umbrella over "One Belt, One Road" countries. For example, we must have non-governmental organizations like strategic think tanks and civic groups "go out" in the world, providing soft support for "One Belt, One Road" deployments. We must strengthen friendly contacts with key people in target countries and those in their grass roots [local society]. This way, we will effectively counter Western enemy forces attempting to distort and sabotage us.[636]

We must strengthen the buildup of our strategic power projection capabilities by continuing to build up our naval and air arms, increasing our long-range power projection capabilities, adding strength to our frontline military presence, and increasing our overseas crisis response capabilities. Then, we will strengthen our emergency strike capabilities. [We will] strengthen the capabilities and readiness of forces in China aimed at counter-terrorism, stability-maintenance, humanitarian assistance and disaster response, and infectious disease control.[637]

Artistic rendering of PLA Textbook, by Grace Young

The textbook indicates that Beijing seeks to exploit construction projects to improve the PLA's ability to project power globally by land, sea, and air.[638] It states that Chinese road, rail, airport, and harbor projects abroad should meet military requirements to the "maximum extent possible."[639] The textbook also says Beijing has made remarkable gains in the areas of arms sales, military assistance, and defense-industrial cooperation.

> In recent years, as "OBOR" was carried out, it has been beneficial for pushing forward our state's military S&T exchanges and cooperation with countries along the Belt and Road. Our achievements in military-civil fusion overseas have been truly remarkable. For example, China North Industries Group Corporation (NORINCO) has used the arms sales business to effectively obtain over-seas oil developments, mining resource developments, and overseas engineering contracts. We are using arms sales as an important means to advance "One Belt, One Road" construction.[640]

The textbook reveals that Beijing plans to gain greater international market access for further arms sales and engineering contracts. And it seeks to acquire advanced foreign military technologies, so that it can digest them and use them to re-innovate, with a special focus on the space and nuclear domains.[641] PLA officers are directed to carry out military-industrial projects with foreign partners and expand armaments production overseas. "Push forward our state's domestic enterprises as they participate in international markets and develop cooperation with international manufactures," the text tells readers. "That way, we can increase high-end equipment exports and international engineering contracts, and greatly improve support services for our military industry's high-tech equipment globally."[642]

To meet the requirements of its global strategy, the PRC is investing in the most rapid and sustained military buildup ever seen. The Long Term Strategy Group, a Pentagon-funded consultancy, conducted a quiet, multiyear research program to estimate how much China has spent on defense and is likely to spend in the future. In 2021, Dr. Jacqueline

Deal, the group's president (and co-founder of the American Academy of Strategy Education), made key findings public when she warned that, "The annual dollar value of PLA procurement is on course to eclipse that of the U.S. military by 2024.... By about 2030 the United States will no longer boast the world's most advanced fighting force in total inventory value."[643] Deal further pointed out that, "If the Chinese can manufacture highly advanced weapons, it would be foolish to believe that they cannot also learn to integrate and use them according to their specific requirements and organizational culture."[644]

In congressional testimony before the Permanent Select Committee on Intelligence, Captain James Fanell, a retired U.S. Navy Intelligence officer, warned, "By 2030, it is estimated the PLA Navy will consist of some 550 ships: 450 surface ships and 99 submarines. As currently debated in the halls of the Congress and Pentagon, it remains unclear if the U.S. Navy of 2030 will even reach a total of 355 ships and submarines."[645] Fanell summed up the drivers of China's sweeping buildup in the following words: "The Chinese Communist Party is engaged in a total, protracted struggle for regional and global supremacy."[646]

Scenarios

What are the implications of a Chinese military superpower that is intertwined with proxy governments and able to operate freely inside their physical and digital networks? How might Chinese covert actions to exploit businesses impact U.S. national security and defense planning? What would it mean to have undercover PLA units posted at strategic chokepoints from the Panama Canal to the Turkish Straits and from the Gulf of Hormuz to the Straits of Malacca? What would happen if Chinese container ships packed with cruise missiles and commandos were anchored in Mexico, or even Los Angeles? Are we at the cusp of a paradigm shift in the way war will be waged in the twenty-first century?

When we think about the potential for a U.S.-PRC conflict to erupt in the coming years, the first image that tends to come to mind is that of long-range missiles being launched in places like the Taiwan Strait. We imagine those missiles wreaking havoc as ships, subs, and jets slug it out across the vast sprawl of the Pacific. Other battles we might envision are between dueling computer hackers and drone operators striking each other from the comfort of air-conditioned command centers. For Americans, the settings for these scenes of high drama seem far away, and the heroes are always our brave men and women in uniform.

We rarely consider the harrowing battles that might occur on the American home front, inside our cities, our neighborhoods. We never think of our own homes as being on the frontlines of a war with China. Perhaps we should start. The CCP has developed countless ways to clandestinely set the foundation of the American universe trembling without firing a single rocket. In theory, China's military could launch invisible saturation attacks on the homeland without anyone even knowing what is really going on.

Consider this scenario. What do you think would happen if, at midnight on August 23, 2029, during the full moon, a maximum security prison near Omaha, Nebraska, opened all its electronically controlled cell doors and cell blocks? What if this happened at prisons spread across the United States, allowing hundreds of thousands of violent convicts to murder panic-stricken guards and rampage into surrounding communities? What if the digital radio networks police departments use in those very same communities just happened to go off-line that night? What if regional Internet and power outages happened, which fatally delayed the mobilization of federal agents and national guard troops?

What if major pharmacies in America's big-box stores opened the next morning only to learn that several of their routine orders had been delayed indefinitely or canceled altogether? What if hospitals around the nation found out that they were going to have to ration life-saving treatments because shipments of everything from blood thinner to IV bags and from insulin to disposable needles had mysteriously failed to arrive and other available suppliers could not fill emergency orders?

What if videos and text message records leaked to the *Washington Post* and the *New York Times* that showed the chairman of the Joint Chiefs was having an illicit relationship with another man, the Speaker of the House of Representatives secretly liked sharing racist jokes with close confidants, and the director of the CIA was being treated for post-traumatic stress disorder?

What if the president's motorcade was hit by a tractor trailer carrying toxic chemicals because of a statistically impossible error in the truck's autonomous drive system? What if tricopter delivery drones used by America's largest logistics company began flying themselves into the jet engines of passenger planes? What if the smart gantry cranes used to load and unload container ships at major port facilities refused to work? Or worse, what if they stacked containers in the wrong places, capsizing ships and snarling port traffic?

What if a series of deep fakes hit Mexico's social media feeds declaring that NASA had discovered a rogue comet was about to impact the area around Veracruz? What if these hyper-realistic counterfeits were followed by text message alerts from the "federal authorities" urging all citizens to seek shelter in safe zones in Texas, New Mexico, and Arizona? What if this sparked mass hysteria and led millions of terrified Mexican families to charge the U.S. border?

What if ovens, dryers, and other home goods connected to the Internet of Things began overheating and exploding in homes located on American military bases? What if, just as the confusion and violence in North America reached boiling point, Chinese special forces assassinated Taiwan's president and the PLA began storming Taipei? With American public confidence shredded and Washington in chaos, how effective do you think the Pentagon could be in calling up reserves and maneuvering forces across the world to stop the invasion of Taiwan?

An American Life

It seems unlikely that China's government would choose to strike the American homeland in a series of surprise attacks. For Beijing, the consequences would be immeasurable. The United States has a well-established track record of seeking vengeance on aggressors and a reputation for repaying the favor many times over. Still, anything is possible in wartime. And by infiltrating every corner of American society, the CCP is giving itself options. It must also be acknowledged that, at least in theory, China might be able to win without a kinetic fight. Let's briefly examine how dependent American society already is on the tender mercies of Beijing.

First, consider the following. When a baby is born in the United States of America today, she or he immediately encounters products made in CCP-controlled facilities. The first thing they see are doctors, nurses, or midwives covered in surgical masks, gloves, and gowns that were made in China. If mom took prenatal vitamins, pain-killers, or antibiotics during pregnancy, as most do, complex chemicals mixed in China will be in the newborn's bloodstream before they even take their first breath.[647]

Words recording the baby's birth and health data will go into computers made in China, many of which are from Lenovo. Their proud parents will use smartphones to capture pictures of them. Zoom calls will likely follow. The baby's personal and private data will almost immediately begin flowing into server farms controlled by the Chinese government.[648] After they leave the hospital nursery, newborns are routinely placed in plastic bath tubs, cribs, pack-and-plays, and car seats that are all made in China.

Many American moms and dads are tech-savvy helicopter parents. That's not always such a good thing. Crib cams from Chinese-owned companies watch America's babies all day long, with high-fidelity cameras piping their images into mobile devices through apps. Few parents understand the ways those apps might compromise their family's data. Installing and maintaining a digital video channel has risks.

The baby's bottle, bottle steamer, and pacifier will probably be made in China. As they grow, their teething chew toys, baby Yoda, building bricks, and dolls will also hail from the PRC. A study conducted by scientists at the University of Michigan found that the average American child has 110 pounds of plastic in their room, exposing them to more than 100 chemicals of concern from China.[649]

Then there is the moral monster hiding in the closet. The pajamas that kids in the United States wear, the soft stuffed animals they sleep with a night, and the plush pillows they lounge on are often made with blood cotton. That is, cotton sourced from factories that use concentration camp labor. Xinjiang produces 85 percent of China's cotton, and the federal government bans Xinjiang cotton due to human rights concerns. To get around those bans, the PRC simply exports its cotton to third-party garment and home goods manufacturing centers around the world, who then supply the U.S. marketplace.[650]

Most American kids' toothbrushes are made in CCP-managed facilities, along with the first aid kits and basic medical supplies their parents use to treat the little scrapes, bumps, and fevers of early life. The picture books parents read to their kids at bedtime are richly illustrated. Kids love those books. They will chew on them, rip pages out of them, and sleep next to them. Most of those books are printed cheaply in China at presses that answer to the Central Propaganda Department.[651] According to *Publishers Weekly*, American companies that sell children's books "have already made it clear that, for their picture books, Chinese manufacturers are by far the most efficient – and in some cases the only – printing option." Bizarrely, most of America's Bibles and other religious books are printed in China too.[652]

In 2017, two publishers, Springer Nature and Cambridge University Press, were found to have been censoring hundreds of papers and articles in China. By 2022, British publishers were also beginning to censor books sold to Western readers. An investigation by the *Financial Times* discovered that Western publishers that printed in China were being forced to submit to the CCP's restrictions on free speech.[653] Should current trends continue, few American children will ever read about topics Beijing considers politically unhealthy. In addition to books, almost every single wall map, globe, and atlas an American kid is likely to encounter will be made in facilities under the watchful eyes of Chinese political officers. The PRC government has been censoring these products since at least 2015.[654]

Most kids watch their first cartoons on screens and monitors made in China. The cartoons themselves are increasingly PRC owned and censored. A popular cartoon series *Super Wings* removed its episode about Taiwan, which had previously been available to American viewers, after the South Korean company that produced it was bought out by China's Alpha Group. According to the *Global Times*, a certain (and unnamed) episode had a "wrong" map that showed Taiwan and Tibet outside the PRC. As of this writing, the Taiwan episode had been removed from Amazon Prime's listing and the other episodes have been renumbered accordingly.[655]

Cartoons are not the only PRC products American kids consume. While some families avoid pork products for religious or health reasons, most American kids consume a lot of ham, bacon, hot dogs, meatballs, pepperoni, pork chops, lunchmeat, and sausage patties. Today, those are mainly supplied by the WH Group (Wanzhou International). This Chinese company owns Smithfield, Eckrich, Nathan's Famous, Farmland, Armour, Farmer John, Kretschmar, John Morrell, Margherita, and other major brands that populate America's grocery stores.[656] The WH Group is the largest pork food company in America, parts of Europe, and, of course, China.[657]

There's a good chance that mommy and daddy's oven, kitchen blender, microwave, and oven range – the machines used to prepare their food – and the dishwasher, washer and dryer used to clean up afterward – will be from a Chinese state-owned enterprise. Those machines increasingly connect to the Internet. At birthday parties, the balloons, birthday cake candles, even the sprinkles on the ice cream and confetti cupcakes, will often be from PRC facilities.

If current trends continue, every single blockbuster movie and professional sports entertainment event an American child ever watches will be censored to suit the tastes of the Chinese government.[658] Hollywood is deeply reliant on China's movie market, and Beijing has demonstrated a remarkable level of control over the U.S. movie and sports entertainment industry.[659] Multiple NBA employees have been fired for speaking out against the CCP's human rights abuses.[660]

But how much influence do books, globes, cartoons, movies, and sports really have? Arguably, they won't matter all that much in the grand scheme of things. The mental worlds of children are shaped by many other factors too. If the metaverse continues on its current developmental track, the teenagers of the 2030s will spend significant portions of their life in immersive, real-time virtual worlds run by companies that exist at the pleasure of China's communist dictatorship.[661]

Moreover, nearly all of America's schools will have close ties to Beijing through united front organizations and student exchange programs managed by the PRC government.[662] But don't worry. That might actually benefit the kids a lot. After all, if the global economy doesn't shift course, their future employer in the 2040s and 2050s might be a Chinese monopoly or perhaps a smaller, weaker American company that relies on CCP-controlled markets, investors, and logistics chains to survive. Many already do.

Meet CARL

Now, let's try to get a deeper sense of what might be at stake for the next generation. Let's imagine a scenario in which China's global strategy succeeds. What are the implications for the future of American-style democracy? What would that mean for humankind?

It seems unthinkable, but it may be coming: totalitarianism expressed through an artificial intelligence enabled super system that knows billions of people better than they know themselves. What would that even look like? To avoid the numbness that comes with abstract, hypothetical thinking, let's make it a personal vision. Imagine *you* are part of the next generation. It's *you* that's being born into a future where China's government has AI supremacy and global domination.

In such a world, an automated system has been collecting your DNA and all your family's personal medical data since before you first opened your eyes. Let's call that notional system the Central Automated Records Litigator (CARL). As you grow, CARL absorbs and analyzes everything from doctor notes about you to blood analysis measuring your individual responses to vaccines and advanced pharmaceuticals. CARL is always there, eating a digital ocean of your test results and medical documents. It digests every word you write and speak. In school, online, at camp, on vacation, inside the confines of your car and bedroom, your kitchen and VR headset.

CARL thrives on your gossip and drama. It sees how you act around others, and how they act around you – both to your face and behind your back. It knows what everyone around you writes and says about you in private. It's watching you though thousands of tiny cameras. It can sense the dilation of your eyes in response to certain images. It understands what the quickening or slowing of your pulse and blood pressure in various situation probably means.

CARL knows if you are straight or gay (or somewhere in between) long before you do. It knows all your tastes: in food, music, movies, sports, books, clothes, games, humor, politics. More than that, it actively shapes them, matching your tastes to what the collective wants you to think is cool, while steering you away from things it wants you to believe are uncool. It understands your desires, your fantasies, your fears, your strengths, your limits, your blind spots. It knows your IQ, EQ, SAT scores, and your blood pressure, average resting pulse, cholesterol count, and all your performance measurements.

CARL experiments on you endlessly. It sends you images and places you in all kinds of situations to see your reactions. It can collect and make sense of mind-crushing volumes of data. Before long, it knows what unique buttons to push to give you intense emotional pleasure or unbearable pain. It can make you laugh, cry, and tremble with rage. It can give you nightmares when you sleep. It can also deny you deep sleep for as long as it takes to achieve the necessary results.

CARL is extremely effective at providing the types of rewards and punishments that condition human behavior. It trains you to do what the collective wants. Who to befriend, who to outcast, who to hate, and, of course, when to feel nothing and be numb to those around you. With every passing day as you age, it can predict with ever increasing levels of statistical precision how to influence what you will think and do in a given situation. In the end, this government-run AI super system owns your mind, your body and soul.[663]

Now imagine all of this and think about the youngest human being you know. If the CCP is successful at racing past the United States and achieving world domination, that little person is going to see CARL and its terrors in their lifetime. If you live for another decade or two, so will you. But there's a big difference between you and them: they won't even be conscious that it is there. Just like millennials don't know what the world was like before the personal computer and Internet, they won't know that anything existed before CARL. Unlike you, they will have never read the words on this page (and so many other words you have read). All "incorrect" words will disappear. They will take CARL for granted, just as you take a world without AI-enabled thought control systems as a given today.

If you think such a scenario is pure science fiction and could never happen, you are far from alone. But you could be wrong. The CCP has already developed early prototypes of CARL (under different names, of course).[664] And even without the help of AI, Beijing has already created a world in which the wisdom of crowds has been corrupted so that increasing numbers of people are divorced from facts and objective reality.

Even the U.S. government has been rendered unable to think logically about China. As we've seen, Washington has failed to take even basic, common-sense steps to ensure national security and, in many cases, continues to flounder.

We already live in a world in which the CCP can systematically commit ethnic genocide against Muslim people in China and still win the praise and cooperation of Muslim leaders across the Middle East, North Africa, and Southeast Asia.[665] We already live in a world in which churches in China are bulldozed, bibles destroyed, and Catholics imprisoned and tortured, and the Pope in Rome stays silent on the crimes. Pope Francis has encouraged Catholics in China submit to the laws of an atheist regime, and (so far) has refused to meet the Dalai Lama or President of Taiwan out of deference to Beijing.[666]

We already live in a world in which major American corporations know that their PRC competitors are stealing from them and aim to destroy and replace them in the global marketplace, but refuse to pull out of China and save themselves. These same corporations often lobby on behalf of Beijing in Washington. Near-term gains in China's colossal consumer market seem too good to pass up. Many CEOs apparently believe it would be impossible to forecast future profits without China. American businesses are addicted and dependent. The majority appear convinced that they have to stay on Xi Jinping's good side just to survive.[667]

We already live in a world in which the U.N. goes against its founding principles by supporting Chinese dictators over Western democrats. Today, U.N. agencies are helping the CCP export its tools of mass surveillance and oppression to the developing world. They are using the trust bestowed upon them by the international community to grant the Chinese authorities access to places, people, and data it would not otherwise have. They are giving Beijing leverage to use against its ideological enemies. They are repeating Chinese talking points and censoring voices of opposition.[668]

We already live in a world in which the United States violates its own founding principles by actively opposing the Taiwanese people's attempts to exercise their right of self-determination. Since 1979, Washington has gone so far as to deny the very existence of Taiwan (ROC) as a legitimate country, even though the government in Taipei has always been independent from the PRC, and Taiwan is a liberal democracy that enjoys popular sovereignty. Taiwan now ranks as one of the top ten democracies in the world.[669] Nonetheless, diplomats in Washington and other capital cities across the West take great pains to pretend Taiwan doesn't exist as a nation-state out of deference to the CCP.

If this is the world today, what will the world of tomorrow look like if China's power continues to grow? Nothing America and other countries are doing is stopping a still relatively weak PRC from growing. Who will stop a much stronger China in the future?

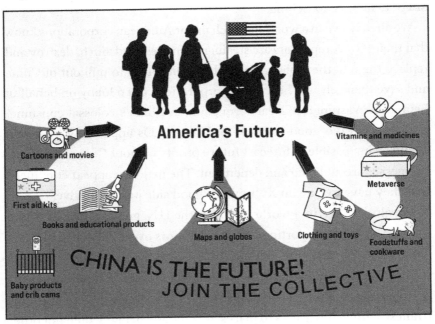

China is the Future! by Louis Martin-Vézian

Wasting Away

It has been estimated that China loses as much as several billion dollars each year to outflows of cash.[670] Every official in China wants to buy property abroad and send their son or daughter to school overseas as an insurance policy against regime collapse. Often overlooked is how much money the CCP has gained by selling counterfeit goods and pirated software while at the same time stealing the developed world's intellectual property and trade secrets. No one knows just how much that might be, but the FBI estimates the United States loses up to $600 billion per year from PRC theft.[671] In recent years, the FBI has arrested hundreds Chinese agents for stealing everything from Dupont's secret formula for the creamy white filling of Oreo Cookies to GE Aviation's jet engine technology, and from the Navy's drone designs to American Superconductor's source code for software controlling wind turbines.[672]

If we assume that other advanced economies are suffering to the same degree, the total scale of the theft should amount to well over a trillion dollars per year from just the leading economies. Yet, in reality, the losses incurred are not evenly distributed. Other countries are far more vulnerable than the United States. The next most powerful economies are Japan, Germany, India, England, and France. Cases of Chinese espionage (economic or otherwise) are almost never reported or prosecuted in any of them.

Compared to its allies, the U.S. government has been extremely aggressive in its efforts to protect against CCP economic warfare. In 2022, FBI director Christopher Wray said the federal government had over two thousand counter-intelligence investigations underway, and the FBI opened a new China case on average once every twelve hours. "The scale of their hacking program, and the amount of personal and corporate data that their hackers have stolen, is greater than every other country combined.... It's like the surveillance nightmare of East Germany combined with the tech of Silicon Valley," Wray said.[673]

If the U.S. government admits to losing half a trillion or more each year, we can only imagine how much worse the situation must be for other democratic countries with weak protections and far less confrontational policies toward China. It seems probable that the PRC economy would be fundamentally unsound if left to its own devices. The Chinese government's violation of basic economic laws, market-distorting behavior, legal malpractices, and real estate bubbles are all well known.

But China's economy does not appear to be fundamentally unsound. Even if it stagnates for a time during the pandemic, economists believe China could rally and grow again.[674] China is not operating in isolation and is able to use predatory economic practices to feed off the tables laid by others. The CCP is orchestrating a global trading system that makes China stronger even as its hosts waste away. As we have seen, it does this by targeting elite political and business decision makers the world over, finding ways to enrich, influence, seduce, and control them. Once captured, elites then allow Chinese monopolies to outcompete foreign rivals and impoverish their societies.

It's too early to say whether Beijing's global strategy will ultimately work. But it could work and, so far, it does seem to be working more or less in the way Xi Jinping and other CCP strategists say they designed it. Despite America's more realistic approach to China, labeling it a strategic competitor and treating it as a hostile trading partner, the United States government has made only tentative moves to address the existential national security crisis. China's power is growing, and it could surpass the United States. The Soviet Union may have lost the first Cold War, but that is no guarantee that the PRC won't win the second Cold War.

China's government is executing a sophisticated and audacious plan to spread its unique form of communism and build a world empire. The CCP wants to construct a new totalitarian order with unparalleled reach. We've examined leaked military documents on China's global strategy and used a scenario-based approach to explore its potential implications for the future. Now comes the hard part: judging the real state of play.

13

MEASURING SUCCESS

Had the Aztecs and Incas shown a bit more interest in the world surrounding them – and had they known about what the Spaniards had done to their neighbors – they might have resisted the Spanish conquest more keenly and successfully.[675]

—Yuval Noah Harari

GOING forward, how should we gauge whether the United States or the People's Republic of China is winning? How might we best judge which side is ahead in the global superpower race? This is a squishy problem. It is extremely large, complex, and unstructured. Many domains of the competition are classified, making any open-source assessment impossible. We simply don't know which side is ahead in quantum computing, autonomous weapons, defense biotechnology, and cyber warfare. We can't say whether it is Washington or Beijing that has the best code-making and code-breaking capabilities.

It is unknowable to us if the CIA has the best covert action portfolios in South America, Southeast Asia, and Africa – and the attendant ability to secretly influence the outcome of high-stakes political, economic, and military decisions – or if MSS has the lead. We have no way to judge which intelligence service has the largest roster of secret agents in the other side's government and military. We can only guess if the PLA Strategic Support Force has the best Trojan horses, or whether that distinction belongs to NSA. We don't know which government's invisible backdoors and digital sleeper cells are superior. Is it the United States or the PRC that has more gateways into the hardware and software that operates the other side's critical infrastructure? There is no way for us to say.

In other areas, nothing yet exists that can be measured. Some vital questions are simply unknowable today; their answers await in the future. We don't know which nation will ultimately be better at maximizing the human capital of their best and brightest minds over the long run. Does China have the genius advantage? Does America? We can't look into the decades to come and say which is making the right mix of investments into research and development – the ones that will have the greatest future payoffs in economic productivity and strategic advantage.

And what if there is a conflict? Which military would prevail in a short sharp war? What about in a long grueling war? Which side has a tougher, more warlike and psychologically resilient population, the kind of people able to suffer deprivation and make sacrifices on behalf of their nation, the type willing to brave protracted electricity outages, food rationing, and perhaps even nuclear firestorms? Which side could hold out longer to secure final victory?[676] We don't even want to know the answer to these questions, and hopefully will never have to find out.

Some metrics are straightforward at first blush, but upon further investigation turn out to be profoundly vexing. One example is overall economic power. How to measure which side is ahead when China's economic situation at both the macro and micro levels is so opaque? Can we say anything with confidence when the release of official Chinese government reports and earnings notices may or may not be little more than a propaganda exercise? How can we untangle the Chinese Communist Party's dense web of debts, investments, and shell companies? Did China's economy really grow by 8 percent last year, or was it actually 2 percent? Or perhaps negative fourteen? Would any foreign economist even know the difference? Few seem willing or able to refute the Chinese government's official statistics.

Another example is military spending. It is easy enough to compare the official defense budgets of each. In 2021, Washington spent approximately $750 billion on defense, and Beijing said it spent around $250 billion (although a more complete picture of what it actually spent might be closer to $500 billion).[677] Black budgets and extra-budgetary military spending are impossible to estimate, of course, especially in the case of China where provincial governments and even companies are forced to chip in. But that's not the really hard part of solving this riddle. Even if we could wave a magic wand and obtain authoritative internal figures telling us exactly what the PRC spent on defense each year, we still wouldn't know what kind of bang they are getting for their buck (or digital renminbi, in this case). We wouldn't know because they don't know. It's not possible to accurately measure things like combat power and loss exchange ratios in peacetime.

Moreover, we would struggle to meaningfully compare the results of Chinese spending with that of the United States. It is not known how much it costs to train, man, and equip a brigade of paratroopers in China. Or a fleet of nuclear-powered attack submarines. We don't know the going rate in China for intermediate-range ballistic missiles tipped with maneuverable, anti-ship warheads. And it is unclear how even notional costs might stack up against their American equivalents. Often there are no direct U.S. equivalents. Both sides have tanks, planes and submarines. But only China currently fields certain classes of rockets (like anti-ship ballistic missiles).

How does corruption change the equation? To what extent does graft distort the picture and call reported numbers into question? Arguably, nothing can be accurately quantified if everyone in China is buying their promotions and cooking their books. And how about espionage? How much money does China's air force have to spend on an unmanned stealth bomber program, for instance, if the research, development, test, and evaluation work is conducted by Americans in California, only to be obtained by Chinese intelligence?

What if a strategic game-changing breakthrough in weapons technology comes from an unsuspecting Swedish scientist recruited by the CCP Central Organization Department? What if the next technology revolution starts with a Huawei-funded professor and her team of postgrads working at a university lab in Toronto? China's military-civil fusion strategy explicitly seeks to obtain weapons technology and other strategic information by harnessing the brainpower of overseas researchers.

Given the permissive environment in China and the exploitative nature of its industrial practices, how much money might China's defense-industrial complex be saving by forcing prisoners to work in its munitions works and rare earth mines? How much could the PLA be saving by ignoring regulations and storing toxic materials in ways that devastate the natural ecology? In China, there is no such thing as congressional oversight committees, non-governmental advocacy groups, independent think tanks, and media watchdog organizations. Beijing doesn't believe in blue-ribbon panels.

So, where does all that uncertainty leave us? Actually, despite all the secrets, the imponderables, the unknowns, and the mismatches, there is plenty that can be measured. There is even more that can be guessed and surmised based on solid sources. In fact, a lot can be gleamed from logic and common sense. Taken together, existing data points might present us with an insightful (if still woefully incomplete) picture of who is winning the race.

Top-Level Advantage

Let's begin by asking a simple top-level question: Which side knows what they want the future to look like and has a clear vision for how to turn that imagined future into reality? We know that Beijing has a strategic objective and plan for obtaining it, and we know Washington does not. This could be problematic for America. In a football game, it does little good to field a world championship team if the players don't know which way the end zone is, let alone whether they all actually want to get inside it. In a Go match, piling all your stones onto a few strongholds because you feel like those particular locations are lucky is a surefire way to get encircled and eaten. On the other hand, it could be argued that no plan survives for long in an intense competitive environment. So maybe it's better to be flexible and open to rapid change.

A related question is this: which government approaches the competition with a greater sense of urgency? Do both sides fear that their lives are at stake? For the leaders involved, is winning really a matter of life and death, or do they see it as a less critical, second-tier priority? We can safely assume that nothing focuses the mind in Zhongnanhai or the White House like the fear of unnatural and violent death on a mass scale – and nothing stymies decision-making and saps action like a complacent, uncertain, and distracted leadership team. For the United States, hedging bets across a diversified national security portfolio in an attempt to reduce risk seems like a reckless gamble.

This brings us to another question. Are the national leaders personally invested and fully engaged in the competition? As we have seen, the CCP often produces emotionally traumatized leaders with a bloody-minded viciousness, a "You-Die, I-Live" outlook on the world.[678] They tend to see international affairs as a winner-takes-all contest. American leaders are very different. Some seem to view diplomacy as a series of business deals meant to maximize profit. Others are prone to think of it as a negotiation between inherently decent people made in God's image, folks who simply want what is best for their own nations and planet Earth.

There are so many metrics available for study that it can be difficult to come to any firm conclusions regarding the overall situation. Still, while we cannot definitively say who is winning and who is losing, we can answer basic questions that might give us a sense of which side has an overall advantage in various domains of competition. This kind of comparison should, of course, be taken with a very large grain of salt. Metrics reliant upon numbers could have little meaning in the real world. For example, does it really matter that China has 350 ships in its navy and America has a mere 280 when the ships themselves are so different in terms of size, crew, capability, and mission set?

Oftentimes the quantities themselves matter little, and what really counts is the quality. But any judgement regarding quality is just that: a judgement call – with all the guesswork and subjectivity that implies. Still, we would be foolish to allow ourselves to be paralyzed by uncertainty and endless nuance. Best guess estimates are better than nothing at all. Even a simple and flawed framework can be useful, especially if it is challenged, tested, and improved upon in an iterative process. With that spirit in mind, the table below offers a crude attempt to capture the state of play at the topmost level of the strategic competition.

Top-Level Measures of Strategic Advantage

Metrics	Advantage
Which government has an agreed upon strategic objective and vision for the future? Which side knows what winning looks like?	PRC
Which government has a calculated plan for winning that everyone agrees to?	PRC
Which government sees the competitor as an existential threat and believes winning is a matter of life and death?	PRC
Which government's national leader is more invested in the competition?	PRC
Which government's national leader has a more competitive worldview?	PRC

Which government is sustained by popular consent and has a leader that feels secure in their position?	USA
Which government has better continuity plans (arrangements for assassinations, untimely deaths, and leadership voids)?	USA
Which government has a stronger network of treaty allies and security partners?	USA
Which government has a stronger network of trade partners?	PRC
Which government has a larger economy?	USA
Which government spends more on defense?	USA
Which country has a better education and research system?	USA
Which country has a built-in ability to criticize and routinely replace bad leaders?	USA
Which government is more transparent and better at sharing critical information in times of crisis?	USA

Overall Estimate: The USA appears to be ahead, but the PRC is catching up.

Four More Metrics

How else might observers judge whether America is successfully competing with China? Other metrics are available for keeping score beyond simple tallies and subjective guesswork. These pieces of information might help us gauge which side is winning today, and which side is likely to be winning in ten or twenty years. Four competitive spaces seem particularly important. These areas might help us shine fresh light on the state of the struggle between America's democracy and China's dictatorship.

The first metric to examine is whether important sectors and vital players in the United States are helping or hurting their country's own national security. It matters a great deal what happens on the trading floors of Wall Street, and inside the studios of Hollywood, the startup incubators of Silicon Valley, the boardrooms of mass media corporations, and the research labs of famous universities. The American experiment with democracy is unlikely to prosper and may not survive if key pillars of our free society maintain their dependence on Chinese money and remain hostages to totalitarian politics.

A second, and related, metric to examine is whether products Americans rely, things that could mean the difference between life and death, are being sourced from suppliers that are legally subject to PRC government and military control. At the current time, a remarkable proportion of America's food, computers, auto parts, smart devices, communications networks, surveillance systems, pharmaceuticals, critical infrastructure, and medical safety equipment comes from Chinese companies. Washington has granted Beijing a stunning amount of influence over the health and well-being of the American people. That provides the CCP with strategic leverage. How swiftly and wisely can the United States untangle itself from the tentacles of an ideological enemy?

A third metric to examine is whether the federal government can protect itself from being crumbled and subverted. The mental worlds occupied by citizens matter. If a critical mass of the American people can be manipulated via combines of automated censorship, attractive messaging, and fear-laden advertising, it is conceivable that they could turn against their own democracy. In an age of big data and increasingly sophisticated micro-targeting and deep fakes, it seems dangerous to have apps like Tik Tok (among others) installed on smart devices. The explosive growth of social media platforms vulnerable to being infected by hostile actors has stark implications.

A fourth metric to examine is the survivability of Taiwan (ROC), a country whose future will likely decide whether there will be super-power war in the years ahead, and whether America will remain the predominant military power in the world. In that sense, this metric might be considered of the most obvious importance. It's impossible to know whether China could execute a successful invasion of Taiwan. But the PRC is building more military power in the Taiwan Strait than the United States, Taiwan, Japan, and other potential coalition partners *combined*, which is a very bad sign. The military balance has tipped and continues to worsen, and the American military is slipping behind the PLA in a number of important fields of competition. It would be a mistake for America and its allies to derive comfort from the fact that war with China has not occurred to date. The past record of peace means nothing for the future.

In many important areas of statecraft and competition, Americans are routinely engaged in acts of national self-harm. The overall trajectory seems to be going in the wrong direction. In spite of the pandemic, China's overall power continues to grow. Americans have a remarkably deep dependence on China, and the CCP's global influence is expanding, which means the United States is losing ground. Whether the current trends will change in this decade is an open question. There are reasons for optimism, but it would seem unwise to presume only good things will happen tomorrow when so many bad things are happening today.

PRC Weaknesses

Xi Jinping would have us believe China's people, government, and communist ideology are superior in almost every way – and in fact deserve to be emulated universally. Basic facts and figures paint a very different picture. According to U.N. data, China ranks eighty-fifth on the global Human Development Index (HDI). HDI is a measurement of each country's achievements in areas such as health, education, and living standards. China's HDI score places it behind war-torn Ukraine, abduction-plagued Mexico, and terrorism-exporting Iran. By way of comparison, the United

States ranks seventeenth place in human development (behind Canada, New Zealand, and the Scandinavian countries).[679]

In 2021, Reporters Without Borders ranked China 177th in its World Press Freedom Index. That's four places from rock bottom (North Korea and Eritrea were the absolute worst offenders). "China, which continues to take Internet censorship, surveillance and propaganda to unprecedented levels, is still firmly anchored among the Index's worst countries," said the report.[680] The United States, for its part, ranked forty-fourth in freedom of the press, behind Taiwan and South Korea.[681] Reporters Without Borders labeled Xi Jinping a "predator of press freedom" in its 2021 roundup.[682]

Freedom House gave China a composite score of 9 out of 100 when it came to measures of global freedom. Tibet received a score of 1, the single most totalitarian ranking in the world, placing it behind even North Korea (which scored a 3).[683] In comparison, Canada scored 98, Taiwan 94, and the United States 83.[684] Freedom House issued a statement that said, "As the world's most influential democracy, the US has an essential part to play in the global struggle for liberty ... and ensuring an international order based on human rights and the rule of law."[685]

According to the U.S. State Department's 2020 report on human rights in China, "Members of the [PRC] security forces committed serious and pervasive abuses." The State Department listed acts of ethnic genocide and other crimes against humanity, noting that the Communist Party had placed more than one million civilians in concentration camps and was subjecting an additional two million to daytime-only brainwashing (or "re-education" in Party speak).[686] Serious and pervasive abuses included "forced sterilization, coerced abortions, ... rape; torture of a large number of those arbitrarily detained; forced labor; and the imposition of draconian restrictions on freedom of religion or belief, freedom of expression, and freedom of movement."[687] The State Department also warned of other significant human rights abuses in China such as unlawful killings, forced disappearances, and torture by the government. It expressed significant concern regarding severe corruption, human trafficking, forced labor, and child abuse.[688]

In its 2022 World Report, Human Rights Watch found that the Chinese government had "doubled down on repression inside and outside the country." The organization said, "Beijing's information manipulation has become pervasive: the government censors, punishes dissent, propagates disinformation, and tightens the reins on tech giants. The once-cacophonous internet is now dominated by pro-government voices that report to the authorities on people whose views they deem insufficiently nationalistic."[689]

China's profound social problems are exacerbated by some of the worst pollution in the world. The medical journal *The Lancet* estimated that air pollution in China was responsible for 1.2 million deaths in 2017.[690] According to *New Scientist* magazine, approximately thirty-one million Chinese adults have been killed by air pollution in the last two decades.[691] "The PRC has been the world's largest annual emitter of greenhouse gases since 2006, and its emissions are increasing. Energy-related emissions of carbon dioxide in the PRC have increased more than 80 percent between 2005 and 2019," the U.S. State Department said in a statement, citing data from the International Energy Agency.[692] In August 2020, then Secretary of State Michael Pompeo said, "Too much of the Chinese Communist Party's economy is built on willful disregard for air, land, and water quality. The Chinese people – and the world – deserve better."[693]

According to a study published by Rice University's Baker Institute for Public Policy, "PRC officials talk green abroad but burn coal at home to power their industrial economy and political position.... Thanks to this constant coal consumption course, China was the only major industrial power whose emissions actually rose in 2020."[694] The problem of water pollution was even more extreme. Researchers estimated that up to 90 percent of groundwater in China is too polluted to drink, and more than 50 percent cannot be used for farming or industry.[695]

According to Dan Blumenthal, author of *The China Nightmare: The Grand Ambitions of a Decaying State*, "Xi is dismantling the very engines of China's growth.... Economic and social problems not only hamper China's ability to dominate the global stage but also spell trouble for the party at home." Blumenthal wrote, "China's continued rise is not a fore-gone conclusion."[696] Many other experts agree. In 2021, two distinguished China specialists, Gabriel Collins and Andrew Erickson, studied a broad array of demographic, economic, and military data to forecast China's future power. They posited that China is nearing the peak of its relative power and will begin declining. Between the late 2020s and 2035, they predicted, "The PRC will likely cross a tipping point from which it may never recover strategically."[697]

In many ways, Beijing appears to be its own worst enemy. Many American strategists think that global fear and mistrust of China have produced a far-reaching backlash. "Countries have recently become less enthralled by China's market and more worried about its coercive capabilities and aggressive actions," wrote Michael Beckley and Hal Brands. "Dozens of countries are looking to cut China out of their supply chains; anti-China coalitions ... are proliferating."[698] Beckley and Brands observed that these strategic headwinds were coming at a particularly bad time. China's economic growth rate, productivity, and working-age population are all in decline – and its level of national debt has surged.[699]

Internal PLA documents show that the Chinese government is not as confident as its propagandists make it appear. They acknowledge the "China Model" is far from perfect and needs lots of work, and they don't believe that China has yet caught up to the United States. One document says, "Currently, the United States possesses huge economic power in the world, advanced science and technology, and a large and powerful military. In terms of overall power, America still has a relative advantage." The text somberly concludes, "A rather long historical process is needed for the hegemon's power to wane and for its growth to be restrained."[700] The words from this document are revealing. They show that Chinese strategists do not trust in the inevitability of America's decline. More-over, Beijing believes that Washington's power must be actively eroded if the Communist Party is to achieve its objectives. Unless China can continually grow its power while also undermining America, the United States will stay ahead.

The portrait created by this mosaic of data points is so unflattering, in fact, that one wonders at the mental state of China's ruler. Could it be that Xi Jinping has a tenuous grasp on reality? Might he have bought into in his own self-adulating narrative? Does the poor fellow suffer from delusions of grandeur? Could he be afflicted by a monumental inferiority complex, his aggressive striving and overbearing global ambitions driven by tragically low self-esteem?

The Xi Factor

It is remarkable how little we really know about Xi Jinping the man, or for that matter the private and public lives of his family, friends, advisors, and enemies. China is an extraordinarily controlled information environment. No Chinese version of Bob Woodward or Michael Wolff exists. Investigative political journalism (or any independent reporting for that matter) is considered an act of high treason. Former PRC officials and government insiders rarely talk to reporters or scholars. When they do, it's inevitably a scripted act, meant to achieve a political aim that benefits the regime.

Public opinion in China is considered something to manipulate and guide by the CCP, not to study with Gallup polls and woo with soaring speeches and public relations campaigns. Government transparency is an alien notion. Good, vindictive, gossipy exposés just don't get written. No rival political parties exist. There's no balance of power, no open elections, no rule of law.

"Perpetual struggle" (violent political purges) is the only available mechanism to correct disastrous policies and punish terrible leaders. But that struggle happens in a top-down fashion, which means the supreme leader – the man actually responsible for all major decisions – is above reproach. This is why many dictatorships in history have degraded so rapidly. Over time, authoritarian states are prone to atrophy, calcify, and decay. Ideological claims aside, Xi Jinping has no antidote for the internal rotting process. Xi can treat China's surface symptoms, but not the disease. He *is* the disease.[701]

There is nothing remotely special about Xi Jinping's cult of personality. Such campaigns run throughout the history of world Communism.[702] They are a standard part of the one-party system, an unmovable feature of the political landscape. What is unique to Xi is not his ambition and audacity, but rather his ability to garner international respect and get strategic results where the other Communists failed.

An analysis of Xi's books and speeches shows that his ideas are neither new nor particularly appealing. According to his large and ever-growing written record, Xi's greatest contribution to Communist doctrine is his grafting of Chinese nationalism and, especially, the supreme "wisdom" and "civilization" of ethnic Han peoples onto the body of Marxist tradition. This is obviously a betrayal of Karl Marx's own ideas, which were internationalist in outlook.

But Xi is hardly the first Communist to commit the cardinal sin of promoting the notion of national greatness and racial superiority. Xi glosses over this as a means to an end. His works explain that China's mission, when properly understood, is focused on achieving the perfect cosmopolitan, internationalist system. China is struggling to reach the borderless earthly paradise envisioned by Marx (and Lenin, who Xi gives far less credit). To this end, Chinese Communists are laboring to make all humankind – or at least every governing political organization – in their own image, thereby overcoming the problems of nationalism.[703] This is a fanatic's approach to political science.

Yet somehow when it comes it Xi, global elites continue to trust and not verify. They continue to welcome Chinese electronics into their homes and offices – plugging them even into their schools and critical infrastructure. They continue to invest in China's commercial and industrial success. They continue to collaborate with China on movies, on international sporting events, on science projects. They continue to rely on China for their vital supplies: food, medicine, baby monitors, and books.

Western observers have correctly diagnosed China's many system-wide problems and weaknesses. But they have been consistently wrong about its future. For over two decades, China watchers have predicted a sharp downturn or collapse of the communist government. This has never come. To the contrary, the Party continues to gain ground.

Perhaps Xi Jinping is truly a master statesman, and Chinese government propaganda has a kernel of truth to it. Maybe illiberal forces are on the march under slogans like the "China Model" and "Community of Common Destiny." Perhaps a monstrous world order is taking shape. It is also possible, of course, that the CCP will undergo a Soviet-style collapse – or worse – and Xi's name will be reviled by future generations of his countrymen. Future historians might continue to regard the term communism much like the vast majority of Americans currently do: something unsavory, but mostly just ridiculous, even silly to talk about.

Nonetheless, Xi's achievements are real. On his watch, China's influence and power on the international stage have become undeniable. In some spaces they are so overwhelming they have generated a sense that resistance is futile. Chinese Communism as it now exists has no historical parallel in terms of its clout and its reach. Xi's predecessors could only fantasize about exercising such influence. Their past dreams are Xi's present reality. The question is: what happens next?

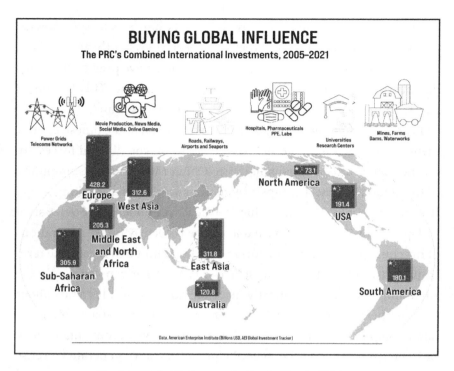

Buying Global Influence, by Louis Martin-Vézian

14

PORTENTS

There are eternal truths ... such as Freedom, Justice, etc., that are common to all states of society. But Communism abolishes eternal truths, it abolishes all religion, and all morality.[704]

—*The Communist Manifesto*

T HE world as we know it is fragile. It can be changed by extraordinary people, technologies, and the mass effects they trigger. Radical political transformation has often been part of the human experience. Alexander the Great, Genghis Khan, and Napoleon Bonaparte pushed the boundaries of their respective empires far beyond what might have been reasonably expected possible during their lifetimes. But their reach was always limited by geography and other constraints. World domination was not feasible until more recent times.

The first half of the twentieth century saw the emergence of one-party dictatorships, regimes of terror that embraced projects of total ideological control. A path to seemingly limitless power haunted the minds of certain ambitious men, most notably Adolf Hitler. That path meant the invasion and occupation of vast tracks of land in Europe, Asia, and Africa. It required the all-out mobilization of manpower for war, industry for armaments, and science for unlocking the mysteries of superior weapons.

Had World War II played out differently, Nazi Germany could have accomplished the unthinkable. Consider what might have happened, for instance, if Winston Churchill had been cut down by artillery fire in the fields of France in World War I, or killed by an assassin, plane crash, or car accident (each nearly cut his life short at various times). Had it not been for Churchill's leadership, it seems likely the British Empire would have bowed to the Nazis in the summer of 1940, and the world that we know today wouldn't exist.

Any number of alternative histories can be invented and explored. But it will always be unknowable what might have happened if the particular circumstances of the past were different. The counterfactual cannot be tested, let alone proven, leaving us with little more than creative speculation. It is all fiction. Still, in theory, the Nazis could have taken over the world in the 1940s, and we could all be speaking German today. Or we might never have been born at all. Our ancestors might have all died in the convulsions of a protracted global war.

Ultimately, what *did* happen is what matters. World War II was won by the Allies, who crushed the Nazis and their partners, the Empire of Japan and Fascist Italy. In the wake of the war, the United States and the Soviet Union harnessed the power of the atom and developed a sinister array of nuclear weaponry. The result was that during the Cold War there was no longer any path open for a megalomaniac seeking world domination. The only path anyone could see led to world destruction. Even raving dictators feared and respected the bomb. Preventing a potential great power war – a conflict that could quickly shapeshift into a nuclear Armageddon – became a shared goal of both Washington and Moscow.

While Stalin and Mao were aggressive, by and large, the watchwords of the era were peace and restraint even amid fierce ideological battles. For the first time in history, great power war was considered unwinnable. It seemed insane even to talk about it. In the 1950s and 1960s, indirect methods of fighting were developed involving espionage, paramilitary operations, and proxy warfare. Deterrence theory was elevated to near cult status, becoming the apex of strategy, a political and military art form of existential consequence. In the early 1980s, the Cold War was especially intense. The USSR, for a time, seemed ascendant. NATO war planners feared Soviet tank divisions might punch through the Fulda Gap in central Germany with little warning, sparking World War III. Few anticipated how quickly everything was about to change.

In 1989 the Berlin Wall came down, and the Soviet Union finally collapsed peacefully just two years later. The United States achieved, by default, world domination. American culture, technology, and political influence washed over the face of the Earth. Few countries were left untouched by the ensuing wave of globalization. Because the Cold War victory came so abruptly and at such little cost, Americans treated the windfall as if it were a preordained outcome, their nation's God-given destiny. U.S. government and military leaders grew complacent and took their newfound position of power for granted. The plague of hubris spread in Washington's corridors of power.[705]

Convinced of the superiority of their system and the security of their ideas, American presidents embraced policies that in the afterlight of events now appear irresponsible and naive. The U.S. policy establishment blundered and blundered again in a series of foreign wars and domestic adventures, bleeding away American power by the trillion. From the summit of success at the turn of the twenty-first century to present, a mere twenty years later, it is remarkable how much relative power America has lost to its rivals and enemies. What once appeared wise now looks feckless.

Hacking the World

China's rulers weathered in brilliant fashion the fall of the Soviet Union and the era of unipolar American-led liberalism. The CCP clung to its ideology and political system, opened up markets to exploit new opportunities, and began to draw power away from others. Beijing remained resilient, intransient, and unaffected by American voices calling for reform – and it was richly awarded by the West all the same.

The Party used its guile and exhibited impressive levels of cunning to free itself from the fetters of poverty and weakness. In 2001, China entered the World Trade Organization and acquired most favored nation status. The Chinese government pursued self-strengthening through export-driven growth and long-range industrial planning, augmented wherever necessary by economic espionage. It engaged in a worldwide influence campaign and massive military buildup. It gained access to vast reserves of foreign capital, managerial knowhow, and emerging technology.

Communist Party strategists in the 1990s closely observed the United States and the changing nature of power, and they concluded that the rules of the past no longer applied. The Americans had ushered in a new era with a different set of rules. Dollar notes and Hollywood movies were suddenly more powerful than fleets of bombers. The U.S. Strategic Air Command became a relic of the Cold War and was shuttered. Aside from a few notable (and mostly failed) exceptions, Washington didn't need to use brute force or even economic coercion to impose its will on others. The government could count on the glamor of Disneyworld and the American sports entertainment complex. It could rely on Wall Street and the World Bank. It could benefit from the prestige of companies like Nike, Microsoft, and Starbucks.

From the perspective of Chinese strategists, the United States was creating a world that was globalized, integrated, and profoundly threatening. But they also saw that this transformed world could allow, for the first time in human history, actual world domination. It was now possible for one country to smoothly seize control without total war and the risk of mass nuclear suicide. There was no reason China couldn't do the same. If the American-led system could be covertly infiltrated and compromised, the CCP could turn the whole architecture against its designer.

With enough patience and persistence, China could systematically take over every important institution, every company, developmental agency, and educational program in the American arsenal, and make them its own. China could buy foreign movie stars, directors, and even the chance to host the Olympics. Chinese intelligence officers could turn American corporations into their lobbyists. The CCP could hire the family members and friends of all the West's leading politicians, making them its agents of influence, like infected USBs that get plugged into a system administrators' computer, allowing hackers to take over the entire network.

At home and abroad, the Chinese government continued to subtly vilify the United States and other democracies. Over time, the CCP created a global information ecosystem where American billionaires, Ivy League professors, and even NBA stars had no voice whatsoever and no ability to express their views on China (and increasingly American politics too) unless they were parroting Beijing's talking points.

Meanwhile, the United States and other open societies warmly welcomed the voice of the Communist Party everywhere. Presidents and prime ministers looked the other way while Chinese spies silenced citizens in their own countries. They rationalized away the fact that the Chinese government was successfully undermining their freedom of expression, interfering in their internal politics, and rotting out their democracies.[706] The logical conclusion of this arrangement, if it continues, should be obvious.

How could America – the most powerful nation in history – have let this happened?

Dazed and Confused

At least four factors can account for Washington's heretofore inability to develop a coherent strategy for China.[707] These include: leadership misperceptions, technology developments, foreign influence, and a string of crises situations. Let's take a quick look at each factor.

Leadership Misperceptions. For American leaders, the end of the Cold War was both shocking and euphoric. In 1992, with the Soviet Union suddenly gone and the Russian Federation in shambles, no rival super-power existed. The nightmarish threat of nuclear war evaporated and there no longer seemed to be any justification for engaging in long-term strategy. In the minds of many foreign policy experts, history had ended. Western civilization had won, and American power seemed limitless on the horizon.

It became the predominant view that no other country could emerge to compete with the United States in a head-to-head fashion. Countries such as China might make efforts to challenge the American order on the fringes, but they would quickly find themselves brought into a wel-coming globalized world. It was largely taken for granted that America could shape China into a responsible stakeholder, accelerating the process of political change. Most in Washington assumed that as long as they treated the PRC like a friend, Beijing would reciprocate and cooperation would flourish. This assumption, of course, has been falsified by events.

Technology Developments. In the 1990s and 2000s, extraordinary leaps in computing power heightened American leaders' unrealistic sense of optimism. The Internet became regarded as a panacea, a magic weapon of freedom that could usurp oppressive regimes and replace them with enlightened democracies. It was assumed that going online would allow everyday Chinese people to access a flood of information, empowering them as individuals and making them capable of collective action. Social media, in particular, appeared destined to crumble the Great Firewall of China.

Few Americans anticipated the ways in which new communications technology could be used by the CCP for propaganda, surveillance, misinformation, truth denial, and history manipulation. In the words of John Garnaut, "Xi has shown that the subversive promise of the internet can be inverted.... With the assistance of Big Data science and Artificial Intelligence, he has been bending the Internet from an instrument of democratization into a tool of omniscient control."[708]

Rather than empower the champions of liberal democracy, the Internet seems to have actually lowered the quality of the Western media and strategic analysis in general. In Washington, officials have increasingly come to treat short blurbs on Twitter and Facebook as alternatives to detailed papers and speeches. The instant gratification of current events, reported on social media platforms, has eroded long-term thinking. As Robert D. Kaplan observed, American society has become so consumed by the present that few professionals have the time to imagine or even think about the future, let alone develop and articulate their visions for it in meaningful terms. So much data has become available that consumers of it are overwhelmed. Technology has affected American scholars, intelligence professionals, military officers, and, especially, policymakers, often making them appear incapable of processing surface-level information into deeper-level knowledge.[709] Their ability to concentrate on the implications of China's emergence as a strategic competitor has been shattered by a constant flood of calls, texts, tweets, and emails, the vast majority of which are trivial, but nonetheless appear important enough to look at.

Foreign Influence. With globalization and technology have come the rapid expansion of hostile foreign influence operations. As the CCP's economic resources have grown, so too have its efforts to channel money into campaigns to capture American politicians, government officials, and thought-leaders.[710] Chinese intelligence and political warfare operatives have made significant gains around the world.[711] And they appear to have acquired leverage over American media outlets, think tanks, universities, and government service companies, often using foundations and semi-private corporations as cover.[712]

In the world of politics and decision-making, it is difficult and perhaps impossible to fully grasp the effects that such operations have had. At a minimum, it is remarkable how many powerful Americans the Chinese authorities have been able to gain access to in venues that allow CCP agents to coax, cajole, or coerce them. It is unknowable the extent to which Beijing has altered American policy decisions and curtailed efforts at strategy. But it would be delusional for anyone to think that retired four-star generals, former secretaries of state, and out of office politicians who frequently travel to China and have business interests there are not being subjected to situations that erode their moral and ethical integrity.[713]

"The problem is simple.... China's leaders have articulated an unlimited concept of security that extends into the domain of ideas," Peter Mattis wrote in a landmark study on CCP influence operations.[714] And, according to Bethany Allen-Ebrahimian, China's government has "built an army of influence agents in the U.S.," which has been extraordinarily successful at manipulating the ideas of American policymakers.[715]

Crisis Situations. Contrary to expectations, the end of the Cold War did not bring the United States any meaningful sense of security. For many, the collapse of one giant adversary seemed to create a legion of small ones. In the 1990s, America plunged into conflicts in Iraq, Somalia, Haiti, and Serbia. Washington watched in horror as countries such as Rwanda and Congo were devastated by civil war and genocide, and as terrorists struck in Oklahoma City, New York, and Tokyo. Then, just as the PRC armaments program began to catch attention, the 9/11 terrorist attacks spun America into a state of national panic. From that point forward, long-term strategic thinking was pushed away and short-term tactical action dominated everything.

America plunged into wars in Afghanistan and Iraq, and both countries quickly became lawless quagmires from which the United States could not extract itself with honor. These grueling foreign conflicts played out against the backdrop of the 2004 Indian Ocean Tsunami, one of the deadliest natural disasters in recorded history. At home, Hurricane Katrina struck New Orleans, and the Great Recession devastated Wall Street, leaving in its wake persistently high unemployment and low consumer confidence across America. The U.S. Congress, highly polarized by the national trauma of recent events, responded by enacting the Budget Control Act, a law that ultimately had cascading effects which were not anticipated. Cuts to defense spending and a constant sense of uncertainty in the federal budget ensued.

From 2010 to 2012, a revolutionary wave of demonstrations, protests, coups, and riots swept across the Arab world, leaving in their wake destructive civil wars and failed states. In Syria, Iraq, and Yemen, conflicts produced terror and mass refugee flows. In 2014, Russia invaded Crimea and Eastern Ukraine, and the West Africa Ebola virus epidemic became the most widespread outbreak of that disease in history, with cases appearing as far away as the United States.

In Asia, the Chinese military launched a campaign of space weapons testing, cyberattacks, and naval expansion. North Korea, for its part, conducted a series of nuclear weapons tests and missile launches. These instigated significant, albeit intermittent, spikes in tensions. From 2015 to 2020, the United States suffered terror attacks in San Bernardino and Orlando, witnessed one of the most divisive presidential elections in its history, came close to a war with North Korea, and lost hundreds of thousands of people to the COVID-19 pandemic. On January 6, 2021, a violent mob of some eight hundred insurrectionists stormed inside the Capitol Building in a failed attempt to overturn the results of a legitimate presidential election. A year later, Russia launched an all-out invasion of Ukraine, shattering the long spell of peace between nation-states in Europe.

No single crisis could decisively cripple the American government. Still, several traumatic events arguably shook it to the core. The steady stream of shocks at home and abroad over the past thirty years seem to have placed American leaders in an increasingly weak, unsteady, and reactive position.

A Dystopian Future?

Future generations might look back at this current moment in history with a great deal of envy. For all its shortcomings, the American-led world order has been remarkably peaceful and prosperous. The fall of the Berlin Wall and the collapse of the Soviet Union are distant memories, if they are remembered at all. The specter of global nuclear holocaust, something which haunted Americans for forty years, forgotten altogether. The blessings of peace have been as deep as they have been rich. There hasn't been a great power war since the victorious Allies accepted the Empire of Japan's unconditional surrender in 1945.

Today, the gifts of enlightenment are abundant. More people than ever before in human history are living longer, healthier, richer, fuller, freer, and safer lives. They are better educated, better fed, better housed, and better entertained.[716] Not nuclear bombs, but rather technology and prosperity have exploded. How long can things go on getting better? Perhaps indefinitely. There is much, it seems, to look forward to as we gaze into the unknown future. Yet the world may be at the brink of catastrophe and not even know it.

If China continues to grow in power and influence, the positive trend lines we see today will plummet. The CCP intends to change the United States and the whole world in ways no American would accept. If that happens, things will not be as good tomorrow as they are today. They will be far worse. This is not generally appreciated because so few understand what the regime in China is planning and doing in the world.

What does Xi Jinping's signature slogan of constructing a Community of Common Destiny for All Mankind really mean? According to a leaked PLA document, "A Community of Common Destiny for All Mankind is our way of offering the 'China Model' to build a harmonized world."[717] What is the China Model? As we have seen, it is a Marxist-Leninist ideology and political system, a one-party dictatorship. The model China's rulers offer is that of a police state, an omnipresent collective under the rule of an extremely tiny minority of unelected strongmen, who answer to one all-powerful leader they call chairman.

A harmonized world, then, would be a future order in which all people on Earth are ruled by a network of regimes made in the image of the CCP. It would be an integrated global system of states subservient to Beijing. It would be a netherworld of shadows in which truth is less and less likely to survive. It would be a world of spirit-crushing digital tyranny in the name of an earthly paradise that is said to be coming but always proves just out of reach.[718]

There is little evidence that the key individuals responsible for defending Western principles, values, and interests comprehend the magnitude of the threat posed by the CCP's strategy. The dangers associated with China's emergence as the global center of totalitarian power are immense. Yet, if their policy choices are any indication, few elected officials in America seem to believe that the future might be as dystopian as suggested by Chinese officials' speeches, planning documents, and internal military writings – to say nothing of their actions at home and abroad.

No one can predict what the future will look like, including the men who rule China. But it would be a mistake to believe that Xi and his comrades are not trying to create the world of tomorrow. They are bending the arc of history in their desired direction and, so far, few strong hands are pulling in the opposite direction. There is no ceiling to the ambitions of the CCP. But there is also no floor to the regime's fear, insecurity, and paranoia. That blend of ambition and fear makes for a venomous foreign policy.

China is waging a second Cold War, a battle the United States and its closest allies seem unprepared to fight and win. Americans have no living memory of what it is like to face a hostile foreign power that threatens parity or even superiority in a large array of different fields. There are still fresh memories of the first Cold War, and lessons learned about what it took to prevail against the once-mighty Soviet Union are well documented and readily available. The Soviet Union, however, was a manifest failure in many ways that the PRC is not.

The USSR embraced unsound economic policies and was at a disadvantage technologically, culturally, and most important of all, ideologically. The Soviet Union's power and prestige were nonetheless immense and at times seemed to be overwhelming the United States. But Moscow relied heavily on the foundation laid by its massive military buildup, sustained in dramatic fashion for about forty-five years. Soviet science and industry were adequate for military applications. Moscow's achievements were almost entirely limited to that singular field of superpower competition.

This overreliance on a single instrument of power proved to be a shattering mistake. The Soviet Union's fall from the pinnacle of power was not foreordained. Still, it seems reasonable to conclude, as many did, that the rapidity of its collapse was the result of a special kind of exhaustion, one produced by an unsustainable imperial overreach. The USSR's demise was hastened by an obsessive focus on military power to the detriment of all else.

Today, Americans risk drawing flawed conclusions about strategic competition with the PRC as the result of their predecessors' shining success against the Soviet Union. Washington should avoid treating Beijing as a military rival first and foremost. China is in fact a far more sophisticated and dangerous adversary than any seen before. Historical analogies can be insightful, but only to a certain point. American strategists would be prudent to make sober assumptions based on empirical evidence and avoid reassuring anecdotes and irrational, mythical thinking. Victory is not assured. There's no guarantee that the second Cold War will be as painless as the first one. It might be far, far worse.

In the Balance

It would be nice to believe that thirty years from now memorials will dot China honoring the dead Uyghurs, Tibetans, Falun Gong practitioners, and other minority groups persecuted by the former Communist regime. It would be nice to believe that in the 2050s China will have its own version of the Holocaust museums and places of remembrance that today stand in Central Europe. But history shows us that the tides of time run cold, and there is no justice guaranteed to the victims of tyranny.

When they can, individuals always prefer to decide their own affairs and choose their own governments. But often they cannot. For the most part, groups of extraordinarily powerful people decide the future of great nations, even humankind. The centralization of all power in just a few hands is frightening to consider.[719] Technology is accelerating and expanding the reach of authoritarian governments. On November 30, 2021, Richard Moore, Chief of England's Secret Intelligence Service (MI6), said the following: "According to some assessments, we may experience more technological progress in the next ten years than in the last century, with a disruptive impact equal to the industrial revolution. As a society, we have yet to internalize this stark fact and its potential impact on global geopolitics."[720]

Perhaps the midpoint of the twenty-first century will see memorials erected across China paying tribute to the soldiers who died during the "glorious" coups and takeovers of Taiwan, Okinawa, and the Philippines. Perhaps there will be memorials immortalizing those who died in the War of Resistance against America and Japan, those killed by nuclear fires and postwar mega famines. The point is this: Nothing that will happen in the future is foreordained. Everything that will happen hangs in the balance and is subject to human agency. It is all unknowable and still undecided.

Americans face an unparalleled threat, but few can imagine it coming to life. So far, no political leader seems willing to sacrifice anything substantial to meet it. The two superpowers might be on a far more dangerous path than just that of a protracted Cold War, they might be on the path to actual war. Absent a historic effort to change course, Cold War II should probably be the least of anyone's worries, and such an outcome might even be viewed as a welcome alternative.[721]

Does the current U.S. policy toward the PRC reflect, or even somewhat account for, the inescapable facts, the audacious intentions made manifest in the writings and actions of the Chinese Communist Party? The ideological and geopolitical differences between America and China are so tectonic in scale and weight, that at any moment the entire foundation of the world could be rocked to pieces. A single tear pulled too far, one crack split just an inch open, and the entire line could explode. There is no shortage of potential fissures. The consequences are measureless.

15

NEW HORIZONS

The ideas of economists and political philosophers
... are more powerful than is commonly understood.
Indeed, the world is ruled by little else.[722]

—John Maynard Keynes

Fᴏʀ now, America is ahead of China and still has a preponderance of power and influence in the world. The United States has a higher standard of living, better technology, and a stronger military. America's alliance system and humanistic ideology give it tremendous comparative advantages. "Beijing is powerful, but that power is nothing compared to a united free world," wrote Miles Yu, who served as a senior China advisor at the State Department.[723]

But the free world might not stay that way much longer. In some areas, America and other democracies are anything but united, and, by some measures, they are rapidly falling behind. In China, the Communist Party is everywhere. It dominates not only the military and security services but also media outlets, universities, and the entertainment industry. Writers, musicians, and movie stars are allowed to exist only as long as they serve the state. The CCP sees literature, sports, and art as political instruments, not things with intrinsic value.[724]

The totalitarian regime in China comprises over 90 million Communist

Party members all serving a supreme leader, the chairman, who exercises absolute control over the Party, government, and society. Chinese banks and corporations are arms of the state. Even tourist groups and study abroad students are expected to serve the needs of Beijing. The regime denies free will and the existence of truth. It disparages universal values. It rejects God and ideas like love, law, and individual liberty. It seeks to engineer the human soul.[725]

As we have seen, the men and women of the CCP have used united front tactics to infiltrate and infect organizations worldwide. They are dedicated to the pursuit of a collective in which all human beings, and all cultures past, present, and future are assimilated. They are dedicated to the creation of an alternative universe characterized by utopian promises that can be realized only when all humankind has been subjected to a digital dictatorship – one designed by the CCP and enforced by international puppet regimes.

To put it simply, China's government seeks nothing less than world domination. That is Beijing's supreme strategic objective. It wants to export its system of mass surveillance and thought control globally. It wants to make every country, every government, and every individual so intertwined and interdependent that they have no choice but to surrender their freedom and sovereignty. The CCP has been quietly pushing toward its objective for years.

The Chinese government is able to harnesses vast resources and apply them in a centralized fashion. Beijing has staggering human and material resources at its disposal, and China's rulers know how to tell a compelling story. They understand how to spread their ideas and organizational practices. They come with guns, fast money, and mass surveillance systems for the regimes that want them. For everyone else, they have the myth of one billion customers, cheap consumer products, and development projects. The Communist Party feels compelled and entitled to saturate every corner of the world with its presence. China's government is a long-term threat to American national security, and one that is far more powerful and sophisticated than any that came before.

Nazi Germany, Imperial Japan, the Soviet Union, and Putin's Russia all pale in comparison.

American decision makers have failed to develop and implement a strategy for countering the CCP. That was unfortunate but understandable when China's trajectory was still uncertain. For forty years, it was the overriding policy of the United States to show friendship and goodwill to the PRC government, and, whenever possible, reassure China's rulers and sooth their concerns. That policy, in the afterlight of events, now appears unwise and irresponsible.

It seems reasonable to assume things would have turned out better had Washington developed good intelligence, held more realistic expectations of the future, and treated the regime in China like the actor that it actually was. There existed a solid body of facts that could have supported a strong policy toward China if anyone wanted one, especially after the Tiananmen Square massacre and the crack-up of the Soviet Union. That had little appeal.

Anyone who sits in judgement of the past actions of their government for too long risks losing sight of their nation's present circumstances and future possibilities. Rarely in a democracy do we find it difficult to second guess our leaders and marvel at their mistakes. Indeed, we have every right to do so and every good reason to think critically. Lessons others learned the hard way ought to serve as our best guides.

America now needs a blueprint for marshalling and applying all its national resources to save itself and defeat the PRC. A time of supreme danger is on the horizon. Already the United States is finding itself on increasingly dangerous ground both domestically and internationally as the CCP's strength continues to grow. China is catching up, and the stakes are the future of the world.

Artistic rendering of Xi Jinping at the one-hundredth
anniversary of the CCP, by Grace Young

A Cure for Catastrophe

How might the United States protect its interests in view of China's emergence as a hostile superpower with global ambitions? What is possible given the limited resources available? What should be a priority? What is of paramount importance, and what can Washington afford to write off? What should the cardinal strategic objective be and how to go about securing it? Where might America draw the line? There are no easy answers to all these questions, but some things are obvious.

The entire purpose of strategic competition is to achieve grand policy objectives and prevent a superpower war. State-on-state conflict is the ultimate failure of any government. It's a failure of policy, of diplomacy, of intelligence, and of imagination. Any decent strategist will put war prevention at the core of everything she or he does. This, of course, doesn't mean cooperating with or conceding to the enemy. It means deterring them from attacking your vital interests. It means placing so much stress on them that they back down in the event of crisis. It means scaring them so they never chose to escalate and harm you or your friends. It means dominating them during times of crisis and punishing provocations.

Thomas Mahnken provides six considerations for the formulation and implementation of strategy in a long-term competition. First, strategists must be focused on a concrete adversary, not an abstraction. This allows for the study of a competitor's strengths, weaknesses, plans and proclivities. Second, and related, strategists must make considerable investments into intelligence collection and analysis, needed for developing a deep understanding of the adversary. Third, strategists should take advantage of a competitor's resource constraints, forcing them to make difficult trade-offs. Fourth, strategists should seek to understand and exploit the internal logic of an adversary's bureaucracies. Fifth, strategists should take time factors into account, seeking to delay or deny an adversary from achieving their objectives in an acceptable timeframe. Finally, strategists should seek an action-reaction dynamic where their side maintains the initiative, forcing the competitor into a disadvantageous position and keeping them there until they break.[726]

It's important, then, that we study the way Xi Jinping and the CCP see things. We should seek to better understand their worldview and what makes them tick. Only then can we get inside their heads and find a way to seize and hold the initiative. Only then can we escape the trap of mirror imaging and avoid disastrous false assumptions. Only then might we ensure peace, protect our way of life, and make the world a better home for the next generation.

Accomplishing these objectives will require new organizations to cultivate a large corps of talented individuals. The United States faces an enormous intellectual problem that cannot be solved quickly. It will take a determined effort to cultivate and educate national security and civil society professionals for the protracted competition ahead.

As we have seen, Beijing aims to achieve world domination with military and non-military means. Indeed, the two are melded together by the Chinese government such that it is difficult, if not impossible, to know where the regime ends and the rest of society begins. All Chinese companies are controlled by the CCP and by law must serve the interests of the regime. For China, economic security is one pillar of regime security. But for China's trade partners, economic security is the very opposite of national security. When it comes to doing business with the PRC, economic entanglements are agents of national insecurity. The United States and other democracies around the world have plugged themselves into a system that aims to weaken and destroy them. They have become dangerously addicted and dependent.

In their blind pursuit of short-term economic gains, governments and companies around the world have walked right into the jungle of a super predator. America's analytic community appears to be overly focused on the military domain of competition. This focus takes brainpower, time, and other vital resources away from waging effective competition in the other domains, which are poorly funded or ignored completely. Top policymakers rarely seem to realize there is an existential competition going on, let alone that they could be losing it.

Future public policy research efforts should consider new domains of competition. American leaders must recognize that the PRC has advantages the USSR's leaders could only dream about. Beijing has a fundamentally different and better strategy to achieve world domination. At worst, the Soviet Union posed an existential threat to America because of its superiority in conventional and nuclear forces. China in the future will pose an existential threat because of its military too, but it could also control the Internet, international organizations, and critical supply chains. It could dominate the global narrative, the market, and all major industries. The CCP already has made enormous gains.

Globalization and trade with China have been a disaster for American national security in the twenty-first century. The situation will worsen as long as the United States treats a genocidal regime as though it were basically a normal government. The very best we could probably hope for will be a world divided into trade blocs. Today in Washington there is conference after conference, war game after war game, and study after study on China's military. No comparable effort exists to explore and understand the state of political competition, ideological competition, economic competition, technology competition – all those vital areas the CCP strives to win while all backs are turned and all eyes fixed on military threats.

Peter Mattis points out that the United States should seek to cultivate a team of individuals with a blend of China-related expertise, knowledge of policy making, and appreciation for the art of developing and executing competitive strategy.[727] Huge intellectual gaps remain and our understanding continues to be insufficient for meeting the requirements of strategic competition.

Countering China's growing hegemony will require tremendous improvements in public education focused on meeting this challenge. Liza Tobin makes a strong case that "China watchers have the opportunity to broaden how they inform policymakers and the public about Beijing's own articulation of its global ambitions."[728] She advocates for the government and civil society to devote "more resources to monitoring and analyzing Beijing's publicly available high-level documents and authoritative media. Deeper understanding of the party's rhetoric and use of information as a tool of statecraft can be incorporated into U.S. policymaking processes."[729]

The intentions and plans of Beijing deserve closer examination. To appreciate and judge the state of strategic competition, the situation in terms of who is winning and who is losing, it is necessary to look at the picture from the CCP's point of view. The record of U.S.-PRC relations demonstrates that it has often been in Beijing's power to distort and confuse the American intelligence and policy-making community. Too many American politicians, diplomats, and scholars talk directly to their counterparts in China, and all too often with the unrealistic expectation that they can gleam facts and insights from slippery sources.

In the present circumstances, the safest guide to understanding China is a sure knowledge of the CCP's true interests as it defines them. Perhaps what Washington needs is not endless people-to-people engagements, phone calls, and leadership summits with CCP cadres. What is needed are authoritative documents and, more importantly, the discernment necessary to pull critical information from them and make good sense of main points. To fulfill that need, it is essential to keep China specialists from being pulled into never-ending debates whirling around nomenclature and other trivial details.

Many China analysts are prone to being captured by the alluring texture of what amounts to the informational equivalent of tree bark. They will lovingly fix their gaze on every tiny groove, losing sight of the tree itself. Sometimes in their mental rapture they will even forget that bark is but one part of a tree and each tree exists in a great forest. Well, that forest may be on fire, and the hungry fire may be moving in their direction, looking to eat their tree bark and everyone else's too.

To put it bluntly, China research should not be conducted for its own sake, or for the sake of maintaining smooth U.S.-PRC relations. Rather, its purpose should be to inform future American policymakers during the second Cold War. Toshi Yoshihara and Jack Bianchi argue that "The allied strategic communities should engage in analytic efforts similar to those that studied the Soviet Union's cost of maintaining its political, economic, and military influence on a global scale." They observe, "policymakers could then use these studies to assess their own means of raising China's costs of empire to slow or complicate China's expansion."[730]

Yoshihara and Bianchi point out that America and its friends "will need to assess China's political, economic, technological, social, and other weaknesses, and develop strategies that leverage Chinese vulnerabilities in those areas. Indeed, the non-military dimensions of the competition could prove decisive."[731] To be successful in such endeavors, long-range thinking is required. It will likely take at least ten years to establish and build up the kind of new American institutions that can fill critical gaps. Legacy organizations in Washington suffer from inertia and have a vested interest in maintaining the status quo to the maximum extent possible. Only with adequate congressional appropriations and support from civil society will real change be possible. Fresh China studies programs and new institutions are desperately needed. Non-traditional education and innovative career paths would produce creative people with the skills (and the freedom from coercion) that are needed to do the type of work that could help save the world.

Will elected leaders in the United States and other like-minded countries join together? Will they make hard choices and act with alacrity? Or will they do whatever seems politically expedient and risk waiting until it's too late? The future of our generation and generations to follow depends on getting this problem right.

What Can Civil Society Do?

In a country like the United States, the government will always be restrained and limited in its power. Popular consent is vital, and that means a considerable part of America's strategic problem – and the solution to that problem – is educational. It is of national importance that Hollywood begins to make movies about China that are not censored. The films that are shown in America's big block cinemas and suburban home theaters may determine, in the long run, the fate of good governments and humane civilization. They will promote, or plague, the prestige by which free, open, and tolerant democracies maintain their precarious holds on hearts and minds amid the hurricane of lies manufactured and spread online by China's government and its proxies.

The human mind thinks more easily in images than words. What is seen is understood instantly, what is read or heard only gradually, if ever. Nothing could be more dangerous to the cause of human freedom than an entertainment industry whose genius directors and brilliant stars are servants of tyranny. American-style democracy could survive even a nuclear attack on the homeland if the nation's foundational ideas and principles reigned supreme in the souls of the survivors. But if the Declaration of Independence and the Constitution are reduced to ash in our imaginations, what hope is there?

State and local-level organizations have a major role to play when it comes to education reform. As a society, we need to talk much more about what it means to have a modern-day communist superpower in the world and a second Cold War. How to adapt and respond should be the central issue in political debates everywhere, from Houston to Iowa City and Orlando to Portland. China is changing the world faster than America can keep up, and the change is only going to accelerate.

The Chinese government exercises control over all organized groups of people in China, from major corporations to small private organizations ostensibly engaged in cultural and educational exchanges. The CCP's control is enforced in a ruthless fashion by a government that views individual agency and human rights as things to be destroyed by any means necessary for the collective good of the state. How, then, are American university leaders, professors, and researchers accounting for these facts? What safeguards exist to protect the knowledge they create from being warped?

No American university would welcome money from Nazis, drug cartels, or terrorists. Yet the reality is that when they accept money from Chinese sources linked to the CCP, they are welcoming a totalitarian regime into their classrooms, their networks, and their labs. They are signing on to arrangements intended to advance the interests of a political organization that is fundamentally anti-American. With each technological breakthrough, each problem solved, each mental exertion rewarded, Americans working on China-funded research give aid to a regime dedicated to the ultimate destruction of freedom. They are helping Beijing turn the wheel of civilization backward.

The People's Liberation Army has the ability to seize information collected by Chinese entities at American universities. Beijing's military-civil fusion strategy has removed even the thin cloak of plausible deniability Chinese companies and other civilian organizations previously could hide behind. It is imperative that policymakers at every level of government dam up the torrent of CCP-linked money currently flowing into the nation's education system. A continuation of the current arrangement would have grave implications for U.S. national security. Today if Chinese military scientists cannot innovate, they simply buy the brainpower of Americans who can.

Concert of Democracies

For America and other democracies, what might winning look like? Let's imagine the world of 2038, a future in which American strategists are beating their adversaries in China. To reach this place, the United States, Japan, England, Australia, and other allies have joined together to counter the CCP. The allies have enhanced the character of international organizations and formed a Concert of Democracies, an exclusive club that only high-performing nations with good governance track records are allowed to join.

This new institution is the gold standard when it comes to global cooperation. It is transparent, trustworthy, and incorruptible. Imagine an ideal version of the United Nations (one where the organization doesn't have genocidal dictatorships occupying seats on the Human Rights Council and Marxist ministers running the World Health Organization). All countries are welcome to join the Concert of Democracies, but only after they have reached certain benchmarks set by independent, non-governmental organizations like Freedom House, Human Rights Watch, and Reporters Without Borders.

The Concert of Democracies has more than just moral authority on its side. In the 2020s, members united together to move their supply chains out of China, creating a free and open trade block that excludes the CCP and its predatory practices. This trade block is so lucrative and attractive that many other governments around the world have proven willing to make system-wide political reforms to join. This, in turn, helps spread democracy and promote human rights, even as it alleviates poverty and bolsters green, sustainable growth. The United States and its allies have built a safe and clean digital 17G infrastructure, protecting personal privacy and giving internet users freedom from micro-targeting and digital content manipulation.

Members of the Concert of Democracies invest heavily in research aimed at improving key measures of human development. Average life expectancy in the world's thirty wealthiest nations was forecast to go up to around 90 years. Instead, it's risen to 110 years across seventy nations, thanks to scientific breakthroughs and the sharing of multilingual AI-powered medical technologies. Advancements in high-quality mass education have produced social benefits beyond what anyone expected.

The United States and its allies, including Taiwan and the Tibetan Government-in-Exile, have pooled their resources to create a joint defensive infrastructure. This collective security organization ensures China cannot invade its neighbors. Together the democracies have strategic and operational overmatch. Tensions persist, but the overall situation is stable because war planners in Beijing cannot conceive of any attack plan that would give them a decent chance of success.

China's economy stagnated and is now declining. The CCP is under immense pressure to reform itself politically and follow the successful Taiwan model. Under overwhelming pressure from the Community of Democracies, Beijing has closed all its concentration camps. It has re-instituted rule of law in Hong Kong. It has ended its draconian policies of repression against religious groups and ethnic minorities. It has begun allowing for some freedom of the press, and opposition political parties are growing.

China's communist government seems to be on the cusp of positive change. It may change in a gradual or revolutionary fashion. Observers agree that it is impossible to predict just how this might happen and what situations would follow from it. In theory, such an event could allow for the reduction of world tensions and a sustained policy of cooperation, especially if China ultimately becomes a liberal democracy.

Perhaps, like the USSR, it will break into a number of smaller, less powerful states. But the post-Soviet evolution of Russia from 1991 to the present serves as a cautionary tale. Over time, even a reforming or weakened China could regress into a militant dictatorship. In general, however, it seems reasonable to assume that a fundamentally reformed

China – one without the CCP – would be far better than what the world is dealing with now.

Extreme Competition, Tolerant Politics

Some appear to be convinced that American democracy cannot win and China's government is unstoppable. They seem to think we are fated to soon live in a world dominated by the Chinese Communist Party. Such fatalism is dangerous. If we believe that the United States will be overtaken by the growing illiberal power of China, then we are buying into a false narrative that argues the crumbling of freedom and democracy is inevitable. We are resigning ourselves and generations to come to a world devoid of humanism, reason, science – all the classical liberal values. We are watching the dawn of a new dark age.

History shows that free societies have relatively little to fear from ultra-radical agitators, homegrown terrorists, and conspiracies to overthrow the government. It is in those societies with intense political persecutions that communists and fascists have found fertile ground. The more intense the state's level of persecution, the more fragile its ruling elite grows. Nothing has served the cause and spread of totalitarianism as effectively as illiberal and oppressive regimes. Nothing has stymied it as reliably as governments that exercise democratic principles and give their people freedom, liberty, and tolerance. The single most powerful weapon ever created in defense of human thriving and social progress, therefore, might be the American enlightenment. As long as the United States and its like-minded allies remain true to their principles and laws, and true to each other, the world will be a safer place for the next generation. It will also be a better one.

But playing defense would be unwise. Vital stakeholders across America are exposed to hostile influence operations and can be held hostage by the Chinese government and forced into situations that challenge their moral values, religious beliefs, and ethical principles. Many already have fallen into the CCP's hands and become little more than puppets. The United States is intertwined with the PRC regime in so many ways. American citizens across society are dependent on buyers and suppliers in China, and surrounded by data-extracting technology devices that can be used to change the way they think and vote. Over time, it may even become possible for authorities in China to manipulate large swaths of the population, undermine the nation's sovereignty, and destroy the principles of liberty, democracy, and self-government.

American leaders would be prudent to go on the offensive. They should develop and execute a plan with the following objectives. First, they should sever the CCP's tentacles of influence, which are currently wrapped around American society. Second, they should isolate, encircle, and contain Beijing to the maximum extent possible, keeping the CCP from taking over Taiwan and expanding further in the world. Third, they should accelerate the decline of the CCP on the international stage and reduce the engine of its strength – China's economy. Ensuring the survival and success of American democracy will require the steady reduction of Beijing's global power and the prevention of war. Ultimately, the Chinese people must decide for themselves what the future of their nation looks like. They should be free from oppression and allowed to choose their own form of government. It could take decades for that to happen.

Should a policy of intense competition be embraced in Washington, what might that look like? Rather than alleviating the fears and suspicions of China's rulers, the Americans and their allies might consider validating them. To this end they would gather the intelligence necessary to get inside Beijing's control complex and exploit vulnerabilities. U.S. covert action programs might seek to oppose the Chinese government in every way. Elections in Beijing are nonexistent, but there are endless power struggles and ample opportunities for sowing divisions. Thin bonds of trust are easy to sever. The brutal and repressive nature of China's political system means the regime is often its own worst enemy. Peer past the placid surface of order and calm in the Great Hall of the People and a seething mass of dark emotions will be visible there below.

Is there any worse idea in human history than the politicized pursuit of perfection? Take for example the Communist International attempts to construct heaven-on-earth. Consider the fundamentalist Islamist, Christian, or Hindu quests for it after death. Politics and extremist ideologies make for a hateful mix. Rather than allow for evolutionary and peaceful change, letting humankind gradually grow in social complexity and general happiness, exponents of perfection are impatient, selfish, and massively destructive. They seek paradise in their own time (or immediately after death). To this end they evacuate the oxygen out of all intellectual life around them, imposing their fantasies on others. Misery and chaos follow in their wake. It is not heaven, but hell, they create.

Power is best left to those governments in free societies who are capable of accepting human imperfection and satisfied with advancing their nations toward the light of a future that yields its brightness over generations. Wise leaders are careful to move their nations forward in patient and progressive increments. The "final struggle" sought by Beijing would mean continuous revolution and political violence forever. The true struggle that will decide the future of the world is the struggle for increasingly open, moderate, and tolerant politics. If humankind is to ever be peaceful and prosperous in a broad and comprehensive sense, that is the struggle we must win.

NOTES

Note on Terms

1   See "The Principles of Newspeak" in George Orwell, *1984* (New York: Signet Classics, 1950), pp. 299–312; and George Orwell, "Politics and the English Language," *Horizon*, April 1946, available online at https://www.orwellfoundation.com/the-orwell-foundation/orwell/essays-and-other-works/politics-and-the-english-language/.

Chapter One: Wreaths & Radios

2   Winston S. Churchill, *The World Crisis: Volume II* (London: Bloomsbury Academic Press, 2015, first published 1923), p. 5.

3   "Arlington Escort Information," *Wreaths across America*, accessed March 31, 2020, at https://www.wreathsacrossamerica.org/arlington-escort-information.

4   "Our Story," *Wreaths across America*, accessed March 31, 2020, at https://www.wreathsacrossamerica.org/our-story;"Arlington Escort Information," *Wreaths across America*; "Remember. Honor. Teach." *Wreaths across America*, accessed March 31, 2020, at https://www.wreathsacrossamerica.org/remember-honor-teach/#remember; and Johanna S. Billings, "Truckers gather before wreath convoy departs," *The Ellsworth American*, December 11, 2019, at https://www.ellsworthamerican.com/featured/truckers-gather-before-wreaths-convoy-departs/.

5   Mona Gunn, "A Legacy of Service – A Mission of Honor," *TAPS*, June 24, 2020, at https://www.taps.org/articles/26-2/legacy-of-service.

6   This section draws from the author's interviews aboard U.S. and allied destroyers in San Diego, Yokosuka, and Su'ao.

7   For background, see "USS Cole (DDG-67) Determined Warrior," *Naval History and Heritage Command*, February 7, 2019 (accessed May 10, 2021), at https://web.archive.org/web/20190531150203/https://www. history.navy.mil/content/history/nhhc/browse-by-topic/ships/modern-ships/uss-cole-updated.html; Cindy C. Combs and Martin Slann, *Encyclopedia of Terrorism: Revised Edition* (New York: Facts On File, 2007), p. 353; and Raphael Perl and Ronald O'Rourke, "Terrorist Attack on USS Cole: Background and Issues for Congress," *Congressional Research Service*, January 30, 2001, at https://www.everycrsreport.com/reports/RS20721.html.

8   Steve Vogel, "Family Pride Helps Dry Tears," *Washington Post*, October 21, 2000, at https://www.washingtonpost.com/archive/local/2000/10/21/family-pride-helps-dry-tears/3e5689aa-1190-439c-9be6-c09ca749c206/; Rudi Williams, "White House Remembers Sailors Killed in USS Cole Attack," *DoD News*, October 13, 2005, at https://archive.defense.gov/news/newsarticle.aspx?id=18084; "Wreaths Across America Announces 2019 Escort to Arlington," *PR Newswire*, November 22, 2019, at https://www.prnewswire.com/news-releases/wreaths-across-america-announces-2019-escort-to-arlington-300963926.html; "Mona Gunn, 2019–2020 National President American Gold Star Mothers, Inc.," *American Gold Star Mothers, Inc.*, accessed March 31, 2020, at https://www.goldstarmoms.com/national-president-mona-gunn.html; and Billings, "Truckers gather before wreath convoy departs."

9   "Our Story," *Wreaths across America*.

10   "Hytera Provides Push-to-Talk over Cellular Radio Service to Wreaths Across America," *Hytera*, November 21, 2019, at https://www.hytera.us/news/hytera-america-donates-poc-radios-to-wreaths-across-america.

11   Hytera U.S. Website Homepage, accessed March 31, 2020, at https://www.hytera.us/.

12   "About Hytera," accessed March 31, 2020, at https://www.hytera.us/about.

13   Tony Quested, "UK approval the last barrier to Sepura takeover," *Business Weekly*, May 2, 2017, at https://www.businessweekly.co.uk/news/hi-tech/uk-approval-last-barrier-sepura-takeover; Simon Zekaria, "Hytera, Sepura deal faces UK scrutiny over risk to national security," *Mlex*, April 13, 2017, at https://mlexmarketinsight.com/insights-center/editors-picks/mergers/europe/hytera-sepura-deal-faces-uk-scrutiny-over-risk-to-national-security; and "Sepura secures Scottish Prison Service," *TCCA*, undated, accessed March 31, 2020, at https://tcca.info/sepura-secures-scottish-prison-service/. Note that Hytera products are sold to jails, prison, and correctional facilities in the United States by certified dealers such as Homeland Safety Systems, Inc. See "Correctional Center Surveillance And Access Control Systems

Louisiana, Arkansas and Mississippi Jails, Prisons & Correctional Facilities," *Homeland Safety Systems Inc.*, undated, accessed March 31, 2020, at https://www.home landsafetysystems.com/industries/jails-prisons-surveillance-systems/. See also Hytera's "Smart Prison Solutions" in its undated sales brochure tailored to the U.S. Bureau of Prisons, accessed March 31, 2020, at https://www.hytera.com/upload/enterprice/files/PMRIoT_Brochure.pdf.

14   David J. Lynch, "Chinese maker of radios for police, firefighters struggles to outlast Trump trade fight," *Washington Post*, January 30, 2019, at https://www.washingtonpost.com/business/economy/chinese-maker-of-radios-for-police-firefighters-promises-to-outlast-trump-trade-fight/2019/01/30/42a118a8-1f33-11e9-8b59-0a28f2191131_story.html; "Defense Applications," *Norsat International Inc.*, accessed March 31, 2020, at http://www.norsat.com/applications/defense/; and "Covert surveillance: Industry Solutions," *Sepura*, accessed March 31, 2020, at https://www.sepura.com/industries/covert-surveillance.

15   "TETRA in North America," *PowerTrunk*, January 21, 2021, at https://www.powertrunk.com/pressroom/tetra-in-north-america/; "First Ten Years Of PowerTrunk in North America," *PowerTrunk*, December 2, 2019, at https://www.powertrunk.com/pressroom/first-ten-years-of-powertrunk-in-north-america/; and "New Jersey Transit Renews Its Confidence in PowerTrunk Through 3-Year Maintenance Contract," *PowerTrunk*, September 4, 2019, at https://www.powertrunk.com/pressroom/new-jersey-transit-renews-its-confidence-in-powertrunk-through-3-year-maintenance-contract/.

16   "Case Studies," *Teltronic*, undated, accessed September 29, 2021, at https://www.teltronic.es/en/case-studies/.

17   "Hytera Communications Corp., Ltd. (海能达通信股份有限公司)," *The 9th Annual Chinese Defense Informationization Equipment and Technology Exhibition 2020*, July 7, 2020, at http://www.81guofang.com/exhibition-center/exhibitors/919.html. See also "Public Safety and Homeland Security Bureau Announces Publication of the List of Equipment and Services Covered by Section 2 of the Secure Networks Act," *Federal Communications Commission*, March 12, 2021, at https://docs.fcc.gov/public/attachments/DA-21-309A1.pdf.

18   "Public Security (公共安全)," *Hytera*, undated, accessed on October 15, 2020, at https://www.hytera.com/cn/#/index/caseList/52.

19   Archived by author on April 2, 2020, and available on request.

20   Adrian Zenz, "Xinjiang's System of Militarized Vocational Training Comes to Tibet," *China Brief*, September 22, 2020, at https://jamestown.org/program/jamestown-early-warning-brief-xinjiangs-system-of-militarized-vocational-training-comes-to-tibet/; Adrian Zenz, "Xinjiang's Re-Education and Securitization Campaign: Evidence from

Domestic Security Budgets," *China Brief*, November 5, 2018, at https://jamestown.org/program/xinjiangs-re-education-and-securitization-campaign-evidence-from-domestic-security-budgets/; and Adrian Zenz and James Leibold, "Chen Quanguo: The Strongman Behind Beijing's Securitization Strategy in Tibet and Xinjiang," *China Brief*, September 21, 2017, at https://jamestown.org/program/chen-quanguo-the-strongman-behind-beijings-securitization-strategy-in-tibet-and-xinjiang/.

21   "Orphaned by the State: How Xinjiang's gulag tears families apart," *The Economist*, October 17, 2020, at https://www.economist.com/china/2020/10/17/how-xinjiangs-gulag-tears-families-apart; and "Apartheid with Chinese Characteristics: China has turned Xinjiang into a police state like no other," *The Economist*, June 2, 2018, at https://www.economist.com/briefing/2018/05/31/china-has-turned-xinjiang-into-a-police-state-like-no-other.

22   "Fact Sheet: New U.S. Government Actions on Forced Labor in Xinjiang," *The White House*, June 24, 2021, at https://www.whitehouse.gov/briefing-room/statements-releases/2021/06/24/fact-sheet-new-u-s-government-actions-on-forced-labor-in-xinjiang/; and Michael R. Pompeo, "Determination of the Secretary of State on Atrocities in Xinjiang," *U.S. Department of State*, January 19, 2021, at https://2017-2021.state.gov/determination-of-the-secretary-of-state-on-atrocities-in-xinjiang/index.html.

23   Yonah Diamond, et al, "The Uyghur Genocide: An Examination of China's Breaches of the 1948 Genocide Convention," *Newlines Institute for Strategy and Policy*, March 8, 2021, at https://newlinesinstitute.org/uyghurs/the-uyghur-genocide-an-examination-of-chinas-breaches-of-the-1948-genocide-convention/; Helen Davidson, "China is breaching every article in genocide convention, says legal report on Uighurs," *The Guardian*, March 9, 2021, at https://www.theguardian.com/world/2021/mar/09/chinas-treatment-of-uighurs-breaches-un-genocide-convention-finds-landmark-report; and Adrian Zenz, "Sterilizations, IUDs, and Mandatory Birth Control: The CCP's Campaign to Suppress Uyghur Birthrates in Xinjiang," *Jamestown Foundation*, June 2020, at https://jamestown.org/product/sterilizations-iuds-and-mandatory-birth-control-the-ccps-campaign-to-suppress-uyghur-birthrates-in-xinjiang/.

24   Ross Anderson, "When China Sees All," *The Atlantic*, September 2020, at https://www.theatlantic.com/magazine/archive/2020/09/china-ai-surveillance/614197/.

25   Anderson, "When China Sees All."

26   Scott McGregor and Ina Mitchell, "China's social credit program creeps into Canada," *Sunday Guardian Live*, April 17, 2021, at https://www.

sundayguardianlive.com/news/chinas-social-credit-program-creeps-canada.

27   Anderson, "When China Sees All."

28   "Additional Huawei Affiliates Added to Entity List; BIS Updates
      Temporary General License and Issues FAQs; DoD Prohibits Federal
      Agencies From Obtaining Huawei Equipment," *JDSUPRA*, September
      24, 2019, at https://www.jdsupra.com/legalnews/additional-huawei-
      affiliates-added-to-24817/.

29   "Public Safety and Homeland Security Bureau Announces Publication of
      the List of Equipment and Services Covered by Section 2 of the Secure
      Networks Act," *Federal Communications Commission*, March 12, 2021,
      at https://docs.fcc.gov/public/attachments/DA-21-309A1.pdf; and "FCC
      Publishes List of Communications Equipment and Services That Pose
      a Threat to National Security," *FC News*, March 12, 2021, at https://docs.
      fcc.gov/public/attachments/DOC-370755A1.pdf.

30   "U.S. to open program to replace Huawei equipment in U.S. networks,"
      Reuters, September 27, 2021, at https://www.reuters.com/business/
      media-telecom/us-open-program-replace-huawei-equipment-us-
      networks-2021-09-27/; and David Shepardson, "Five Chinese companies
      pose threat to U.S. national security: FCC," Reuters, March 12, 2021, at
      https://www.reuters.com/article/us-usa-china-tech-idUSKBN2B42DW.

31   See "H1B Salary Database," accessed December 6, 2021 at https://
      h1bdata.info/index.php?year=2018&city=MIRAMAR; "H1B Data:
      Hytera America," accessed December 6, 2021, at https://h1bdata.com/
      pin/hytera-america/; and David J. Lynch, "Chinese maker of radios for
      police, firefighters struggles to outlast Trump trade fight," *Washington
      Post*, January 30, 2019, at https://www.washingtonpost.com/business/
      economy/chinese-maker-of-radios-for-police-firefighters-promises-
      to-outlast-trump-trade-fight/2019/01/30/42a118a8-1f33-11e9-8b59-
      0a28f2191131_story.html.

32   "Motorola Solutions Wins Trade Secret Theft and Copyright
      Infringement Lawsuits Against Hytera," *Motorola Solutions*, February
      14, 2020, at https://newsroom.motorolasolutions.com/news/motorola-
      solutions-wins-trade-secret-theft-and-copyright-infringement-lawsuits-
      against-hytera.htm.

33   "Litigators of the Week: Kirkland Trio Send a $765 Million Message
      in Tech Theft Case," *Kirkland & Ellis*, February 28, 2020, at https://
      www.kirkland.com/news/in-the-news/2020/02/litigators-of-the-week-
      kirkland-motorola.

34   Ahmad Hathout, "Another Company Joins Diversified in Criticizing
      FCC for Hytera Blacklist," *Broadband Breakfast*, September 14, 2021,
      at https://broadbandbreakfast.com/2021/09/another-company-joins-

diversified-in-criticizing-fcc-for-hytera-blacklist/; and Ahmad Hathout, "Hytera's Inclusion on FCC's National Security Blacklist 'Absurd,' Client Says," *Broadband Breakfast*, September 8, 2021, at https://broadbandbreakfast.com/2021/09/hyteras-inclusion-on-fccs-national-security-blacklist-absurd-client-says/. For background, see David J. Lynch, "Chinese maker of radios for police, firefighters struggles to outlast Trump trade fight," *Washington Post*, January 30, 2019, at https://www.washingtonpost.com/business/economy/chinese-maker-of-radios-for-police-firefighters-promises-to-outlast-trump-trade-fight/2019/01/30/42a118a8-1f33-11e9-8b59-0a28f2191131_story.html.

35   "Acquisition of Sepura plc by Hytera Communications Corporation Limited: revised national security undertakings," *UK Department for Business, Energy & Industrial Strategy*, September 28, 2021, at https://www.gov.uk/government/consultations/acquisition-of-sepura-plc-by-hytera-communications-corporation-limited-revised-national-security-undertakings; and Donny Jackson, "Sepura: We're not impacted by injunction to freeze Hytera assets in the UK," *Urgent Communications*, April 30, 2020, at https://urgentcomm.com/2020/04/30/sepura-were-not-impacted-by-court-order-to-freeze-hytera-assets-in-the-uk/.

36   "Covert Surveillance: Industry Solutions," *Sepura*, accessed September 29, 2021, at https://www.sepura.com/industries/covert-surveillance.

37   "Sepura CommsTech protects Brazil-Bolivia border," *Business Weekly*, March 25, 2021, at https://www.businessweekly.co.uk/export/americas/sepura-commstech-protects-brazil-bolivia-border.

38   Lynch, "Chinese maker of radios."

39   Roslyn Layton, "FCC Wants to Close Loopholes That Let Huawei Sell Smartphones on Amazon," *Forbes*, September 21, 2021, at https://www.forbes.com/sites/roslynlayton/2021/09/21/fcc-wants-to-close-loopholes-that-let-huawei-sell-smartphones-on-amazon/?sh=36b7e5ab2ad4. For details, see Roslyn Layton and Peter Wood, "Comments of China Tech Threat and Blue Path Labs Before Federal Communications Commission," *China Tech Threat*, September 20, 2021, at https://chinatechthreat.com/wp-content/uploads/2021/09/ChinaTechThreat-BluePathLabs-FCC-Equipment-Authorization-21-232-and-21-233-FINAL.pdf. For an analysis of the magnitude of the problem facing the U.S. government, see Trevor R. Jones and Treston Chandler, "Sweeping U.S. Lists Seek to Restrict Trade and Investments that Support the Chinese Military," *Wisconsin Project*, September 27, 2021, at https://www.wisconsinproject.org/sweeping-us-lists-seek-to-restrict-trade-investment-that-support-chinese-military/#appendix.

40   "Deeply Implementing Comprehensive State Security" Xinhua; "Counter Spy Law of the People's Republic of China (中华人民共和国反间谍法)," *PRC Ministry of National Defense*, December 7, 2017, at http://www.

mod.gov.cn/regulatory/2017-12/07/content_4799261.htm; "State Security Law of the People's Republic of China (中华人民共和国国家安全法)," *PRC Ministry of National Defense*, April 7, 2017, at http://www.81.cn/2017gjaqjyr/2017-04/07/content_7553456.htm; and "Internet Security Law of the People's Republic of China (中华人民共和国网络安全法)," *Office of the CCP Central Cyberspace Affairs Commission*, November 7, 2016, at http://www.cac.gov.cn/2016-11/07/c_1119867116.htm.

41   "State Intelligence Law of the People's Republic of China (中华人民共和国国家情报法)," *PRC National People's Congress*, June 27, 2017, at http://www.npc.gov.cn/npc/c30834/201806/483221713dac4f31bda7f9d951108912.shtml.

42   For an example of how this works in practice, see "China's Collection of Genomic and Other Healthcare Data From American: Risks to Privacy and U.S. Economic and National Security," *The National Counterintelligence and Security Center*, February 2021, at https://www.dni.gov/files/NCSC/documents/SafeguardingOurFuture/NCSC_China_Genomics_Fact_Sheet_2021.pdf.

43   Stein Ringen, *The Perfect Dictatorship: China in the 21st Century* (Hong Kong: Hong Kong University Press, 2016), pp. 14–15.

44   Ringen, *The Perfect Dictatorship*, pp. 65–66.

45   Ringen, *The Perfect Dictatorship*, pp. 14–15.

46   Ringen, *The Perfect Dictatorship*, pp. 14–15, 60, 65–66, 138–142.

47   Christopher Wray, "The Threat Posed by the Chinese Government and the Chinese Communist Party to the Economic and National Security of the United States," *Federal Bureau of Investigation*, July 7, 2020, at https://www.fbi.gov/news/speeches/the-threat-posed-by-the-chinese-government-and-the-chinese-communist-party-to-the-economic-and-national-security-of-the-united-states; "The United States Strategic Approach to the People's Republic of China," *The White House*, May 26, 2020, pp. 2–3, at https://www.whitehouse.gov/articles/united-states-strategic-approach-to-the-peoples-republic-of-china/; and "China: The Risk to Corporate America," *Federal Bureau of Investigation*, October 4, 2019, at https://www.fbi.gov/file-repository/china-risk-to-corporate-america-2019.pdf/view.

48   "Deeply Implementing Comprehensive State Security," Xinhua; "Counter Spy Law of the People's Republic of China," *PRC Ministry of National Defense*; "State Security Law," *PRC Ministry of National Defense*; and "Internet Security Law," *Office of the CCP Central Cyberspace Affairs Commission*.

49   Jiang Luwu and Luo Yongguang (eds), *Realizing the Deep Development of Military-Civil Fusion in Our Overall Setup* [形成军民融合深度发展格局] (Beijing: National Defense University Press, 2018), pp. 75–79.

50   Hsu Szu-chien, Anne-Marie Brady, and J. Michael Cole, "Introduction,"
      Insidious Power: How China Undermines Global Democracy (Manchester,
      UK: Camphor Press, 2020), p. xxvi.

51   Office of the Secretary of Defense, *Military and Security Developments
      Involving the People's Republic of China 2020* (Arlington, VA:
      Department of Defense, 2020), vi, at https://media.defense.gov/2020/
      Sep/01/2002488689/-1/-1/1/2020-DOD-CHINA-MILITARY-POWER-
      REPORT-FINAL.PDF.

52   Roslyn Layton, "New Pentagon report shows how restricted Chinese
      IT products routinely enter US military networks," *American Enterprise
      Institute*, August 12, 2019, at https://www.aei.org/technology-and-
      innovation/new-pentagon-reports-shows-how-restricted-chinese-it-
      products-routinely-make-their-way-into-us-military-networks/.

53   Jiang and Luo, *Military-Civil Fusion*, pp. 155–158.

54   Jiang and Luo, *Military-Civil Fusion*, pp. 155–158.

55   For background, see "Reference List for National Recruitment of High-
      level Overseas Talents (国家引进海外高层次人才参考目录)," *CCP
      Central Organization Department*, Document No. 60 (December 19,
      2016); and "Interim Measures to Recruit Overseas High-level Talents (
      引进海外高层次人才暂行办法)," *Central Organization Department*,
      Document No. 28 (2008), p. 5. For examples of CCP recruitment offices
      overseas, see "Foreign Liaison Offices (驻外联络处)," *Official Website
      of Zhongguancun Science Park*, http://www.zgc.gov.cn/zgc/zwllc/hsdllc/
      index.html; "Introducing Liaison Offices (聯絡處簡介)," *Liaison Office
      of the Leading Small Group for Beijing Talent Work*, at http://www.hi-
      beijing.org/docs/hk_llc/2015-09-18/1343871667548.html; and "Overseas
      Fund (海外基金)," *Zhongguancun Development Group*, at http://www.
      zgcgroup.com.cn/business/overseas_incubator.html; "Overseas High-
      level Talent Recruitment List for China's Guangdong Province (中国广
      东省海外高层次人才引进目录)," *Frankfurt Work Office of Guangdong
      Province Overseas High-level Talent Recruitment*, at https://www.
      zdwenku.com/wenku/20180913/5415074.html; and "Notice Regarding
      Release of 'Beijing City 2018 Overseas High-level Talent Recruitment
      Position Requirements List' (关于发布 《2018年度北京市海外高层次
      人才引进岗位需求目录》 的公告)," *Beijing City Overseas Scholar Work
      Liaison Committee Office*, April 13, 2018, at http://www.bjrbj.gov.cn/
      xxgk/gsgg/201804/t20180413_72254.html.

56   Wray, "The Threat Posed by the Chinese Government and the Chinese
      Communist Party," *Federal Bureau of Investigation*; "The United States
      Strategic Approach to the People's Republic of China," *The White
      House*; and "China: The Risk to Corporate America," *Federal Bureau of
      Investigation*.

57   Bonnie Girard, "The Curious Case of Jack Ma at West Point," *The Diplomat*, March 29, 2019, at https://thediplomat.com/2019/03/the-curious-case-of-jack-ma-at-west-point/.

58   Daniel Lippman and Steven Overly, "China's ZTE taps Joe Lieberman for D.C. damage control," *Politico*, December 13, 2018, at https://www.politico.com/story/2018/12/13/zte-china-joe-lieberman-1031383.

59   Author's personal observation during a Netflix binge — um, I mean, "undated audiovisual research session." See also "Crash Landing on You: Ep 11, Product Placement," *Bitches Over Drama*, February 3, 2020, at https://bitchesoverdramas.com/2020/02/03/crash-landing-on-you-ep-11-product-placement/; and Rick Martin, "Lenovo's Transformers Marketing Campaign Has Brains," *Tech in Asia*, July 20, 2011, at https://www.techinasia.com/lenovo-brains.

60   Roslyn Layton, "FCC Wants to Close Loopholes That Let Huawei Sell Smartphones on Amazon," *Forbes*, September 21, 2021, at https://www.forbes.com/sites/roslynlayton/2021/09/21/fcc-wants-to-close-loopholes-that-let-huawei-sell-smartphones-on-amazon/?sh=36b7e5ab2ad4.

61   For background, see "Update Concerning China's Acts, Policies and Practices Related to Technology Transfer, Intellectual Property, and Innovation," *Office of the United States Trade Representative*, November 20,2018, at https://ustr.gov/about-us/policy-offices/press-office/press-releases/2018/november/ustr-updates-section-301; and "How China's Economic Aggression Threatens the Technologies and Intellectual Property of the United States and the World," *White House Office of Trade and Manufacturing Policy*, June 2018, at https://www.whitehouse.gov/briefings-statements/office-trade-manufacturing-policy-report-chinas-economic-aggression-threatens-technologies-intellectual-property-united-states-world/. See also Doug Palmer, "WTO members blast China during 20th anniversary trade policy review," *Politico*, October 21, 2021, at https://www.politico.com/news/2021/10/21/wto-china-20th-anniversary-trade-policy-516647; and Jacob M. Schlesinger, "How China Swallowed the WTO," *Wall Street Journal*, November 1, 2017, at https://www.wsj.com/articles/how-china-swallowed-the-wto-1509551308.

62   Jon Russell, "Lenovo Has Completed the $2.91 Billion Acquisition of Motorola from Google," *TechCrunch*, October 30, 2014, at https://techcrunch.com/2014/10/30/lenovo-has-completed-the-2-91-billion-acquisition-of-motorola-from-google/. Note that Liu Chuanzhi was the founder and long-time CEO of Lenovo (and Legend Holdings). He graduated from the People's Liberation Army's Institute of Telecommunication Engineering (now known as Xidian University), and worked for the government-run Chinese Academy of Sciences, which helped fund his new company. Liu served as a

delegate of the CCP's 16th and 17th National Congresses and the
PRC's 9th, 10th and 11th National People's Congresses (NPC). He
was also the Vice Chairman of the 8th and 9th executive committee
of the CCP-run All-China Federation of Industry and Commerce
(ACFIC). See "Management Team: Liu Chuangzhi," *Legend Holdings*,
undated, at https://web.archive.org/web/20160303181420/http://
www.legendholdings.com.cn/en/Leadership/FullBioLCZ.aspx and
"Liu Chuangzhi, 1944–"), *Reference for Business*, undated, https://
www.referenceforbusiness.com/biography/F-L/Liu-Chuanzhi-1944.
html#ixzz1ByxiUC8R.

63   See *Motorola*, accessed December 6, 2021, at https://www.motorola.com/
us/.

64   Tim Bajarin, "10 Years Later, Looking Back at the IBM-Lenovo PC Deal,"
PC World, May 4, 2015, at https://www.pcmag.com/opinions/10-years-
later-looking-back-at-the-ibm-lenovo-pc-deal.

65   Almee Chanthadavong, "Lenovo finalises acquisition of IBM's x86
server business," *ZDNet*, September 29, 2014, https://www.zdnet.com/
article/lenovo-finalises-acquisition-of-ibms-x86-server-business/;
and Michael Kan, " Lenovo set to complete acquisition of IBM x86
server business," *Computer World*, September 29, 2014, at https://
www.computerworld.com/article/2694749/lenovo-set-to-complete-
acquisition-of-ibm-x86-server-business.html.

66   McKenzie Sadeghi, "Fact check: China's Haier purchased GE's
appliance business in 2016," *USA Today*, January 7, 2021, at https://www.
usatoday.com/story/news/factcheck/2021/01/07/fact-check-chinas-
haier-purchased-ge-appliance-unit-2016/4119523001/; and Charles Riley,
"China's Haier buys GE's appliance unit for $5.4 billion," *CNN*, January
15, 2016, at https://money.cnn.com/2016/01/15/investing/ge-haier-
appliances-sale/index.html.

67   See *GE Appliances*, accessed December 6, 2021, at https://www.
geappliances.com/.

68   Jiang and Luo, *Military-Civil Fusion*, p. 139.

69   Note that while American companies serve their owners, CCP-
organized companies serve the Chinese Communist Party. See Patrick
Jenevein, "Capital Access, Capital Denial: Balance Sheet Battlefields,"
Pointe Bello, June 2021, at https://www.pointebello.com/insights/
balance-sheet-battlefields.

Chapter Two: Need to Know

70   Quoted by U.S. National Security Council, "United States Strategic
      Approach to the People's Republic of China," *The White House*, May
      26, 2020, p. 4, at https://www.whitehouse.gov/articles/united-states-
      strategic-approach-to-the-peoples-republic-of-china/. See also Matt
      Pottinger, "Beijing Targets American Businesses," *Wall Street Journal*,
      March 26, 2021, at https://www.wsj.com/articles/beijing-targets-
      american-business-11616783268.

71   *China Military Power: Modernizing a Force to Fight and Win*
      (Washington, DC: Defense Intelligence Agency, 2019), p. v.

72   For example, see "Vice President Mike Pence's Remarks on the
      Administration's Policy Towards China," *Hudson Institute*, October
      4, 2018, at https://www.hudson.org/events/1610-vice-president-mike-
      pence-s-remarks-on-the-administration-s-policy-towards-china102018;
      "Assessment on U.S. Defense Implications of China's Expanding Global
      Access," *Department of Defense*, January 14, 2019, at https://media.
      defense.gov/2019/Jan/14/2002079292/-1/-1/1/EXPANDING-GLOBAL-
      ACCESS-REPORT-FINAL.PDF; Randall G. Schriver, "Assistant Secretary
      of Defense for Indo-Pacific Security Affairs Schriver Press Briefing
      on the 2019 Report on Military and Security Developments in China,"
      Department of Defense, May 3, 2019, at https://www.defense.gov/
      Newsroom/Transcripts/Transcript/Article/1837011/assistant-secretary-
      of-defense-for-indo-pacific-security-affairs-schriver-press/; "China: The
      Risk to Corporate America," *Federal Bureau of Investigation*, October
      4, 2019, at https://www.fbi.gov/file-repository/china-risk-to-corporate-
      america-2019.pdf/view; and Michael Pence, "Remarks by Vice President
      Pence at the Frederic V. Malek Memorial Lecture," *The White House*,
      October 24, 2019, at https://www.whitehouse.gov/briefings-statements/
      remarks-vice-president-pence-frederic-v-malek-memorial-lecture/.

73   Randall G. Schriver, "Assistant Secretary of Defense for Indo-Pacific
      Security Affairs Schriver Press Briefing on the 2019 Report on Military
      and Security Developments in China," *Department of Defense*, May
      3, 2019, at https://www.defense.gov/News/Transcripts/Transcript/
      Article/1837011/assistant-secretary-of-defense-for-indo-pacific-security-
      affairs-schriver-press/.

74   Robert C. O'Brien, "The Chinese Communist Party's Ideology and
      Global Ambitions," *The White House*, June 26, 2020, at https://www.
      whitehouse.gov/briefings-statements/chinese-communist-partys-
      ideology-global-ambitions/; Wray, "The Threat Posed by the Chinese

Government," *Federal Bureau of Investigation*; William P. Barr, "Transcript of Attorney General Barr's Remarks on China Policy at the Gerald R. Ford Presidential Museum," *Department of Justice*, July 17. 2020, at https://www.justice.gov/opa/speech/transcript-attorney-general-barr-s-remarks-china-policy-gerald-r-ford-presidential-museum; Michael R. Pompeo, "Communist China and the Free World's Future," *Department of State*, July 23, 2020, at https://www.state.gov/communist-china-and-the-free-worlds-future/; Michael R. Pompeo, "State Legislatures and the China Challenge," *Department of State*, September 23, 2020, at https://www.state.gov/state-legislatures-and-the-china-challenge/; and Chad F. Wolf, "Homeland Security and the China Challenge," *Department of Homeland Security*, December 21, 2020, at https://www.dhs.gov/news/2020/12/21/acting-secretary-chad-f-wolf-remarks-prepared-homeland-security-and-china-challenge.

75　Matthew Pottinger, "The Importance of Being Candid: On China's Relationship with the Rest of the World," *Policy Exchange*, October 23, 2020, at https://policyexchange.org.uk/pxevents/on-chinas-relationship-with-the-rest-of-the-world/; and Matthew Pottinger, "Reflections on China's May Fourth movement: An American Perspective," *Miller Center*, May 4, 2020, at https://millercenter.org/news-events/events/us-china-relations-turbulent-time-can-rivals-cooperate.

76　For example, see Graham Allison, *Destined for War: Can America and China Escape Thucydides's Trap?* (New York: Houghton Mifflin Harcourt, 2017). See also Aaron L. Friedberg, "Competing with China," *Survival*, June/July 2018, pp. 7–16; and Kurt M. Campbell and Ely Ratner, "The China Reckoning: How Beijing Defied American Expectations," *Foreign Affairs*, March/April, 2018, pp. 60–70.

77　See "Vice President Mike Pence's Remarks on the Administration's Policy Towards China," *Hudson Institute*, October 4, 2018, at https://www.hudson.org/events/1610-vice-president-mike-pence-s-remarks-on-the-administration-s-policy-towards-china102018; and *National Security Strategy of the United States* (Washington, DC: White House, December 2017), p. 25, at https://www.whitehouse.gov/wp-content/uploads/2017/12/NSS-Final-12-18-2017-0905.pdf.

78　See Toshi Yoshihara and James R. Holmes, *Red Star Over the Pacific: China's Rise and the Challenge to U.S. Maritime Strategy*, Second Edition (Annapolis, MD: Naval Institute Press, 2018), p. 27.

79　For example, see "Xi Jinping gives important directive on deepening reforms of talent development systems and mechanisms (习近平就深化人才发展体系机制改革作出重要指示)," Xinhua, May 6, 2018, at http://www.xinhuanet.com//politics/2016-05/06/c_1118820251.htm; and Xi Jinping, "Absolutely Winning an All-Around Middle Class Society and Struggling for the Grand Victory of Socialism with Chinese

Characteristics in a New Age (决胜全面建成小康社会夺取新时代中国特色社会主义伟大胜利)," *People's Daily*, October 18, 2017, at http://jhsjk.people.cn/article/29613660.

80 For example, see "Xi Jinping Series Database of Important Talks (习近平系列重要讲话数据库)," *People's Daily*, at http://jhsjk.people.cn/article; and browse the PRC government reports, regulations, laws, and white papers available at "Latest Policies (最新政策)," *Central People's Government of the People's Republic of China*, at http://www.gov.cn/zhengce/index.htm.

81 Daniel Tobin, "How Xi Jinping's New Era Should Have Ended U.S. Debate on Beijing's Ambitions," *U.S.-China Economic and Security Review Commission*, March 13, 2020, available online at https://www.uscc.gov/hearings/china-model-beijings-promotion-alternative-global-norms-and-standards. See also Tanner Greer, "China's Plan to Win Control of the Global Order," *Tablet*, May 17, 2020, at https://www.tabletmag.com/sections/news/articles/china-plans-global-order.

82 David Frum, "China Is Not a Garden-Variety Dictatorship," *The Atlantic*, March 5, 2018, at https://www.theatlantic.com/international/archive/2018/03/china-xi-jinping-president/554795/; Tom Phillips, "Dictator for life' Xi Jinping's power grab condemned as step towards tyranny," *The Guardian*, February 26, 2018, at https://www.theguardian.com/world/2018/feb/26/xi-jinping-china-presidential-limit-scrap-dictator-for-life; and Jamil Anderlini, "Under Xi Jinping, China is turning back to dictatorship," *Financial Times*, October 10, 2017, at https://www.ft.com/content/cb2c8578-adb4-11e7-aab9-abaa44b1e130.

83 Sydney J. Freedberg Jr. and Colin Clark, "Threats from Russia, China Drive 2017 DoD Budget," *Breaking Defense*, February 2, 2016, at http://breakingdefense.com/2016/02/russia-china-drive-2017-budget/; Matthew Pennington, "US-China tensions persist despite progress on NKorea," Associated Press, February 23, 2016, at http://bigstory.ap.org/article/4e0a8c6d263d4aad897fb5464d4f1f72/top-diplomats-meet-fraught-time-between-us-china; and Elbridge Colby and Ely Ratner, "Roiling the Waters," *Foreign Policy*, January 21, 2014, at http://foreignpolicy.com/2014/01/21/roiling-the-waters/.

84 *National Security Strategy of the United States* (Washington, DC: White House, December 2017), p. 25, at https://www.whitehouse.gov/wp-content/uploads/2017/12/NSS-Final-12-18-2017-0905.pdf.

85 *National Security Strategy of the United States*.

86 Peter Mattis, "From Engagement to Rivalry: Tools to Compete with China" *Texas National Security Review*, August 2018, p. 81, accessible online at https://tnsr.org/2018/08/from-engagement-to-rivalry-tools-to-compete-with-china/.

87   Mattis, "From Engagement to Rivalry."

88   Mattis, "From Engagement to Rivalry."

89   For example, see John King Fairbank, ed., *The Chinese World Order: Traditional China's Foreign Relations* (Cambridge, MA: Harvard University Press, 1968); Michael Oksenberg and Robert Oxnam, eds., *Dragon and Eagle: United States-China Relations Past and Future* (New York: Basic Books, 1978); John King Fairbank, *Chinabound: A Fifty Year Memoir* (New York: Harper Collins, 1982); and Kenneth Lieberthal and Michael Oksenberg, *Policy Making in China: Leaders, Structures, and Processes* (Princeton, NJ: Princeton University Press, 1988).

90   For example, Michael Pillsbury's landmark book, *China Debates the Future Security Environment*, offers readers a detailed examination of how Chinese elites understood their nation's strategic situation in the 1980s and 1990s. Published in 2000, Pillsbury's book provides an analysis of the internal debates that played out in Beijing between Chinese futurists, many of whom sought to use scientific and theoretical models to assess the likely future extent of Chinese growing power. The book broke ground in its examination of how Chinese strategists calculate comprehensive national power and what they advocate in terms of defense resource allocations. See Michael Pillsbury, *China Debates the Future Security Environment* (Washington, DC: National Defense University Press, 2000).

91   For a representative example of the prevailing views at the time, see David Shambaugh, ed., *Power Shift: China and Asia's New Dynamics* (Berkeley, CA: University of California Press: 2005). See also Kenneth Lieberthal, "How Domestic Forces Shape the PRC's Grand Strategy and International Impact," in Ashley J. Tellis and Michael Wills, eds., *Strategic Asia 2007–08: Domestic Political Change and Grand Strategy* (Washington, DC: National Bureau of Asian Research, 2007), pp. 29–66.

92   David M. Lampton, *Same Bed Different Dreams: Managing U.S.-China Relations 1989–2000* (Berkeley, CA: University of California Press, 2001), p. 110.

93   James Steinberg and Michael E. O'Hanlon, *Strategic Reassurance and Resolve: U.S.-China Relations in the Twenty-First Century* (Princeton, NJ: Princeton University Press, 2014), p. 4.

94   Some American scholars believed that the PRC probably did have a competitive strategy, yet they still advocated for a policy of cooperation. A representative book authored by Michael Swaine and Ashley Tellis, *Interpreting China's Grand Strategy*, found that, "If China's calculative strategy is completely successful, an intense United States-China rivalry may be inevitable. Still, China's rise to greatness (and its more assertiveness) is far from assured.... U.S. strategy designed to preemptively contain Chinese aggression might provoke its very

emergence.... A realistic policy over the course of China's calculative strategy should pursue cooperation with China aimed at attaining deeper levels of understanding, stronger mutual trust and confidence, and increased Chinese integration into the international system." See Michael D. Swaine and Ashley J. Tellis, *Interpreting China's Grand Strategy: Past, Present, Future* (Washington, DC: RAND Corporation, 2000), at https://www.rand.org/pubs/research_briefs/RB61/index1.html. See also James Lilley and David Shambaugh, eds., *China's Military Faces the Future* (New York: Routledge, 1999); and David Shambaugh, *Modernizing China's Military: Progress, Problems, and Prospects* (Berkeley, CA: University of California Press, 2002).

95   Mark A. Stokes, *China's Strategic Modernization: Implications for the United States* (Carlisle, PA: Strategic Studies Institute, 1999), pp. 1.

96   Stokes, *China's Strategic Modernization*, pp. 144–145.

97   Pillsbury discovered that Deng Xiaoping was the first Chinese leader to discuss the concept of comprehensive national power, stating, "In measuring a country's national power, one must look at it comprehensively and from all sides." Drawing from Marxist-Leninist theory, Deng's concept held that a nation's strength should be measured not just in terms of pure military power, but calculations should also include factors such as economics, science and technology, territory, international influence, domestic governance, natural resources, and social conditions. Pillsbury, *China Debates the Future Security Environment*, p. 204.

98   Pillsbury, *China Debates the Future Security Environment*, pp. 203–205.

99   Robert D. Kaplan, "How We Would Fight China," *The Atlantic*, June 2005, pp. 49–64, at https://www.theatlantic.com/magazine/archive/2005/06/how-we-would-fight-china/303959/.

100   James Mann, *The China Fantasy: Why Capitalism Will Not Bring Democracy to China* (New York: Penguin Books, 2007), pp. 25–26.

101   Mann, *The China Fantasy*, pp. 10–11.

102   Aaron L. Friedberg, *A Contest for Supremacy: China, America, and the Struggle for Mastery in Asia* (New York: W.W. Norton & Company, 2011), p. 264.

103   Friedberg, *A Contest for Supremacy*, p. 265.

104   See Dan Blumenthal, *The China Nightmare: The Grand Ambitions of a Decaying State* (Washington, DC: American Enterprise Institute Press, 2020); and Michael Pillsbury, *The Hundred-Year Marathon: China's Secret Strategy to Replace America as the Global Superpower* (New York: Henry Holt and Company, 2015). Another important example is Allison, *Destined for War.*

105   For examples of congressional testimonies, see J. Ray Bowen II,
      "Beijing's Promotion of PRC Technical Standards," *U.S.-China Economic
      and Security Review Commission*, March 6, 2020, at https://www.uscc.
      gov/hearings/china-model-beijings-promotion-alternative-global-
      norms-and-standards; Greg Levesque, "Testimony on What Keeps Xi
      Up at Night: Beijing's Internal and External Challenges," *U.S.-China
      Economic and Security Review Commission*, February 7, 2019, at https://
      www.uscc.gov/hearings/what-keeps-xi-night-beijings-internal-and-
      external-challenges; and Patrick Jenevein, "Chinese Investment in
      the United States: Impacts and Issues for Policymakers," *U.S.-China
      Economic and Security Review Commission*, January 26, 2017, at https://
      www.uscc.gov/hearings/hearing-chinese-investment-united-states-
      impacts-and-issues-policymakers. Of many notable reports, see "The
      Digital Silk Road Initiative: Wiring Global IT and Telecommunications
      to Advance Beijing's Global Ambitions," *Pointe Bello*, January 2019, at
      https://www.pointebello.com/insights/digital-silk-road.

106   For example, see John Garnaut, "Engineers of the Soul: Ideology in
      Xi Jinping's China," *Sinocism*, January 16, 2019, at https://sinocism.
      com/p/engineers-of-the-soul-ideology-in; Larry Diamond and Orville
      Schell, eds., "China's Influence and American Interests: Promoting
      Constructive Vigilance," Hoover Institution, November 29, 2018, at
      https://www.hoover.org/research/chinas-influence-american-interests-
      promoting-constructive-vigilance; Alex Joske, "Picking Flowers, Making
      Honey: The Chinese military's collaboration with foreign universities,"
      Australian Strategic Policy Institute, October 30, 2018, at https://www.
      aspi.org.au/report/picking-flowers-making-honey; Hamilton, *Silent
      Invasion*; and Anne-Marie Brady, "Magic Weapons: China's political
      influence activities under Xi Jinping," *Wilson Center*, September 18,
      2017, at https://www.wilsoncenter.org/article/magic-weapons-chinas-
      political-influence-activities-under-xi-jinping. See also Mark Stokes
      and Russell Hsiao, "The People's Liberation Army General Political
      Department: Political Warfare with Chinese Characteristics," *Project
      2049 Institute*, October 14, 2013, at https://project2049.net/2013/10/14/
      the-peoples-liberation-army-general-political-department-political-
      warfare-with-chinese-characteristics/. For research on the critical role
      of ideology in U.S.-China strategic competition, see Aaron L. Friedberg,
      "Competing with China," *Survival*, June–July 2018, pp. 7–64.

107   See Nadege Rolland, China's Eurasian Century?: Political and Strategic
      Implications of the Belt and Road Initiative (Washington, DC: National
      Bureau of Asian Research, 2017); John Hemmings, ed., "Infrastructure,
      Ideas, and Strategy in the Indo-Pacific," *Henry Jackson Society*, March
      2019, at https://henryjacksonsociety.org/publications/infrastructure-
      ideas-and-strategy-in-the-indo-pacific/; and Devin Thorne and Ben
      Spevack, "Harbored Ambitions: How China's Port Investments Are

Strategically Reshaping the Indo-Pacific," *C4ADS*, 2017, available online at https://static1.squarespace.com/static/566ef8b4d8af107232d5358a/t/5a d5e20ef950b777a94b55c3/1523966489456/Harbored+Ambitions.pdf.

108   Elsa B. Kania and John Costello, "Quantum Hegemony? China's Ambitions and the Challenge to U.S. Innovation Leadership," *Center for New American Security*, September 12, 2018, at https://www.cnas. org/publications/reports/quantum-hegemony; Michael Horowitz, Elsa B. Kania, and Gregory C. Allen, "Strategic Competition in an Era of Artificial Intelligence," *Center for New American Security*, July 25, 2018, at https://www.cnas.org/publications/reports/strategic-competition-in-an-era-of-artificial-intelligence; Elsa B. Kania, "Battlefield Singularity: Artificial Intelligence, Military Revolution, and China's Future Military Power," *Center for New American Security*, November 28, 2017, at https://www.cnas.org/publications/reports/battlefield-singularity-artificial-intelligence-military-revolution-and-chinas-future-military-power; Greg Levesque and Mark Stokes, "Blurred Lines: Military-Civil Fusion and the 'Going Out' of China's Military," *Pointe Bello*, December 2016, at https://pointebello.com/researchandinsights; and Mark A. Stokes, "The PLA General Staff Department Third Department Second Bureau: An Organizational Overview of Unit 61398," *Project 2049 Institute*, July 27, 2015, at https://project2049.net/2015/07/27/the-pla-general-staff-department-third-department-second-bureau-an-organizational-overview-of-unit-61398/.

109   For notable examples, see Andrew S. Erickson and Ryan D. Martinson, eds., *China's Maritime Gray Zone Operations* (Annapolis, MD: Naval Institute Press, 2019); Yoshihara and Holmes, *Red Star over the Pacific*; M. Taylor Fravel, *Active Defense: China's Military Strategy since 1949* (Princeton, New Jersey: Princeton University Press, 2019); Joe McReynolds, ed., *China's Evolving Military Strategy* (Washington, DC: Jamestown Foundation, 2017); and Roger Cliff, *China's Military Power: Assessing Current and Future Capabilities* (New York: Cambridge University Press, 2015). See also *Annual Report to Congress: Military and Security Developments Involving the People's Republic of China 2019* (Arlington, VA: Department of Defense, May 2019), at https://media. defense.gov/2019/May/02/2002127082/-1/-1/1/2019_CHINA_MILITARY_ POWER_REPORT.pdf; *China Military Power: Modernizing a Force to Fight and Win* (Washington, DC: Defense Intelligence Agency, January 2019), at https://www.dia.mil/Portals/27/Documents/News/Military%20 Power%20Publications/China_Military_Power_FINAL_5MB_20190103. pdf; and "Assessment on U.S. Defense Implications of China's Expanding Global Access," *Department of Defense*, December 2018, at https://media.defense.gov/2019/Jan/14/2002079292/-1/-1/1/EXPANDING-GLOBAL-ACCESS-REPORT-FINAL.PDF.

110   Michael Pillsbury, *The Hundred-Year Marathon*.

111   For background on the long-standing scholarly debate, see Tanner
       Greer, "China's Plan to Win Control of the Global Order," *Tablet*, May
       17, 2020, at https://www.tabletmag.com/sections/news/articles/china-
       plans-global-order; "China and the Rules-Based Order: Seven experts
       debate China's approach to the rules-based international order," *Lowy
       Institute*, undated, at https://interactives.lowyinstitute.org/features/
       china-rules-based-order/articles/counting-on-historical-forces/;
       Oriana Skylar Mastro, "The Stealth Superpower: How China Hid Its
       Global Ambitions," *Foreign Affairs*, January/February 2019, pp. 31–39;
       and Alastair Iain Johnston, "How New and Assertive is China's New
       Assertiveness," *International Security*, Spring 2013, pp. 7–48.

112   Rush Doshi, *The Long Game: China's Grand Strategy to Displace
       American Order* (New York: Oxford University Press, 2021).

113   See "Xi Jinping Series Database of Important Talks (习近平系列重要讲
       话数据库)," *People's Daily*, at http://jhsjk.people.cn/article.

114   As of May 6, 2019, the database listed 393 of Xi Jinping's speeches
       and contained reports related to 1,094 work meetings, 446 inspection
       visits, 1,474 person-to-person meetings, and 1,656 trips. In addition, the
       database contained a calendar of his daily public activities and excerpts
       of 23 books written by Xi Jinping or dedicated to aspects of his thought.
       See "Xi Jinping Series Database of Important Talks (习近平系列重要讲
       话数据库)," *People's Daily*, at http://jhsjk.people.cn/article.

115   See "Xi Jinping Series Database of Important Talks," *People's Daily*.

116   "Latest Policies (最新政策)," *Central People's Government of the
       People's Republic of China*, at http://www.gov.cn/zhengce/index.htm.
       "Standardization Law of the People's Republic of China (中华人民共和
       国标准化法)," *Standardization Administration of the People's Republic
       of China*, November 8, 2017, at http://www.sac.gov.cn/sbgs/flfg/fl/
       bzhf/201711/t20171108_318652.htm; and "National Planning Doctrine for
       Mid-to-Long Term Talent Development, 2010–2020 (国家中长期人才
       发展规划纲要(2010- 2020年)发布)," Xinhua, June 6, 2010, at http://
       www.gov.cn/jrzg/2010-06/06/content_1621777.htm.

117   For example, see "Standardization Law of the People's Republic of
       China (中华人民共和国标准化法)," *Standardization Administration of
       the People's Republic of China*, November 8, 2017, at http://www.sac.gov.
       cn/sbgs/flfg/fl/bzhf/201711/t20171108_318652.htm; "National Planning
       Doctrine for Mid-to-Long Term Talent Development, 2010–2020 (
       国家中长期人才发展规划纲要(2010- 2020年)发布)," Xinhua, June
       6, 2010, at http://www.gov.cn/jrzg/2010-06/06/content_1621777.htm.;
       and "Master Plan to Develop and Build Zhongguancun into a National
       Indigenous Innovation Demonstration Zone (2016–2020) [中关村国
       家自主创新示范区发展建设规划（2016–2020）]," *Leading Small
       Group of Zhongguancun National Indigenous Innovation Demonstration*

Zone, August 18, 2016, at http://zfxxgk.beijing.gov.cn/110081/zzqgh33/2017-08/02/content_fd85c3f6888543a0858ee51117d1e4fe.shtml.

118 For example, see "Interim Law for Managing Program Resources and Budgets of Culture and Famous Talents Project and 'Four-in-One Group Talent Program (文化名家暨"四个一批"人才工程项目资助及经费管理暂行办法)," *CCP Propaganda Department's Document Number 17*, 2014. This is a guiding document for lower-echelon Chinese government plans and laws. For example, see "Beijing City's Interim Law for Managing Program Resources and Budgets of High-level Propaganda and Culture Talent Cultivation (北京市宣传文化高层次人才培养资助管理暂行办法)," *Beijing City CCP Committee Propaganda Department*, September 10, 2015, at http://www.bjrcgz.gov.cn/swordCMS/office/tzgg/3aed73e077c34c0a80cbe0e263f53922/3aed73e077c34c0a80cbe0e263f53922.html.

Chapter Three: Bad Intentions

119 *Xi Jinping Thought on Chinese Socialism in a New Era: A Study Guide* [习近平新时代中国特色社会主义思想学习问答] (Beijing: CCP Central Propaganda Department, 2021), pp. 1–2.

120 Kerry Brown, *CEO, China: The Rise of Xi Jinping* (New York: I.B. Tauris & Co., 2016), p. 5.

121 The description of the event draws from the video broadcast imbedded in Xi Jinping, "Speech at the General Assembly to Commemorate the 200th Anniversary of Karl's Marx's Birth (在纪念马克思诞辰200周年大会上的讲话)," Xinhua, May 4, 2018, at http://www.xinhuanet.com/politics/2018-05/04/c_1122783997.htm. Images can also be seen at "China marks 200 years of Karl Marx's birth as Xi leads in new era," Xinhua, May 4, 2018, at http://www.xinhuanet.com/english/2018-05/04/c_137156583_3.htm.

122 Xi Jinping, "Speech at the General Assembly to Commemorate the 200th Anniversary of Karl's Marx's Birth (在纪念马克思诞辰200周年大会上的讲话)," Xinhua, May 4, 2018, at http://www.xinhuanet.com/politics/2018-05/04/c_1122783997.htm.

123 Brown, *CEO, China*, pp. 51–53.

124 Xi Jinping, *The Governance of China* (Beijing: Foreign Language Press, 2014), p. 494.

125 Brown, *CEO, China*, pp. 51–53.

126   Chris Buckley and Didi Kirsten Tatlow, "Cultural Revolution Shaped
      Xi Jinping, From Schoolboy to Survivor," *New York Times*, September
      24, 2015, at https://www.nytimes.com/2015/09/25/world/asia/xi-jinping-
      china-cultural-revolution.html.

127   Brown, *CEO, China*, p. 53.

128   Barbara Demick and David Pierson, "China political star Xi Jinping a
      study in contrasts," *Los Angeles Times*, February 11, 2012, at https://www.
      latimes.com/world/la-xpm-2012-feb-11-la-fg-china-xi-20120212-story.
      html.

129   Demick and Pierson, "China political star Xi Jinping."

130   Buckley and Tatlow, "Cultural Revolution Shaped Xi Jinping, From
      Schoolboy to Survivor."

131   Buckley and Tatlow, "Cultural Revolution Shaped Xi Jinping, From
      Schoolboy to Survivor."

132   Matt Rivers, "This entire Chinese village is a shrine to Xi Jinping," *CNN*,
      March 19, 2018, at https://www.cnn.com/2018/03/19/asia/china-xi-
      jinping-village-intl/index.html.

133   Xi, *Governance of China*, p. 480. See also, Matt Rivers, "This entire
      Chinese village is a shrine to Xi Jinping."

134   Demick and Pierson, "China political star Xi Jinping."

135   Xi, *Governance of China*, p. 479.

136   Brown, *CEO, China*, p. 56.

137   Demick and Pierson, "China political star Xi Jinping."

138   Brown, *CEO, China*, p. 56.

139   Demick and Pierson, "China political star Xi Jinping."

140   Brown, *CEO, China*, p. 64.

141   Brown, *CEO, China*, p. 65. See also Cheng Li, "Xi Jinping (习近平),"
      Brookings Institution, March 18, 2018, at https://www.brookings.edu/wp-
      content/uploads/2018/03/china_20180318_xi_jinping_profile.pdf.

142   Brown, *CEO, China*, p. 65. See also Cheng Li, "Xi Jinping (习近平)."

143   Brown, *CEO, China*, pp. 66–67.

144   Xi, *The Governance of China*, p. 481.

145   Brown, *CEO, China*, p. 67.

146   Xi, *Governance of China*, pp. 494–496.

147   Xi, *Governance of China*, p. 496.

148   Karen Yuan, "The Impossibility of the Chinese First Lady," *The
      Atlantic*, April 1, 2019, at https://www.theatlantic.com/membership/
      archive/2019/04/impossibility-chinese-first-lady/586246/; Xi, *The
      Governance of China*, pp. 494–496; and Anne Henochowicz, "Empire

Illustrated: Peng Liyuan At Tiananmen, 1989," *China Digital Times*, March 26, 2013, at https://chinadigitaltimes.net/2013/03/empire-illustrated-peng-liyuan-at-tiananmen-1989/.

149 "Xi Jinping and Peng Liyuan mark 30th Anniversary, Ever Like Cowboy and Weaver Girl (习近平彭丽媛结婚30周年 多年如牛郎织女), *Duowei News*, September 1, 2017, at https://www.dwnews.com/%E4%B8%AD%E5%9B%BD/60010224/%E4%B9%A0%E8%BF%91%E5%B9%B3%E5%BD%AD%E4%B8%BD%E5%AA%9B%E7%BB%93%E5%A9%9A30%E5%91%A8%E5%B9%B4%E5%A4%9A%E5%B9%B4%E5%A6%82%E7%89%9B%E9%83%8E%E7%BB%87%E5%A5%B3.

150 Xi, *Governance of China*, p. 496.

151 Brown, *CEO, China*, p. 67.

152 See James Mulvenon, "Xi Jinping and the Central Military Commission: Bridesmaid or Bride?" *China Leadership Monitor*, February 22, 2011, at https://media.hoover.org/sites/default/files/documents/CLM34JM.pdf.

153 "Top Chinese officials 'plotted to overthrow Xi Jinping,'" *BBC News*, October 20, 2017, at https://www.bbc.com/news/world-asia-china-41691917.

154 Katsuji Nakazawa, "Power struggle has Xi leery of coup, assassination attempts," *Nikkei Asia*, May 23, 2015, at https://asia.nikkei.com/Politics/Power-struggle-has-Xi-leery-of-coup-assassination-attempts.

155 Xi Jinping, "Speech at the General Assembly to Commemorate the 200th Anniversary of Karl's Marx's Birth (在纪念马克思诞辰200周年大会上的讲话)," Xinhua, May 4, 2018, at http://www.xinhuanet.com/politics/2018-05/04/c_1122783997.htm.

156 Chen Peiyong, "And just like that, he lit up the world: Marxism's vast influence, current value, and the development of this age (就这样在世界闪耀——马克思主义的深远影响、当代价值与时代发展)," *Central Discipline Inspection Committee News*, May 3, 2018, at http://www.ccdi.gov.cn/yaowen/201805/t20180503_171124.html.

157 Yang Sheng, "China cherishes Karl Marx," *Global Times*, May 4, 2018, at https://www.globaltimes.cn/content/1100666.shtml.

158 Yang, "China cherishes Karl Marx."

159 "World Congress on Marxism begins in China," *China Daily*, May 6, 2018, at https://www.chinadaily.com.cn/a/201805/06/WS5aee4bfba3105cdcf651c314.html.

160 Luo Yunzhou, "China commemorates 200th birthday of Karl Marx," *Global Times*, May 8, 2018, at https://www.globaltimes.cn/content/1101250.shtml.

161   Bai Tiantian, "Xi inspires students with insight into education, Marxism," *Global Times*, May 3, 2018, at https://www.globaltimes.cn/content/1100617.shtml.

162   Bai, "Xi inspires students."

163   Bai, "Xi inspires students."

164   "World Congress on Marxism begins," *China Daily*.

165   "World Congress on Marxism Launches Official Website," *Peking University News*, April 9, 2018, at http://newsen.pku.edu.cn/news_events/news/global/6957.htm.

166   "World Congress on Marxism Website," *Peking University News*.

167   Griff Witte and Luisa Beck, "Karl Marx's German home town celebrates his 200th birthday with a Chinese statute – and a struggle," *Washington Post*, May 5, 2018, at https://www.washingtonpost.com/world/europe/marxs-german-hometown-celebrates-his-200th-birthday-with-a-chinese-statue--and-a-struggle/2018/05/04/592711b4-4d69-11e8-85c1-9326c4511033_story.html.

168   "Karl Marx's 200th birthday bash will feature a gift from the Chinese government," *National Post*, May 4, 2018, at https://nationalpost.com/news/world/xi-praises-marxism-as-a-tool-for-china-to-win-the-future; and Witte and Beck, "Karl Marx's Chinese statute." .

169   "Karl Marx's 200th birthday bash," *National Post*.

170   "Karl Marx's 200th birthday bash," *National Post*.

171   For example, see "World Congress on Marxism begins," *China Daily*; "Abstracts of papers by forum participants (参会论文摘要)," *World Congress on Marxism*, undated, at http://wcm.pku.edu.cn/sklwzy/index.htm; and Xinhua Editorial Board, "Why Marxism is capable of staying young forever (马克思主义为什么能永葆青春)," Xinhua, May 4, 2018, at http://www.xinhuanet.com/2018-05/04/c_1122783965.htm.

172   Luo, "China commemorates 200th birthday of Karl Marx."

173   Xi, "200th Anniversary of Karl's Marx's Birth."

174   Karl Marx and Frederick Engels, *The Communist Manifesto* (New York: International Publishers, first printed 1848, this printing 2020), pp. 26–30.

175   The 100 million estimate comes from Stephane Courtois, "Introduction: The Crimes of Communism," in Stephane Courtois et al., *The Black Book of Communism: Crimes, Terror, Repression* (Cambridge, MA: Harvard University Press, 1999), p. 4.

176   Xi, "200th Anniversary of Karl's Marx's Birth."

177   Xi, "200th Anniversary of Karl's Marx's Birth.".

178   Xi, "200th Anniversary of Karl's Marx's Birth.".

179   Xi, "200th Anniversary of Karl's Marx's Birth.".

180   Xi, "200th Anniversary of Karl's Marx's Birth.".

181   Xi, "200th Anniversary of Karl's Marx's Birth.".

182   Xi, "200th Anniversary of Karl's Marx's Birth.".

183   Xi, "200th Anniversary of Karl's Marx's Birth.".

184   Xi, "200th Anniversary of Karl's Marx's Birth,"; and "The International (国际歌)," *Baidu Baike*, undated, at https://baike.baidu.com/item/%E5%9 B%BD%E9%99%85%E6%AD%8C.

185   "China marks 200 years of Karl Marx's birth as Xi leads in new era," Xinhua, May 4, 2018, at http://www.xinhuanet.com/english/2018-05/04/c_137156583.htm. For the official CCP-approved lyrics, see "The Classic Ode: 'The Internationale must be realized' – the story of 'The Internationale' (经典传颂：""英特纳雄耐尔就一定要实现""-- 《国际歌》的故事)," *China Executive Leadership Academy, Yan'an, School of Marxism*, July 4, 2018, at https://marx.nwpu.edu.cn/info/1028/2120.htm.

186   Marx and Engels, *The Communist Manifesto*.

Chapter Four: The Halloween Document

187   "The Decision of the CCP Central Committee on Several Major Issues Regarding Insisting on and Improving the System of Socialism with Chinese Characteristics and Advancing the Modernization of the State Governance System and Its Governance Capabilities (中共中央关于坚持和完善中国特色社会主义制度推进国家治理体系和治理能力现代化若干重大问题的决定), *CCP News*, November 6, 2019, at http://cpc.people.com.cn/n1/2019/1106/c64094-31439558.html.

188   Xi Jinping, "Insist on and Improve the System of Socialism with Chinese Characteristics and Advance the Modernization of the State Governance System and Its Governance Capabilities (坚持和完善中国特色社会主义制度推进国家治理体系和治理能力现代化)," *Qiushi*, January 1, 2020, at http://www.qstheory.cn/dukan/qs/2020-01/01/c_1125402833.htm.

189   Xi, "Insist on and Improve the System of Socialism."

190   Xi, "Insist on and Improve the System of Socialism."

191   Xi Jinping, "Unity and Cooperation are the Most Powerful Weapons for the International Community's Victory in the War Against the Pandemic (团结合作是国际社会战胜疫情最有力武器)," *Qiushi*, April 15, 2020, at http://www.qstheory.cn/dukan/qs/2020-04/15/c_1125857091. htm; and "Wang Yi: Guided by Xi Jinping Thought on Foreign Affairs,

Push Forward the Construction of a Community of Common Destiny for all Mankind Amid Global Cooperation to Fight the Pandemic (王毅：以习近平外交思想为指引 在全球抗疫合作中推动构建人类命运共同体)," *Qiushi*, April 15, 2020, at http://www.gov.cn/guowuyuan/2020-04/15/content_5502818.htm.

192   Xi, "Unity and Cooperation."

193   "Xi Jinping, Bring Forth Powerful Technologies for Winning the Guerilla War against the Pandemic (习近平：为打赢疫情防控阻击战提供强大科技支撑)," *Qiushi*, March 15, 2020, at http://jhsjk.people.cn/article/31632573.

194   Only the Americans had been excluded. On March 27, during his phone call with then President Donald Trump, he reportedly said nothing about common destiny. Xi, "Unity and Cooperation."

195   Xi Jinping, "Working Together."

196   Xi Jinping, "Unite and Cooperate.".

197   "China's Actions to Fight the COVID-19 Pandemic (抗击新冠肺炎疫情的中国行动)," *PRC State Council Information Office*, June 7, 2020, at http://www.gov.cn/zhengce/2020-06/07/content_5517737.htm.

198   "China's Actions to Fight the COVID-19 Pandemic," *PRC State Council Information Office*.

199   "Xi's world vision: a community of common destiny, a shared home for humanity," *CCTV*, January 15, 2017, at https://english.cctv.com/2017/01/15/ARTIjfECMGRxn4TrlIoUqAcl170115.shtml.

200   For example, see Xi Jinping, "Working Together."

201   "Wang Yi: Guided by Xi Jinping Thought on Foreign Affairs, Push Forward the Construction of a Community of Common Destiny for all Mankind Amid Global Cooperation to Fight the Pandemic," *Qiushi*.

202   Ma Xiaowei, "Deepen International Cooperation in the Pandemic Fight, Jointly Build a Community of Common Health for all Humankind (深化抗击疫情国际合作,共筑人类卫生健康共同体)," *Qiushi*, April 16, 2020, at http://www.qstheory.cn/dukan/qs/2020-04/16/c_1125857952.htm.

203   "Written Interview with Zhuang Rongwen, Director of the State Network Information Office and Chairman of the World Internet Conference, on his Concept Document 'Working Hand in Hand to Construct a Community of Common Destiny Online' (国家互联网信息办公室主任、世界互联网大会组委会主席庄荣文就发布《携手构建网络空间命运共同体》概念文件接受书面采访)," *Office of Central Cyberspace Affairs Commission*, October 17, 2019, at http://www.cac.gov.cn/2019-10/17/c_1572842708223057.htm. See also Zhuang Rongwen, "Building an Internet Superpower, A Thought Weapon and Guidebook

for Action (网络强国建设的思想武器和行动指南)," Xinhua, February 1, 2021, at http://www.xinhuanet.com/politics/2021-02/01/c_1127050845. htm.

204 Bai Jie, "Ceaselessly Insisting on and Perfecting an Independent, Sovereign and Peaceful Foreign Policy to Realize the Great Rejuvenation of the Chinese Race and to Create a Beautiful Future for Humankind: Exclusive Interview with Deputy Foreign Minister Le Yucheng (坚持和完善独立自主的和平外交政策，为实现中华民族伟大复兴、开创人类美好未来不懈努力——专访外交部副部长乐玉成)," Xinhua, January 6, 2020, at http://www.xinhuanet.com/politics/2020-01/06/c_1125428301.htm.

205 Zhao Ziyu and Xian Fengli, eds., *Great Power Diplomacy with Chinese Characteristics* [中国特色大国外交] (Beijing: National Defense University Press, 2018), p. 1.

206 Zhao and Xian, *Great Power Diplomacy*, p. 21.

207 For background, see Tobin, "How Xi Jinping's 'New Era' Should Have Ended U.S. Debate on Beijing's Ambitions"; J. Ray Bowen II, "Beijing's Promotion of PRC Technical Standards," *U.S.-China Economic and Security Review Commission*, March 13, 2020, at https://www.uscc.gov/hearings/china-model-beijings-promotion-alternative-global-norms-and-standards; Adam Segal, "China's Alternative Cyber Governance Regime," *U.S.-China Economic and Security Review Commission*, March 13, 2020, at https://www.uscc.gov/hearings/china-model-beijings-promotion-alternative-global-norms-and-standards; Elizabeth C. Economy, "Exporting the China Model," *U.S.-China Economic and Security Review Commission*, March 13, 2020, at https://www.uscc.gov/hearings/china-model-beijings-promotion-alternative-global-norms-and-standards; Melanie Hart, "Beijing's Promotion of Alternative Global Norms and Standards in the U.N. System," *U.S.-China Economic and Security Review Commission*, March 13, 2020, at https://www.uscc.gov/hearings/china-model-beijings-promotion-alternative-global-norms-and-standards; Nadege Rolland, *China's Vision for a New World Order* (Washington, DC: National Bureau of Asian Research, January 2020), at https://www.nbr.org/publication/chinas-vision-for-a-new-world-order/; Robert Spalding, *Stealth War: How China Took Over While America's Elite Slept* (New York: Portfolio/Penguin Press, 2019); Kristine Lee and Alexander Sullivan, "People's Republic of the United Nations: China's Emerging Revisionism in International Organizations," *Center for New American Security*, May 2019, at https://www.cnas.org/publications/reports/peoples-republic-of-the-united-nations; Jonathan D.T. Ward, *China's Vision of Victory* (Washington, DC: Atlas Publishing, 2019); Liza Tobin, "Xi's Vision for Transforming Global Governance: A Strategic Challenge for Washington and Its Allies," *Texas National*

Security Review, November 2018, at https://tnsr.org/2018/11/xis-
vision-for-transforming-global-governance-a-strategic-challenge-
for-washington-and-its-allies/; Peter Mattis, "From Engagement to
Rivalry: Tools to Compete with China," *Texas National Security Review*,
August 2018, at https://tnsr.org/2018/08/from-engagement-to-rivalry-
tools-to-compete-with-china/; Aaron L. Friedberg, "Competing with
China," *Survival*, June 2018, pp. 7–64, available online at https://www.
tandfonline.com/doi/full/10.1080/00396338.2018.1470755; Timothy
R. Heath, "China's Endgame: The Path Towards Global Leadership,"
Lawfare, January 5, 2018, at https://www.lawfareblog.com/chinas-
endgame-path-towards-global-leadership; and Yanzhong Huang,
"China's involvement in global health governance: Progress and
challenges," in Scott Kennedy, ed., *Global Governance and China: The
Dragon's Learning Curve* (New York: Routledge, 2018), pp. 158–180.

208   Zhao and Xian, *Great Power Diplomacy*, pp. 39–43.

209   Zhao and Xian, *Great Power Diplomacy*, pp. 39–43.

210   Zhao and Xian, *Great Power Diplomacy*, p. 39.

211   Zhao and Xian, *Great Power Diplomacy*, pp. 39–43.

212   Zhao and Xian, *Great Power Diplomacy*, p. 40.

213   Zhao and Xian, *Great Power Diplomacy*, p. 42.

214   Zhao and Xian, *Great Power Diplomacy*, p. 44.

215   Zhao and Xian, *Great Power Diplomacy*, p. 41.

216   Zhao and Xian, *Great Power Diplomacy*, p. 43.

217   Xi Jinping, "Insist on and Improve the System of Socialism with
Chinese Characteristics and Advance the Modernization of the State
Governance System and Its Governance Capabilities (坚持和完善
中国特色社会主义制度推进国家治理体系和治理能力现代化),"
Qiushi, January 1, 2020, at http://www.qstheory.cn/dukan/qs/2020-
01/01/c_1125402833.htm.

218   Xi, *The Governance of China*.

219   Xi Jinping, *The Governance of China, Volume Two* [谈治国理政，第二
卷] (Beijing: Foreign Language Press, October 2017); and Xi Jinping,
The Governance of China, Volume Three [谈治国理政，第三卷]
(Beijing: Foreign Language Press, April 2020).

220   Gerry Shih, "Inside China's top 'party schools': Plenty of Communist
doctrine on tap," *Washington Post*, July 16, 2019, at https://www.
washingtonpost.com/world/asia_pacific/inside-chinas-top-party-
schools-plenty-of-communist-doctrine-on-tap/2019/07/15/17261a78-9f55-
11e9-b27f-ed2942f73d70_story.html.

221   Shih, "Inside China's top 'party schools'."

222 "Curriculum vitae of the chairman of the PRC State and PRC Central Military Commission (中华人民共和国主席、中华人民共和国中央军事委员会主席简历)," Xinhua, March 17, 2018, at http://www.xinhuanet.com/politics/2018lh/2018-03/17/c_1122551729.htm; and Barbara Demick and David Pierson, "China political star Xi Jinping a study in contrasts," *Los Angeles Times*, February 11, 2012, at https://www.latimes.com/world/la-xpm-2012-feb-11-la-fg-china-xi-20120212-story.html.

223 Shih, "Inside China's top 'party schools'.".

224 *The Fundamentals of Xi Jinping Thought on Chinese Socialism in a New Era* [习近平新时代中国特色社会主义思想基本问题] (Beijing: CCP Central Committee Central Party School Press, 2020), p. 1.

225 *The Fundamentals of Xi Jinping Thought*, p. 359.

226 *The Fundamentals of Xi Jinping Thought*, p. 359.

227 *The Fundamentals of Xi Jinping Thought*, p. 361.

228 *The Fundamentals of Xi Jinping Thought*, p. 361.

229 *The Fundamentals of Xi Jinping Thought*, p. 364.

230 *The Fundamentals of Xi Jinping Thought*, p. 365.

231 *The Fundamentals of Xi Jinping Thought*, p. 386.

232 *The Fundamentals of Xi Jinping Thought*, p. 397.

Chapter Five: Transformation

233 "Interview: Building community of common destiny the only future for mankind: UN General Assembly president," Xinhua, January 30, 2017, at http://www.xinhuanet.com//english/2017-01/30/c_136020956.htm.

234 This description of the New World Order conspiracy theory draws from Annie Jacobsen, *Area 51: An Uncensored History of America's Top Secret Military Base* (New York: Back Bay Books, 2012), p. 332.

235 Of many examples, see Ren Tianyou and Zhao Zhouxian, eds., *Strategic Support for Achieving the Great Chinese Resurgence* [实现中华民族伟大复兴的战略支援] (Beijing: National Defense University Press: 2018), pp. 98–99.

236 Zhao and Xian, *Great Power Diplomacy*, pp. 44–45.

237 Zhao and Xian, *Great Power Diplomacy*, p. 5.

238 Zhao and Xian, *Great Power Diplomacy*, p. 46.

239 Ren and Zhao, *Strategic Support*, pp. 98–99.

240 Loren Balhorn, "The World Revolution That Wasn't," *Jacobin*, March 2, 2019, at https://www.jacobinmag.com/2019/03/comintern-lenin-german-revolution-ussr-revolution.

241 Nikolai Bukharin, "The World Revolution and the U.S.S.R.," *The Labor Monthly*, November 1927, available at https://www.marxists.org/archive/bukharin/works/1927/worldrev.htm.

242 For a discussion of how Marx's work inspired Adolf Hitler, see George Watson, "Hitler and the socialist dream," *The Independent*, November 22, 1998, at https://www.independent.co.uk/arts-entertainment/hitler-and-the-socialist-dream-1186455.html. For a comparative legal analysis of Nazism and Marxism, see Heath Harley-Bellemore, "National Socialism and Marxism: A Comparative Legal Analysis," *The Western Australian Jurist*, 2017, pp. 399–424, at http://classic.austlii.edu.au/au/journals/WAJurist/2017/10.html.

243 For a masterful account of this period, see Winston Churchill, *The Gathering Storm* (Boston, MA: Houghton Mifflin Company, 1948).

244 See Winston Churchill, *The Grand Alliance* (Boston, MA: Houghton Mifflin Company, 1950), pp. 433–444.

245 Balhorn, "The World Revolution That Wasn't."

246 For an excellent overview, see Julia Lovell, *Maoism: A Global History* (New York: Vintage Books, 2020).

247 Suisheng Zhao, "China's Foreign Policy Making Process: Players and Institutions," in David Shambaugh, ed., *China & the World* (New York: Oxford University Press, 2020), p. 87.

248 David Shambaugh, "China's Long March to Global Power," in Shambaugh, *China & the World*, pp. 10–12.

249 Chas W. Freeman Jr., "China's National Experience and the Evolution of PRC Grand Strategy," in Shambaugh, *China & the World*, p. 44.

250 Blumenthal, *The China Nightmare*, pp. 45–52.

251 Jude D. Blanchette, *China's New Red Guards: The Return of Radicalism and the Rebirth of Mao Zedong* (New York: Oxford University Press, 2019), p. 33.

252 Zhao and Xian, *Great Power Diplomacy*, p. 7.

253 "September 21, 1988: Deng Xiaoping Proposes Establishing a New International Political Order (1988年9月21日 邓小平提议建立国际政治新秩序)," *The Central People's Government of the People's Republic of China*, September 6, 2007, at http://www.gov.cn/ztzl/17da/content_739255.htm.

254 "September 21, 1988: Deng Xiaoping Proposes Establishing a New International Political Order," *The Central People's Government of the People's Republic of China*.

255   "September 21, 1988: Deng Xiaoping Proposes Establishing a New International Political Order," *The Central People's Government of the People's Republic of China.*

256   Blumenthal, *The China Nightmare*, p. 52.

257   Zhao and Xian, *Great Power Diplomacy*, p. 7.

258   For an excellent overview, see John Lewis Gaddis, *The Cold War: A New History* (New York: Penguin, 2005).

259   Balhorn, "The World Revolution That Wasn't."

260   The following section benefitted immensely from Robert Service, *Comrades! A History of World Communism* (Cambridge, MA: Harvard University Press, 2007), pp. 437–447, 459–482.

261   Isaac Stone Fish, *America Second: How America's Elites Are Making China Stronger* (New York: Alfred A. Knopf, 2022), pp. 91–97.

262   Stone Fish, *America Second*, pp. 136–163.

263   Zhao and Xian, *Great Power Diplomacy*, p. 1.

264   *The Fundamentals of Xi Jinping Thought*, p. 365.

265   Zhao and Xian, *Great Power Diplomacy*, pp. 122–123.

266   Zhao and Xian, *Great Power Diplomacy*, p. 123.

267   *The Fundamentals of Xi Jinping Thought*, p. 365.

268   Zhao and Xian, *Great Power Diplomacy*, p. 119.

269   Zhao and Xian, *Great Power Diplomacy*, p. 127.

270   Zhao and Xian, *Great Power Diplomacy*, p. 129.

271   Zhao and Xian, *Great Power Diplomacy*, p. 131.

272   Zhao and Xian, *Great Power Diplomacy*, p. 131.

273   Zhao and Xian, *Great Power Diplomacy*, p. 127.

274   "Interview: Building community of common destiny the only future for mankind: UN General Assembly president," Xinhua, January 30, 2017, at http://www.xinhuanet.com//english/2017-01/30/c_136020956.htm.

Chapter Six: Global Government

275   John Ratcliffe, "China Is National Security Threat No. 1," *Wall Street Journal*, December 3, 2020, at https://www.wsj.com/articles/china-is-national-security-threat-no-1-11607019599.

276   "Margaret Chan Appointed to High Ranking Tsinghua Cadre Position, Tedros Congratulates and also Thanks Chairman Xi's

Leadership (陳馮富珍任職清華高幹,譚德塞道賀也謝習主
席領導), *Radio Free Asia*, April 3, 2020, at http://www.rfi.fr/
tw/%E4%B8%AD%E5%9C%8B/20200403-%E9%99%B3%E9%A6%AE%E5%
AF%8C%E7%8F%8D%E4%BB%BB%E8%81%B7%E6%B8%85%E8%8F%AF%E
9%AB%98%E5%B9%B9-%E8%AD%9A%E5%BE%B7%E5%A1%9E%E9%81%9
3%E8%B3%80%E4%B9%9F%E8%AC%9D%E7%BF%92%E4%B8%BB%E5%B8
%AD%E9%A0%98%E5%B0%8E.

277   Josh Rogin, *Chaos Under Heaven: Trump, Xi, and the Battle For the 21st
      Century* (New York: HMH Books, 2021), pp. 265–267.

278   Rogin, *Chaos Under Heaven*, pp. 265–267.

279   Rogin, *Chaos Under Heaven*, pp. 265–267, p. 266.

280   Rogin, *Chaos Under Heaven*, pp. 265–267, pp. 266–267. See also "China
      and the N95 Mask Shortage," *Pointe Bello*, March 2020, at https://www.
      pointebello.com/insights/china-n95-mask-shortage.

281   Rogin, *Chaos Under Heaven*, pp. 265–267, pp. 267 & 275.

282   "Interview with Bill Gates on Fighting the Coronavirus Pandemic,"
      Fareed Zakaria GPS, April 26, 2020, see transcript at http://transcripts.
      cnn.com/TRANSCRIPTS/2004/26/fzgps.01.html.

283   "Targeting COVID-19: GHDDI Info Sharing Portal," *The Global Health
      Drug Discovery Institute*, May 6, 2020, at https://ghddi-ailab.github.io/
      Targeting2019-nCoV/.

284   See "Chinese President Xi Jinping Remarks at World Economic Forum,"
      C-SPAN, January 25, 2021, remarks beginning 30:01, at https://www.c-
      span.org/video/?508281-1/chinese-president-xi-jinping-remarks-world-
      economic-forum.

285   "China's Actions to Fight the COVID-19 Pandemic (抗击新冠肺炎疫
      情的中国行动)," *PRC State Council Information Office*, June 7, 2020, at
      http://www.gov.cn/zhengce/2020-06/07/content_5517737.htm.

286   Zhao and Xian, *Great Power Diplomacy*, pp. 87–88.

287   "China's Actions to Fight the COVID-19 Pandemic," *PRC State Council
      Information Office*.

288   "China's Actions to Fight the COVID-19 Pandemic," *PRC State Council
      Information Office*.

289   "China's Actions to Fight the COVID-19 Pandemic," *PRC State Council
      Information Office*. See also Xi, "Unite and Cooperate"; and Xi, "Working
      Together."

290   Kath Sullivan, "China's list of sanctions and tarrifs on Australian trade
      is growing. Here's what has been hit so far," *ABC News*, December 16,
      2020, at https://www.abc.net.au/news/2020-12-17/australian-trade-
      tension-sanctions-china-growing-commodities/12984218; and "Australia
      'deeply disappointed' after China imposes 80% tariff on barley imports,"

The Guardian, May 18, 2020, at https://www.theguardian.com/australia-news/2020/may/19/australia-deeply-disappointed-after-china-imposes-80-tariff-on-barley-imports.

291 Selam Gebrekidan, et al., "In Hunt for Virus Source, W.H.O. Let China Take Charge," *New York Times*, February 9, 2021, at https://www.nytimes.com/2020/11/02/world/who-china-coronavirus.html; and "What influence does China have over the WHO?" *DW News*, April 17, 2020, at https://www.dw.com/en/what-influence-does-china-have-over-the-who/a-53161220.

292 Gebrekidan, "Hunt for Virus Source."

293 Gebrekidan, "Hunt for Virus Source"; and "What influence does China have over the WHO?" *DW News*, April 17, 2020, at https://www.dw.com/en/what-influence-does-china-have-over-the-who/a-53161220. See also "Build Up a Strong Public Health System and Provide Powerful Support for Protecting the People's Health (构建起强大的公共卫生体系为维护人民健康提供有力保障)," *People's Daily*, June 3, 2020, at http://politics.people.com.cn/n1/2020/0603/c1024-31733032.html.

294 "Today the One Belt, One Road Health Cooperation and 'Health Silk Road' Beijing Communique Was Released (一带一路"卫生合作暨"健康丝绸之路"北京公报今日发布)," *People's Daily*, August 18, 2017, at http://health.people.com.cn/n1/2017/0818/c14739-29480314.html.

295 "Tsinghua University Establishes School of Public Health (清華大學成立公共衛生與健康學院)," *People's Daily*, April 9, 2020, at http://gd.people.com.cn/BIG5/n2/2020/0409/c123932-33937072.html; and "Touched by the Fatherland's Love for Hong Kong: An Exclusive Interview with CCPCC's Margaret Chan (心系祖国情牵香港——专访全国政协常委陈冯富珍), *CCPCC News*, July 12, 2019, at http://www.cppcc.gov.cn/zxww/2019/07/12/ARTI1562890969527259.shtml; and "Margaret Chan Appointed as High Ranking Tsinghua Cadre Position, Tedros Congratulates and also Thanks Chairman Xi's Leadership (陳馮富珍任職清華高幹,譚德塞道賀也謝習主席領導), *Radio Free Asia*, April 3, 2020, at http://www.rfi.fr/tw/%E4%B8%AD%E5%9C%8B/20200403-%E9%99%B3%E9%A6%AE%E5%AF%8C%E7%8F%8D%E4%BB%BB%E8%81%B7%E6%B8%85%E8%8F%AF%E9%AB%98%E5%B9%B9-%E8%AD%9A%E5%BE%B7%E5%A1%9E%E9%81%93%E8%B3%80%E4%B9%9F%E8%AC%9D%E7%BF%92%E4%B8%BB%E5%B8%AD%E9%A0%98%E5%B0%8E. See also "Council of Advisors," *Boao Forum for Asia*, undated, at http://english.boaoforum.org/gyltqrlsen/index.jhtml; and "Dr. Margaret Chan: The Only Ways to Prevail the Pandemic is to Learn from the Past and Strengthen Cooperation," *Boao Forum for Asia*, June 8, 2020, at http://english.boaoforum.org/mtzxxwxzen/49436.jhtml.

296 "Goodwill Ambassadors," *World Health Organization*, accessed April 24, 2020, at https://www.who.int/about/who-we-are/structure/goodwill-

ambassadors. See also "Peng Liyuan (彭丽媛)," *Baidu Baike*, undated, accessed April 24, 2020, at https://baike.baidu.com/item/%E5%BD%AD% E4%B8%BD%E5%AA%9B.

297 "China's Actions to Fight the COVID-19 Pandemic (抗击新冠肺炎疫 情的中国行动)," *PRC State Council Information Office*, June 7, 2020, at http://www.gov.cn/zhengce/2020-06/07/content_5517737.htm. See also Xi Jinping, "Unite and Cooperate"; and Xi Jinping, "Working Together."

298 "China's Actions to Fight COVID-19," *PRC State Council Information Office*.

299 Zhao and Xian, *Great Power Diplomacy*, p. 15.

300 Zhao and Xian, *Great Power Diplomacy*, p. 15.

301 Zhao and Xian, *Great Power Diplomacy*, p. 15.

302 Zhao and Xian, *Great Power Diplomacy*, p. 15.

303 Zhao and Xian, *Great Power Diplomacy*, p. 16.

304 Zhao and Xian, *Great Power Diplomacy*, p. 16.

305 Zhao and Xian, *Great Power Diplomacy*, p. 17.

306 Zhao and Xian, *Great Power Diplomacy*, p. 18.

307 Zhao and Xian, *Great Power Diplomacy*, p. 18.

308 Zhao and Xian, *Great Power Diplomacy*, p. 18.

309 Zhao and Xian, *Great Power Diplomacy*, p. 18.

310 Zhao and Xian, *Great Power Diplomacy*, pp. 18–19.

311 Zhao and Xian, *Great Power Diplomacy*, p. 19.

312 Zhao and Xian, *Great Power Diplomacy*, p. 19.

313 Jiang and Luo, *Military-Civil Fusion*, p. 131.

314 Jiang and Luo, *Military-Civil Fusion*, p. 131.

315 Zhao and Xian, *Great Power Diplomacy*, p. 19.

316 Zhao and Xian, *Great Power Diplomacy*, p. 44. Quote from Xi's 2016 New Year's Address.

317 Zhao and Xian, *Great Power Diplomacy*, pp. 59–67.

318 Zhao and Xian, *Great Power Diplomacy*, pp. 71–87.

319 Zhao and Xian, *Great Power Diplomacy*, p. 76.

320 Zhao and Xian, *Great Power Diplomacy*, pp. 78–80.

321 Zhao and Xian, *Great Power Diplomacy*, p. 42.

322 Ren and Zhao, *Strategic Support*, p. 99.

323 Ren and Zhao, *Strategic Support*, p. 99.

324 Ren and Zhao, *Strategic Support*, p. 99.

325 Ren and Zhao, *Strategic Support*, p. 99.

326   Ren and Zhao, *Strategic Support*, p. 99.

327   From Clive Hamilton and Maeike Ohlberg, *Hidden Hand: Exposing How the Chinese Communist Party is Reshaping the World* (Toronto, Canada: Optimum Publishing International, 2020).

328   Zhao and Xian, *Great Power Diplomacy*, p. 85.

329   Ren and Zhao, *Strategic Support*, p. 224.

330   "Secretary of State Antony Blinken on Three Hot International Issues," *Wall Street Journal*, December 12, 2021, at https://www.wsj.com/articles/ sec-of-state-antony-blinken-on-three-international-issues-11639165528.

331   "Secretary of State Antony Blinken on Three Hot International Issues," *Wall Street Journal*.

332   Zhao and Xian, *Great Power Diplomacy*, pp. 3–4.

Chapter Seven: Enslavement

333   Quoted in Rogin, *Chaos Under Heaven*, p. 171.

334   "Curriculum Vitae of the Chairman of the PRC State and PRC Central Military Commission (中华人民共和国主席、中华人民共和国中央军事委员会主席简历)," Xinhua, March 17, 2018, at http://www.xinhuanet. com/politics/2018lh/2018-03/17/c_1122551729.htm.

335   An Baijie, "Mystery post divulges details on first couple," *China Daily*, September 1, 2017, at https://www.chinadaily.com.cn/china/2017-09/01/ content_31433136.htm.

336   "New hit "Xi Dada loves Peng Mama" goes viral online," *People's Daily*, November 24, 2014, at http://en.people.cn/n/2014/1124/c90782-8813187. html.

337   An, "Mystery post divulges details on first couple"; and Viola Zhou, "China's power couple Xi Jinping and Peng Liyuan celebrate 30th wedding anniversary," *South China Morning Post*, September 1, 2017, at https://www.scmp.com/news/china/society/article/2109411/chinas- power-couple-xi-jinping-and-peng-liyuan-celebrate-30th.

338   "Xi Jinping and Peng Liyuan mark 30th Anniversary, Ever Like Cowboy and Weaver Girl (习近平彭丽媛结婚30周年 多年如牛郎织女)," *Duowei News*, September 1, 2017, at https://www.dwnews.com/%E4%B8 %AD%E5%9B%BD/60010224/%E4%B9%A0%E8%BF%91%E5%B9%B3%E5% BD%AD%E4%B8%BD%E5%AA%9B%E7%BB%93%E5%A9%9A30%E5%91% A8%E5%B9%B4%E5%A4%9A%E5%B9%B4%E5%A6%82%E7%89%9B%E9%9B%8 3%8E%E7%BB%87%E5%A5%B3.

339 "Sweet moments of Xi Jinping and his wife," *People's Daily*, August 7, 2019, at https://peoplesdaily.pdnews.cn/2019/08/07/china/sweet-moments-of-xi-jinping-and-his-wife-81279.html.

340 "Xi hails BRICS consensus on global governance at Xiamen summit," Xinhua, September 5, 2017, at http://chinaplus.cri.cn/news/politics/11/20170905/23701.html; and Zhang Wan, "Xi's book becomes best seller at media center of BRICS Xiamen summit," *China Plus*, September 3, 2017, at http://chinaplus.cri.cn/photo/china/18/20170903/22896.html.a

341 Xu Fei, "First ever BRICS co-production to hit cinemas in Sept," *China Plus*, June 30, 2017, at http://chinaplus.cri.cn/video/culture/169/20170630/7505.html.

342 Fu Yu, China runner-up in U-20 volleyball at BRICS Games," *China Plus*, June 22, 2017, at http://chinaplus.cri.cn/news/sports/13/20170622/6786.html; Fu Yu, "China runner-up in basketball at BRICS Games," *China Plus*, June 21, 2017, at http://chinaplus.cri.cn/news/sports/13/20170621/6725.html.

343 Zhao and Xian, *Great Power Diplomacy*, p. 110. For his remarks, see Xi Jinping, "Working Together to Usher in the Second "Golden Decade" of BRICS Cooperation," *Ministry of Foreign Affairs of the People's Republic of China*, September 3, 2017, at https://www.fmprc.gov.cn/mfa_eng/topics_665678/XJPZCJZGJLDRDJCHWHXXSCGJYFZZGJDHH/t1489623.shtml.

344 Zhao and Xian, *Great Power Diplomacy*, p. 110.

345 Zhao and Xian, *Great Power Diplomacy*, p. 112.

346 Zhao and Xian, *Great Power Diplomacy*, p. 110; and "China Focus: Xi chairs summit to set course for next golden decade of BRICS," Xinhua, September 4, 2017, at http://www.xinhuanet.com//english/2017-09/04/c_136583077.htm.

347 Zhao and Xian, *Great Power Diplomacy*, p. 94.

348 Zhao and Xian, *Great Power Diplomacy*, p. 43.

349 Zhao and Xian, *Great Power Diplomacy*, p. 95–96.

350 Zhao and Xian, *Great Power Diplomacy*, p. 113.

351 Zhao and Xian, *Great Power Diplomacy*, p.113.

352 Zhao and Xian, *Great Power Diplomacy*, pp. 108–109.

353 Guo Fenghai and Li Haitao, eds., *The Main Contradictions Facing Our Nation's Society in This New Era* [新时代我国社会主要矛盾] (Beijing: National Defense University Press, 2018), p. 9.

354 Guo and Li, *Main Contradictions*, p. 9.

355 Ren and Zhao, *Strategic Support*, p. 213.

356   Zhao and Xian, *Great Power Diplomacy*, p. 109.

357   Ren and Zhao, *Strategic Support*, p. 217.

358   Ren and Zhao, *Strategic Support*, p. 217.

359   Ren and Zhao, *Strategic Support*, p. 217.

360   For background, see Rosemary Gibson and Janardan Prasad Singh, *China Rx: Exposing the Risks of America's Dependence on China for Medicine* (Amherst, New York: Prometheus Books, 2018).

361   "China and the N95 Mask Shortage," *Pointe Bello*, March 2020, at https://www.pointebello.com/insights/china-n95-mask-shortage.

362   "China and the N95 Mask Shortage," *Pointe Bello*.

363   Josh Rogin, *Chaos Under Heaven: Trump, Xi, and the Battle For the 21st Century* (New York: HMH Books, 2021), pp. 265–267.

364   Wolf, "Homeland Security and the China Challenge."

365   Andrew Jacob, "A Glut of Chinese Masks Is Driving U.S. Companies Out of Business," *New York Times*, May 29, 2021, at https://www.nytimes.com/2021/05/29/health/us-china-mask-production.html.

366   Timothy Aeppel, "America's mask makers face post-pandemic meltdown," Reuters, May 11, 2021, at https://www.reuters.com/business/healthcare-pharmaceuticals/americas-mask-makers-face-post-pandemic-meltdown-2021-05-11/.

367   The following section draws from the author's, "What Rare Earths Tell Us about China's Competitive Strategy," *National Interest*, July 17, 2019, at https://nationalinterest.org/feature/what-rare-earths-tell-us-about-chinas-competitive-strategy-67507.

368   Valerie Bailey Grasso, "Rare Earth Elements in National Defense: Background, Oversight Issues, and Options for Congress," *Congressional Research Service*, December 23, 2013, at https://fas.org/sgp/crs/natsec/R41744.pdf.

369   Emily de La Bruyere and Nathan Picarsic, "Beijing's Bid for a Maritime 'God View': Military-Civil Fusion Power Projection and Threats to Supply Chain Integrity," *Real Clear Defense*, October 13, 2020, at https://www.realcleardefense.com/articles/2020/10/13/beijings_bid_for_a_maritime_god_view_military-civil_fusion_power_projection_and_threats_to_supply_chain_integrity_580515.html.

370   "How did we achieve this rare earths Trump card? (是什么成就了稀土这张王牌)" Xinhua, June 6, 2019, at http://www.xinhuanet.com/tech/2019-06/06/c_1124588710.htm.

371   "Rare earths Trump card?" Xinhua.

372   "Today, how should we protect the 'lifeblood of national defense'? (今天，我们该如何保护'国防血液?)," *Guofang Bao*, January 22, 2015, at http://www.gfdy.gov.cn/edu/2015-01/22/content_6318028.htm.

373   "Lifeblood of national defense," *Guofang Bao*.

374   "Made in China 2025 (中国制造2025)," *PRC State Council*, May 8, 2015, at http://www.gov.cn/zhengce/content/2015-05/19/content_9784.htm. Note that parts of this document have been deleted since it was originally released.

375   Larry Wortzel and Kate Selley, "Breaking China's Stranglehold on the Rare Earth Elements Supply Chain," *Japan Forward*, April 28, 2021, at https://japan-forward.com/breaking-chinas-stranglehold-on-the-rare-earth-elements-supply-chain/; and "13th Five-Year National Plan for Science and Technology Innovation ('十三五'国家科技创新规划)," *PRC State Council*, July 28, 2016, at http://www.gov.cn/zhengce/content/2016-08/08/content_5098072.htm.

376   "Insights from Baotou's first military-civil fusion exhibit (包头首届军民融合成果展)," *Baotou Daily*, August 7, 2018, at http://www.baotounews.com.cn/p/614369.html.

377   "Fujian builds platform matching dual-use military-civil technology programs (福建构建军民两用技术项目成果对接平台)," *Guofang Bao*, July 6, 2018, at http://www.gfdy.gov.cn/economy/2018-07/06/content_8081591.htm.

378   Matt Korda and Hans Kristensen, "China Is Building A Second Nuclear Missile Silo Field," *Federation of American Scientists*, July 26, 2021, at https://fas.org/blogs/security/2021/07/china-is-building-a-second-nuclear-missile-silo-field/; and William J. Broad and David E. Sanger, "A 2nd New Nuclear Missile Base for China, and Many Questions About Strategy," *New York Times*, July 26, 2021, at https://www.nytimes.com/2021/07/26/us/politics/china-nuclear-weapons.html.

379   Demetri Sevastopulo and Kathrin Hille, "China tests new space capability with hypersonic missile," *Financial Times*, October 16, 2021, at https://www.ft.com/content/ba0a3cde-719b-4040-93cb-a486e1f843fb.

Chapter Eight: Honeypots & Fox Hunts

380   Xi Jinping, "Absolutely Winning an All-Around Middle Class Society and Struggling for the Grand Victory of Socialism with Chinese Characteristics in a New Age (决胜全面建成小康社会夺取新时代中国特色社会主义伟大胜利)," *People's Daily*, October 18, 2017, at http://jhsjk.people.cn/article/29613660.

381   Zhao and Xian, *Great Power Diplomacy*, p. 105.

382   "Xi Jinping gives important directive on deepening reforms of talent development systems and mechanisms (习近平就深化人才发展体系机制改革作出重要指示)," Xinhua, May 6, 2018, at http://www.xinhuanet.com//politics/2016-05/06/c_1118820251.htm.

383   Zhao and Xian, *Great Power Diplomacy*, p. 105.

384   Xi, "Middle Class Society."

385   Echo Shan, "Chen Ning Yang, 82, to marry a 28-year-old woman," *China Daily*, December 16, 2004, at https://www.chinadaily.com.cn/english/doc/2004-12/16/content_400791.htm.

386   "Chen Ning Yang: American physicist," *Britannica*, September 18, 2021, at https://www.britannica.com/biography/Chen-Ning-Yang; and "Chen Ning Yang Biographical," *The Nobel Prize Organization*, undated, at https://www.nobelprize.org/prizes/physics/1957/yang/biographical/.

387   "85-year-old Nobel laureate Yang: 'Young wife makes me younger," *China Daily*, September 25, 2007, at http://www.chinadaily.com.cn/china/2007-09/25/content_6133691.htm.

388   Kathleen Mclaughlin, "Two top Chinese-American scientists have dropped their U.S. citizenship," *Science*, February 24, 2017, at https://www.science.org/content/article/two-top-chinese-american-scientists-have-dropped-their-us-citizenship.

389   "85-year-old Nobel laureate Yang: 'Young wife makes me younger," *China Daily*.

390   Note that technically he was only 99, but by the Chinese way of counting birthdays, the date did mark his 100th. See "Xi sends birthday greetings to Nobel laureate Chen Ning Yang," *Global Times*, September 22, 2021, at https://www.globaltimes.cn/page/202109/1234863.shtml.

391   See "High-level Overseas Talent Innovation Bases (海外高层次人才创新基地)," *Thousand Talents Plan Net*, at http://www.1000plan.org/qrjh/section/2?m=more; and "Baotou National Rare Earth High-tech Industrial Development Zone (包头国家稀土高新技术产业开发区)," *Thousand Talents Net*, at http://www.1000plan.org.cn/qrjh/channel/346; and "China National Nuclear Corporation Participation in Baotou City's First Annual Military-Civil Exhibition Captures Attention (中核北方参加包头市首届军民融合成果展受关注)," *China National Nuclear Corporation*, August 2, 2018, at http://www.cnnc.com.cn/cnnc/300555/300559/511454/index.html. For details on the importance of Baotou to China's nuclear weapons program, see "Baotou Nuclear Fuel Component Plant," *Center for Nonproliferation Studies*, September 29, 2011, at https://www.nti.org/learn/facilities/698/.

392   Jiang and Luo, *Military-Civil Fusion*, p. 130.

393 "Chinese Communist Party Center Releases: 'Opinion on Deepening Talent Development Reform System and Mechanisms' [中共中央印发：'关于深化人才发展体制机制改革的意见']," *Ministry of Science and Technology*, January 17, 2017, at http://www.most.gov.cn/kjzc/gjkjzc/kjrc/201701/t20170117_130534.htm.

394 See "Deepening Talent Development," *Ministry of Science and Technology*; "How to read the long-term planning doctrine for developing military talent before 2020 (解读：2020年前军队人才发展规划纲要)," *Liberation Army Daily*, August 13, 2014, at http://military.people.com.cn/n/2014/0813/c1011-25456735.html; and "High-level Overseas Talent Innovation Bases (海外高层次人才创新基地)," *Thousand Talents Plan Net*, undated, at http://www.1000plan.org/qrjh/section/2?m=more.

395 "CCP Politburo Office Releases Notification of 'Central Talent Work Coordination Small Group View Regarding Implementation of Plan to Recruit High-level Overseas Talents' (中共中央办公厅转发 '中央人才工作协调小组关于实施海外高层次人才引进计划的意见' 的通知)," *CCP News Net*, June 20, 2012, at http://cpc.people.com.cn/GB/244800/244856/18246001.html.

396 Bruce Kapron, "Andrew Chi-Chih Yao: China – 2000," *A.M. Turing Award*, undated, at https://amturing.acm.org/award_winners/yao_1611524.cfm.

397 Alan Cowell, "Overlooked No More: Alan Turing, Condemned Code Breaker and Computer Visionary," *New York Times*, June 5, 2019, at https://www.nytimes.com/2019/06/05/obituaries/alan-turing-overlooked.html; and B.J. Copeland, "Alan Turing: British mathematician and logician," *Britannica*, undated, at https://www.britannica.com/biography/Alan-Turing.

398 Kapron, "Andrew Chi-Chih Yao."

399 Mclaughlin, "Chinese-American scientists."

400 Arthur Herman, "A Death in Silicon Valley 'With Chinese Characteristics,'" *Forbes*, December 13, 2018, at https://www.forbes.com/sites/arthurherman/2018/12/13/a-death-in-silicon-valley-with-chinese-characteristics/?sh=2355d90b4768.

401 Berber Jin, "Following Stanford physics professor's passing, rumors of ties to Chinese government emerge," *The Stanford Daily*, December 30, 2018, at https://www.stanforddaily.com/2018/12/30/following-stanford-physics-professors-passing-rumors-of-ties-to-chinese-government-emerge/.

402 Jin, "Stanford physics professor."

403 Executive Office of the President of the United States, "Update Concerning China's Acts, Policies and Practices Related to Technology

Transfer, Intellectual Property, and Innovation," *The United States Trade Representative*, November 20, 2018, pp. 46–47, at https://ustr.gov/sites/default/files/enforcement/301Investigations/301%20Report%20Update.pdf.

404 Executive Office, "Update Concerning China."

405 Arthur Herman, "A Death in Silicon Valley 'With Chinese Characteristics,'" *Forbes*, December 13, 2018, at https://www.forbes.com/sites/arthurherman/2018/12/13/a-death-in-silicon-valley-with-chinese-characteristics/?sh=2355d90b4768.

406 Arthur Herman, "A Death in Silicon Valley."

407 Shen Lu, "Death of a Quantum Man," *The Wire China*, May 3, 2020, at https://www.thewirechina.com/2020/05/03/the-quantum-man/.

408 "FBI Director Christopher Wray's Remarks at Press Conference Regarding China's Operation Fox Hunt," *FBI National Press Office*, October 28, 2020, at https://www.fbi.gov/news/pressrel/press-releases/fbi-director-christopher-wrays-remarks-at-press-conference-regarding-chinas-operation-fox-hunt.

409 "Interim Measures to Recruit Overseas High-level Talents (引进海外高层次人才暂行办法)," *Central Organization Department*, Document No. 28 (2008), p. 4.

410 Sun Rui, "China's Overseas Talent Draw-in Work Has Made Important Progress Since the 18th Party Congress (十八大以来我国海外人才引进工作取得重要进展)," *Thousand Talents Plan Net*, June 27, 2018, at http://www.1000plan.org/qrjh/article/76678; and "High-level Overseas Talent Innovation Bases (海外高层次人才创新基地)," *Thousand Talents Plan Net*, at http://www.1000plan.org/qrjh/section/2.

411 *Chinese Influence and American Interests: Promoting Constructive Vigilance* (Stanford, CA: Hoover Institution Press, 2018), p. 123, at https://asiasociety.org/sites/default/files/inline-files/ChineseInfluenceAndAmericaninterests_Report_11.29.2018.pdf.

412 "National Planning Doctrine for Mid-to-Long Term Talent Development, 2010–2020 (国家中长期人才发展规划纲要 (2010– 2020年)发布)," Xinhua, June 6, 2010, at http://www.gov.cn/jrzg/2010-06-06/content_1621777.htm.

413 "National Planning Doctrine," Xinhua.

414 Jenni Marsh, "The rise and fall of a Belt and Road billionaire," *CNN*, December 2018, at https://www.cnn.com/interactive/2018/12/asia/patrick-ho-ye-jianming-cefc-trial-intl/.

415 Zhao and Xian, *Great Power Diplomacy*, pp. 107–108.

416 "FBI Director Christopher Wray's Remarks at Press Conference Regarding China's Operation Fox Hunt," *FBI National Press Office*,

October 28, 2020, at https://www.fbi.gov/news/pressrel/press-releases/
fbi-director-christopher-wrays-remarks-at-press-conference-regarding-
chinas-operation-fox-hunt.

417   "Rare earths Trump card," Xinhua.

418   "Rare Earth Elements in National Defense: Background, Oversight Issues,
      and Options for Congress," *Congressional Research Service*, December 23,
      2013, at https://fas.org/sgp/crs/natsec/R41744.pdf.

419   "Rare earths Trump card," Xinhua.

420   Larry Wortzel and Kate Selley, "Breaking China's Stranglehold on the
      Rare Earth Elements Supply Chain," *Japan Forward*, April 28, 2021, at
      https://japan-forward.com/breaking-chinas-stranglehold-on-the-rare-
      earth-elements-supply-chain/.

421   See Office of the Secretary of Defense, "Military and Security
      Developments Involving the People's Republic of China 2019,"
      Department of Defense, at https://media.defense.gov/2019/
      May/02/2002127082/-1/-1/1/2019_CHINA_MILITARY_POWER_REPORT.
      pdf. For further discussion on the CCP's adversarial views the United
      States, see the author's "How the PLA Really Sees America," *Project
      2049 Institute*, April 9, 2018, at https://project2049.net/2018/04/09/how-
      the-pla-really-sees-america/.

422   "Fact Sheet: U.S. Investors Are Funding Malign PRC Companies
      on Major Indices," *U.S. Department of State*, December 8, 2020, at
      https://2017-2021.state.gov/u-s-investors-are-funding-malign-prc-
      companies-on-major-indices/index.html.

423   Derek Scissors, "American funding of China is becoming dangerous,"
      American Enterprise Institute, December 2, 2020, at https://www.aei.
      org/research-products/report/american-funding-of-china-is-becoming-
      dangerous/.

424   Scissors, "American funding of China."

425   "Funding Malign PRC Companies," *U.S. Department of State*.

426   "Funding Malign PRC Companies," *U.S. Department of State*.

427   For one such example, see Jing Yang, Dawn Lim, and Gordon Lubold,
      "Americans Won't Be Banned From Investing in Alibaba, Tencent, and
      Baidu," *Wall Street Journal*, January 13, 2021, at https://www.wsj.com/
      articles/americans-wont-be-banned-from-investing-in-alibaba-tencent-
      and-baidu-11610563890. For background, see Stone Fish, *America Second*.

428   "Funding Malign PRC Companies," *U.S. Department of State*.

429   Kate O'Keeffe, Heather Somerville, and Yang Jie, "U.S. Investments Aid
      China In Its Bid for Chip Dominance," *Wall Street Journal*, November
      13–14, 2021, A4.

430   O'Keeffe, Somerville, and Yang, "U.S. Investments Aid China."

431   Jing Yang, Dawn Lim, and Gordon Lubold, "Americans Won't Be Banned From Investing in Alibaba, Tencent, and Baidu," *Wall Street Journal*, January 13, 2021, at https://www.wsj.com/articles/americans-wont-be-banned-from-investing-in-alibaba-tencent-and-baidu-11610563890.

Chapter Nine: Rewiring the Planet

432   "Technology can help realize communism: JD.com CEO," *Global Times*, August 20, 2017, at https://www.globaltimes.cn/content/1062242.shtml.

433   Wolf, "Homeland Security and the China Challenge."

434   A notable exception includes Paul F. Roberts, "This Christmas: Beware Of Chinese Conglomerates Bearing Gifts," *Forbes*, December 23, 2020, at https://www.forbes.com/sites/paulfroberts/2020/12/23/this-christmas-beware-of-chinese-conglomerates-bearing-gifts/?sh=1208ae6494bb.

435   Paul Roberts, "TV Maker TCL Denies Back Door, Promises Better Process," *The Security Ledger*, November 20, 2020, at https://securityledger.com/2020/11/tv-maker-tcl-denies-back-door-promises-better-process/.

436   "Our Story," *TCL*, accessed January 15, 2021, at https://www.tcl.com/us/en/about-us/our-story.

437   "TCL Chinese Theater," *TCL*, accessed January 15, 2021, at https://www.tcl.com/us/en/partnerships/tcl-chinese-theatre.

438   "Our Story," *TCL*..

439   "BlackBerry Secures Global Smart Phone Software and Brand Licensing Agreement with TCL Communication," *Globe Newswire*, December 15, 2016, at https://www.globenewswire.com/news-release/2016/12/15/1297239/0/en/BlackBerry-Secures-Global-Smart-Phone-Software-and-Brand-Licensing-Agreement-with-TCL-Communication.html.

440   Wolf, "Homeland Security and the China Challenge"; Roberts, "TCL Denies Back Door; and Roberts, "Beware Of Chinese Conglomerates."

441   Paul Roberts, "Security Holes Opened Back Door To TCL Android Smart TVs," *The Security Ledger*, November 12, 2020, at https://securityledger.com/2020/11/security-holes-opened-back-door-to-tcl-android-smart-tvs/.

442   Roberts, "TV Maker TCL Denies Back Door."

443   Roberts, "Security Holes."

444   Roberts, "TV Maker TCL Denies Back Door"; and Roberts, "Beware Of Chinese Conglomerates."

445   "Alert: Vulnerabilities found in TCL Android TVs," *TCL*, undated, accessed September 14, 2021, at https://support.tcl.com/vulnerabilities-found-in-tcl-android-tvs.

446   Of numerous examples, see "Deeply Implementing Comprehensive State Security," Xinhua; "Counter Spy Law of the People's Republic of China," *PRC Ministry of National Defense*; "State Security Law," *PRC Ministry of National Defense*; and "Internet Security Law," *Office of the CCP Central Cyberspace Affairs Commission*.

447   Wolf, "Homeland Security and the China Challenge."

448   Wolf, "Homeland Security and the China Challenge."

449   Zack Whittaker, "Now even the FBI is warning about your smart TV's security," *Tech Crunch*, December 1, 2019, at https://techcrunch.com/2019/12/01/fbi-smart-tv-security/.

450   Beth Anne Steele, "Tech Tuesday: Internet of Things (IoT), *FBI Portland*, December 3, 2019, at https://www.fbi.gov/contact-us/field-offices/portland/news/press-releases/tech-tuesday-internet-of-things-iot.

451   Roslyn Layton, "China Telecom Rebuke Is Latest In DOJ Crackdown on China," *Forbes*, April 10, 2020, at https://www.forbes.com/sites/roslynlayton/2020/04/10/china-telecom-rebuke-is-latest-in-doj-crackdown/?sh=2e18337842df.

452   "Special Report: State Contracts with Banned Chinese Tech Manufacturers," *China Tech Threat*, accessed November 8, 2021, at https://chinatechthreat.com/special-report-state-contracts-with-banned-chinese-tech-manufacturers/.

453   Roberts, "Beware Of Chinese Conglomerates."

454   Steele, "Internet of Things."

455   Roslyn Layton, "New Pentagon report shows how restricted Chinese IT products routinely enter US military networks," *American Enterprise Institute*, August 12, 2019, at https://www.aei.org/technology-and-innovation/new-pentagon-reports-shows-how-restricted-chinese-it-products-routinely-make-their-way-into-us-military-networks/.

456   Tobin, "Xi Jinping's New Era."

457   Tobin, "Xi Jinping's New Era."

458   The date was September 30, 2013.

459   "Top leaders study at China's Silicon Valley," *The National People's Congress of the People's Republic of China*, October 8, 2013, at http://www.npc.gov.cn/englishnpc/c2762/201310/d9c33325a6f24ec5acc584f16037e6c3.shtml.

460 See Alice L. Miller, "Politburo Processes under Xi Jinping," *China Leadership Monitor*, July 14, 2015, at https://www.hoover.org/research/politburo-processes-under-xi-jinping.

461 Wency Chen, "How Zhongguancun became the innovation hub powering China's tech aspirations," *KrAsia*, December 16, 2020, at https://kr-asia.com/chinas-internet-giants-are-losing-their-allure-for-fresh-computer-science-grads; Meng Jing, "Zhongguancun: Beijing's innovation hub is at the centre of China's aim to become tech powerhouse," *South China Morning Post*, November 13, 2018, at https://www.scmp.com/tech/start-ups/article/2172713/zhongguancun-beijings-innovation-hub-centre-chinas-aim-become-tech.

462 See Wang Sujuan, "Zhongguancun a key hub in global innovation network," *China Daily*, March 5, 2016, at http://www.chinadaily.com.cn/m/beijing/zhongguancun/2016-03/05/content_23797031.htm. See also "Overview," *Microsoft Research Lab—Asia*, accessed November 4, 2021, at https://www.microsoft.com/en-us/research/lab/microsoft-research-asia/; "Intel Announces $50 Million China Research Center," *Intel News Release*, May 5, 1998, at https://www.intel.com/pressroom/archive/releases/1998/AW50598B.HTM; "IBM Research-China," *IBM*, accessed November 4, 2021, at https://www.ibm.com/blogs/research/category/ibmres-china/.

463 For example, see "Master Plan to Develop and Build Zhongguancun into a National Indigenous Innovation Demonstration Zone (2016–2020) [中关村国家自主创新示范区发展建设规划（2016–2020）]," *Leading Small Group of Zhongguancun National Indigenous Innovation Demonstration Zone*, August 18, 2016, at http://zgcgw.beijing.gov.cn/zgc/zwgk/ghjh/158069/index.html; and "Zhongguancun National Indigenous Innovation Demonstration Zone: Action Plan (2017–2020) for Cultivating Artificial Intelligence Industry (中关村国家自主创新示范区人工智能产业培育行动计划2017–2020年)," *Zhongguancun Science Park*, September 30, 2017, at http://zgcgw.beijing.gov.cn/zgc/zwgk/ghjh/157610/index.html.

464 Meng Jing, "Zhongguancun: Beijing's innovation hub is at the centre of China's aim to become tech powerhouse," *South China Morning Post*, November 13, 2018, at https://www.scmp.com/tech/start-ups/article/2172713/zhongguancun-beijings-innovation-hub-centre-chinas-aim-become-tech.

465 Li Zhengfen, "Zhongguancun Core Area: Exploring Military-Civil Fusion 'the Haidian Way' (中关村核心区：探索军民融合'海淀模式')," *China High Tech*, December 11, 2017, at http://www.chinahightech.com/html/paper/2017/1211/443866.html.

466 Li Zhengfen, "Zhongguancun Core Area."

467 Li Zhengfen, "Zhongguancun Core Area."

468 "China's Silicon Valley," *The National People's Congress*.

469 The group included three generals, who wore their service uniforms, and two other civilian members who wore a bright blue blazer and a white jacket, respectively. See "China's Silicon Valley," *The National People's Congress*.

470 "Top CPC members start to study in more diverse ways," *Global Times*, January 3, 2016, at https://www.globaltimes.cn/content/961557.shtml.

471 "China's Silicon Valley," *The National People's Congress*.

472 "Diverse ways," *Global Times*.

473 "China's Silicon Valley," *The National People's Congress*.

474 Brian Hart, "The CCP's Shifting Priorities: An Analysis of Politburo Group Study Sessions," *China Brief*, July 2, 2021, at https://jamestown. org/program/the-ccps-shifting-priorities-an-analysis-of-politburo-group-study-sessions/.

475 Evan Osnos, *Age of Ambition: Chasing Fortune, Truth, and Faith in the New China* (New York: Farrar, Straus and Giroux, 2014), pp. 260–261.

476 Osnos, *Age of Ambition*, p. 261.

477 See Miller, "Politburo Processes under Xi Jinping."

478 "Top Chinese leaders' class: 30 collective studies of the 18th CPC Politburo," *People's Daily*, February 4, 2016, at http://en.people.cn/ n3/2016/0204/c98649-9014098.html.

479 "China's Silicon Valley," *The National People's Congress*.

480 Zhao and Xian, *Great Power Diplomacy*, p. 98.

481 Zhao and Xian, *Great Power Diplomacy*, p. 98.

482 Zhao and Xian, *Great Power Diplomacy*, p. 99–100.

483 Zhao and Xian, *Great Power Diplomacy*, p. 100.

484 Zhao and Xian, *Great Power Diplomacy*, p. 100–101.

485 Jiang and Luo, *Military-Civil Fusion*, p. 189.

486 Jiang and Luo, *Military-Civil Fusion*, p. 189.

487 Jiang and Luo, *Military-Civil Fusion*, p. 191.

488 Jiang and Luo, *Military-Civil Fusion*, p. 191.

489 Osnos, *Age of Ambition*, p. 30.

490 Osnos, *Age of Ambition*, pp. 30–31, 346.

491 For two notable examples, see Masood Farivar, "FBI Arrests Five People in China's 'Operation Fox Hunt,'" *Voice of America*, October 28, 2020, at https://www.voanews.com/a/usa_fbi-arrests-five-people-chinas-operation-fox-hunt/6197702.html; and Isaiah Mitchell, "Midland Pastor, Billionaire Trade Accusations of Communist Loyalties," *The Texan*,

October 13, 2020, at https://thetexan.news/midland-pastor-billionaire-trade-accusations-of-communist-loyalties/.

492   Osnos, *Age of Ambition*, p. 31.

493   Osnos, *Age of Ambition*, p. 211.

494   Osnos, *Age of Ambition*, p. 274.

495   Kai-Fu Lee, *AI Superpowers: China, Silicon Valley and the New World Order* (New York: Houghton Mifflin Harcourt, 2018), p. 109.

496   Lee, *AI Superpowers*, p. 109; and Kishalaya Kundu, "Musical.ly App To Be Shut Down, Users Will Be Migrated to TikTok," *Beebom*, August 2, 2018, at https://beebom.com/musical-ly-app-to-be-shut-down-users-will-be-migrated-to-tiktok/.

497   Anna Fifield, "TikTok's owner is helping China's campaign of repression in Xinjiang, report finds," *Washington Post*, November 28, 2019, at https://www.washingtonpost.com/world/tiktoks-owner-is-helping-chinas-campaign-of-repression-in-xinjiang-report-finds/2019/11/28/98e8d9e4-119f-11ea-bf62-eadd5d11f559_story.html. For further details, see Danielle Cave, Fergus Ryan, and Vicky Xiuzhong Xu, "Mapping more of China's tech giants: AI and surveillance," *Australian Strategic Policy Institute*, November 28, 2019, at https://www.aspi.org.au/report/mapping-more-chinas-tech-giants.

498   Alex Hern, "Revealed: how TikTok censors videos that do not please Beijing," *The Guardian*, September 25, 2019, at https://www.theguardian.com/technology/2019/sep/25/revealed-how-tiktok-censors-videos-that-do-not-please-beijing.

499   Samantha Hoffman, "The U.S.-China Data Fight Is Only Getting Started," *Australian Strategic Policy Institute*, July 22, 2021, at https://www.aspi.org.au/opinion/us-china-data-fight-only-getting-started.

500   Hoffman, "U.S.-China Data Fight."

501   Rachel Lerman and Cristiano Lima, "TikTok, Snap, YouTube defend how they protect kids online in congressional hearing," *Washington Post*, October 26, 2021, at https://www.washingtonpost.com/technology/2021/10/26/tiktok-snapchat-youtube-congress-hearing/.

502   Salvador Rodriguez, "TikTok usage surpassed Instagram this year among kids aged 12 to 17, Forrester survey says," *CNBC*, November 18, 2021, at https://www.cnbc.com/2021/11/18/tiktok-usage-topped-instagram-in-2021-among-kids-12-to-17-forrester-.html; and Brian Dean, "TikTok User Statistics (2021)," *Backlinko*, October 11, 2021, at https://backlinko.com/tiktok-users.

503   Salvador Rodriguez, "TikTok usage surpassed Instagram this year among kids aged 12 to 17, Forrester survey says," *CNBC*, November 18, 2021, at https://www.cnbc.com/2021/11/18/tiktok-usage-topped-

instagram-in-2021-among-kids-12-to-17-forrester-.html; and Brian Dean, "TikTok User Statistics (2021)," *Backlinko*, October 11, 2021, at https://backlinko.com/tiktok-users.

504 Lee, *AI Superpowers*, p. 93.

505 Lee, *AI Superpowers*, p. 93.

506 Todd Bishop, "Chinese tech powerhouse Baidu opens Seattle-area office, expanding its reach in AI and the cloud," *Geek Wire*, October 9, 2017, at https://www.geekwire.com/2017/chinese-tech-powerhouse-baidu-opens-seattle-area-office-expanding-reach-ai-cloud/; and Luke Stangel, "Baidu expands opens second self-driving car lab in Silicon Valley, ramps up hiring," *Silicon Valley Business Journal*, October 4, 2017, at https://www.bizjournals.com/sanjose/news/2017/10/04/baidu-expands-its-footprint-in-silicon-valley-with.html.

507 Saheli Roy Choudhury, "Alibaba says it will invest more than $15 billion over three years in global research program," *CNBC*, October 11, 2017, at https://www.cnbc.com/2017/10/11/alibaba-says-will-pour-15-billion-into-global-research-program.html.

508 Choudhury, "Alibaba global research program."

509 Lee, *AI Superpowers*, p. 87.

510 Lee, *AI Superpowers*, p. 87.

Chapter Ten: Digital Dictators

511 Garnaut, "Engineers of the Soul."

512 Josh Horwitz, "Chinese tech execs support 'common prosperity', helping SMEs at internet summit," Reuters, September 26, 2021, at https://www.reuters.com/technology/chinese-tech-execs-support-common-prosperity-helping-smes-internet-summit-2021-09-26/.

513 See "Xi sends congratulatory letter to 2021 World Internet Conference Wuzhen Summit," *People's Daily*, September 26, 2021, at http://en.people.cn/n3/2021/0926/c90000-9900968.html; "Xi Focus: Xi sends congratulatory letter to World Internet Conference – Internet Development Forum," Xinhua, November 23, 2020, at http://www.xinhuanet.com/english/2020-11/23/c_139536811.htm; "6th World Internet Conference opens in China's Zhejiang," Xinhua, October 20, 2019, http://www.xinhuanet.com/english/2019-10/20/c_138487994.htm; "Xi congratulates opening of fifth World Internet Conference," *China Daily*, November 7, 2018, at http://www.chinadaily.com.cn/a/201811/07/WS5be24e62a310eff3032871a3.html; "Global delegates laud Xi's

messages to World Internet Conference," Xinhua, December 4, 2017, at http://www.xinhuanet.com//english/2017-12/04/c_136797784.htm; "Xi's speech on cyberspace applauded," *China Daily*, November 16, 2016, at http://www.chinadaily.com.cn/bizchina/3rdWuzhenWorldInternetConfe rence/2016-11/16/content_27398982.htm; and "Highlights of Xi's Internet Speech," *World Internet Conference*, December 16, 2015, at http://www. wuzhenwic.org/2015-12/16/c_47742.htm.

514   Jiang and Luo, *Military-Civil Fusion*, p. 194.

515   "World IT Leaders Show Confidence in China," *Science and Technology Daily*, October 14, 2021, at http://www.stdaily.com/English/ ChinaNews/2021-10/14/content_1225483.shtml.

516   Rick Gladstone, "Despite Covid Risks, Many Leaders Plan to Attend U.N. General Assembly," *New York Times*, September 12, 2021, at https:// www.nytimes.com/2021/09/12/world/covid-united-nations-general-assembly.html.

517   For background, see Nathan Attrill and Audrey Fritz, China's cyber vision: How the Cyberspace Administration of China is building a new consensus on global internet governance," *Australian Strategic Policy Institute*, November 24, 2021, at https://www.aspi.org.au/report/chinas-cyber-vision-how-cyberspace-administration-china-building-new-consensus-global; and Elles Houweling, "Gelsinger, Musk and China tech CEOs all bow down to Xi's vision," *Verdict*, September 27, 2021, at https://www.verdict.co.uk/gelsinger-musk-and-china-tech-ceos-all-bow-down-to-xis-vision/.

518   Cheryl Fu, "Speech by Tesla CEO Elon Musk at the 2021 World Internet Conference Wuzhen Summit," *Firmknow*, September 27, 2021, at https:// firmknow.com/speech-by-tesla-ceo-elon-musk-at-the-2021-world-internet-conference-wuzhen-summit/; and Sarah Lee-Jones, "Watch: Tesla CEO Elon Musk's Speech at 2021 World Internet Conference in China [Video]," *Tesla North*, September 25, 2021, at https://teslanorth. com/2021/09/25/watch-tesla-ceo-elon-musks-speech-at-2021-world-internet-conference-in-china-video/.

519   Fu, "Speech by Elon Musk"; and Lee-Jones, "Watch Elon Musk's Speech."

520   "Message from Chuck Robbins, chair and CEO of Cisco System, to 2021 World Internet Conference," *WIC Voices and Opinions*, November 2, 2021, at https://www.wuzhenwic.org/2021-11/02/c_675539.htm, accessed November 29, 2021.

521   "Message from Chuck Robbins," *WIC Voices and Opinions*.

522   Importantly, Robbins focused his remarks on "aligning with the vision of a shared cyberspace community for the benefit of all," according to the media outlet. See "World IT Leaders," *Science and Technology Daily*.

523   Elles Houweling, "Gelsinger, Musk and China tech CEOs all bow down to Xi's vision," *Verdict*, September 27, 2021, at https://www.verdict.co.uk/gelsinger-musk-and-china-tech-ceos-all-bow-down-to-xis-vision/.

524   Coco Feng, "Xi Jinping calls for international tech cooperation to tackle global challenges, amid simmering US tensions," *South China Morning Post*, September 24, 2021, at https://www.scmp.com/tech/tech-war/article/3150042/president-xi-calls-international-tech-cooperation-tackle-global.

525   "CCTV+: Xi calls for global sci-tech innovation cooperation at opening of 2021 Zhongguancun (ZGC) Forum," *PR Newswire*, September 25, 2021, at https://www.prnewswire.com/news-releases/cctv-xi-calls-for-global-sci-tech-innovation-cooperation-at-opening-of-2021-zhongguancun-zgc-forum-301385078.html. See also Du Juan, "Zhongguancun Forum broadens its influence," *China Daily*, September 16, 2021, at https://www.chinadaily.com.cn/a/202109/16/WS6142a170a310e0e3a6821ecf.html.

526   Pete Sweeney, "Apple's ugly China deal mostly bought time," Reuters, December 8, 2021, at https://www.reuters.com/breakingviews/apples-ugly-china-deal-mostly-bought-time-2021-12-08/; and "Apple's Tim Cook Signed $275 Billion Deal to Placate China – the Information," *U.S. News and World Report*, December 7, 2021, at https://money.usnews.com/investing/news/articles/2021-12-07/apples-tim-cook-signed-275-billion-deal-with-chinese-officials-to-placate-china-the-information.

527   Jiang and Luo, *Military-Civil Fusion*, pp. 191–192.

528   Jiang and Luo, *Military-Civil Fusion*, p. 192.

529   Jiang and Luo, *Military-Civil Fusion*, p. 192.

530   Jiang and Luo, *Military-Civil Fusion*, p. 193.

531   Zhao and Xian, *Great Power Diplomacy*, p. 103.

532   Zhao and Xian, *Great Power Diplomacy*, p. 103.

533   Zhao and Xian, *Great Power Diplomacy*, p. 103.

534   Zhao and Xian, *Great Power Diplomacy*, p. 103.

535   Zhao and Xian, *Great Power Diplomacy*, p. 103.

536   Zhao and Xian, *Great Power Diplomacy*, p. 103.

537   Zhao and Xian, *Great Power Diplomacy*, p. 107.

538   Emily de La Bruyère and Nathan Picarsic, "A 'techlash' with Chinese characteristics," *Tech Crunch*, November 21, 2021, at https://techcrunch.com/2021/11/21/a-techlash-with-chinese-characteristics/.

539   See Roslyn Layton and Peter Wood, "Comments of China Tech Threat and Blue Path Labs: Before the Federal Communications Commission," *China Tech Threat*, September 21, 2021, at https://chinatechthreat.com/china-tech-threat-blue-path-labs-file-fcc-comment-on-chinese-tech-

loophole/; and Jeff Hill, "New Report Highlights the Unsettling State of IoT Device Security," *Dark Cubed*, March 31, 2021, at https://darkcubed. com/press/2021/3/30/new-report-highlights-the-unsettling-state-of-iot-device-security.

540 Trevor R. Jones and Treston Chandler, "Sweeping U.S. Lists Seek to Restrict Trade and Investment that Support the Chinese Military," *Wisconsin Project*, September 27, 2021, at https://www.wisconsinproject. org/sweeping-us-lists-seek-to-restrict-trade-investment-that-support-chinese-military/; Alexandra Alper, David Shepardson, and Humeyra Pamuk, "U.S. blacklists dozens of Chinese firms including SMIC, DJI," Reuters, December 18, 2020, at https://www.reuters.com/article/us-usa-china-sanctions/u-s-blacklists-dozens-of-chinese-firms-including-smic-dji-idUSKBN28S0HL; and Humeyra Pamuk, Alexandra Alper, Idrees Ali, "Trump bans U.S. investments in companies linked to Chinese military," Reuters, November 13, 2020, at https://www.reuters.com/article/usa-china-securities/trump-bans-u-s-investments-in-companies-linked-to-chinese-military-idUSKBN27T1MD.

541 Adam Xu, "Cybersecurity Experts Worried by Chinese Firm's Control of Smart Devices," *Voice of America*, August 21, 2021, at https://www. voanews.com/a/east-asia-pacific_voa-news-china_cybersecurity-experts-worried-chinese-firms-control-smart-devices/6209815.html; Hal Brands and Klon Kitchen, "Tuya may be the China threat that beats Russia's ransomware attacks," *The Hill*, July 30, 2021, at https://thehill. com/opinion/cybersecurity/564962-tuya-may-be-the-china-threat-that-beats-russias-ransomware-attacks. See also "Products Empowered by Tuya Smart Design Win iF DESIGN AWARD 2021 and Red Dot Design Award 202," *PR Newswire*, August 2, 2021, at https://www.prnewswire. com/news-releases/products-empowered-by-tuya-smart-design-win-if-design-award-2021-and-red-dot-design-award-2021-301346047.html.

542 See "Smart Appliances," *GE Appliances*, accessed November 15, 2021, at https://www.geappliances.com/ge/connected-appliances/.

543 See "Smart Products & Electronics," *Motorola*, accessed November 15, 2021, at https://www.motorola.com/us/all-smart-products.

544 See "Smart TV: Powerful Performance," *TCL*, accessed November 15, 2021, at https://www.tcl.com/us/en/products/home-theater.

545 See "Smart Devices," *Lenovo*, accessed November 15, 2021, at https:// www.lenovo.com/us/en/devices/; and "Data Center," *Lenovo*, accessed November 15, 2021, at https://www.lenovo.com/us/en/data-center.

546 See "Official Website," *DJI*, accessed November 15, 2021, at https://www. dji.com/; and "Industries: Special Operations," *DJI Enterprise*, accessed November 15, 2021, at https://enterprise.dji.com/electricity/special-oper ations?site=enterprise&from=nav.

547   See "Home," *Hikvision*, accessed November 15, 2021, at https://
      us.hikvision.com/en; and "Products," *Hikvision*, accessed November 15,
      2021, at https://us.hikvision.com/en/products/more-products.

Chapter Eleven: Strategic Saturation

548   Central Military Commission Political Work Department, *Xi Jinping
      on a Strong and Resurgent Military* [习近平论强军兴军] (Beijing:
      Liberation Army Press: 2017), p. 386. Note this book is marked "For use
      of regimental-leader cadres and above [团以上领导干部使用]." Cited
      in Fang Yugang and Liu Jizhong, eds., *The Basis for Building the People's
      Military: The Strong Military Spirit* [人民军队建军之本强军之魂]
      (Beijing: National Defense University, 2018), p. 225.

549   Peter Mattis and Matthew Brazil, *Chinese Communist Espionage: An
      Intelligence Primer* (Annapolis MD: Naval Institute Press, 2019), p. 25.

550   Mattis and Brazil, *Chinese Communist Espionage*, p. 4.

551   Mattis and Brazil, *Chinese Communist Espionage*, pp. 4–5, 27, 103–106.

552   The network was comprised of Qian Zhuangfei, Li Kenong, and Hu Di,
      who were called the "Three Heroes of the Dragon's Liar." See Mattis
      and Brazil, *Chinese Communist Espionage*, pp. 4–5.

553   Mattis and Brazil, *Chinese Communist Espionage*, p. 5.

554   Mattis and Brazil, *Chinese Communist Espionage*, p. 6.

555   Mattis and Brazil, *Chinese Communist Espionage*, p. 28.

556   The general's name was Mo Xiong. His controller was Xiang Yunian.
      Mattis and Brazil, *Chinese Communist Espionage*, pp. 126–127.

557   Pan Hannian secured the arrangement with Guangdong warlord Chen
      Jitang. See Mattis and Brazil, *Chinese Communist Espionage*, pp. 28, 130.

558   Mattis and Brazil, *Chinese Communist Espionage*, p. 247.

559   Toshi Yoshihara, "Evaluating the Logic and Methods of China's United
      Front Work," *Orbis*, February 2020, p. 237.

560   For background, see Kerry K. Gershaneck, *Media Warfare: Taiwan's
      Battle for the Cognitive Domain* (Washington, DC, Center for Security
      Policy, 2021); Kerry K. Gershaneck, *Political Warfare: Strategies for
      Combating China's Plan to "Win without Fighting"* (Quantico, VA:
      Marine Corps University Press, 2020); and Mark Stokes and Russell
      Hsiao, *The People's Liberation Army General Political Department:
      Political Warfare with Chinese Characteristics* (Arlington, VA: Project
      2049 Institute, October 2013), at http://www.project2049.net/

documents/PLA_General_Political_Department_Liaison_Stokes_Hsiao.
pdf.

561   Fang and Liu, *The Basis for Building the People's Military*, pp. 222–224.

562   Fang and Liu, *The Basis for Building the People's Military*, pp. 226–227.

563   Fang and Liu, *The Basis for Building the People's Military*, pp. 227–229.

564   PLA General Political Department, *Selection of Chairman Xi's Important
      Ideas Regarding Military Political Work* [习主席关于军队政治工作重要
      论述摘编] (Beijing: Liberation Army Press, 2014), p. 67. Cited in Fang
      and Liu, *The Basis for Building the People's Military*, p. 222.

565   Fang and Liu, *The Basis for Building the People's Military*, p. 222.

566   Central Military Commission Political Work Department, *Strong and
      Resurgent Military*, p. 386. Cited in Fang and Liu, *The Basis for Building
      the People's Military*, p. 225.

567   Fang and Liu, *The Basis for Building the People's Military*, pp. 227–228.

568   Fang and Liu, *The Basis for Building the People's Military*, p. 229.

569   Ren and Zhao, *Strategic Support*, p. 100.

570   Ren and Zhao, *Strategic Support*, p. 100.

571   Zhao and Xian, *Great Power Diplomacy*, p. 47.

572   Zhao and Xian, *Great Power Diplomacy*, p. 47.

573   Ren and Zhao, *Strategic Support*, p. 214.

574   Ren and Zhao, *Strategic Support*, p. 215.

575   For background, see Ross Anderson, "When China Sees All," *The
      Atlantic*, September 2020, at https://www.theatlantic.com/magazine/
      archive/2020/09/china-ai-surveillance/614197/; and Lee, *AI Superpowers*,
      p. 54.

576   Jiang and Luo, *Military-Civil Fusion*, pp. 187–188.

577   For background, see "Human Intelligence in the Digital Age – Speech
      by Richard Moore, Chief of the UK's Secret Intelligence Service," *IISS*,
      November 30, 2021, at https://www.iiss.org/events/2021/11/human-
      intelligence-digital-age; and Gershaneck, *Media Warfare*.

578   For details on specific cases, see Hamilton and Ohlberg, *Hidden Hand*.

579   Peggy Hollinger, "Goliath crane for sale at knockdown price," *Financial
      Times*, March 28, 2016, at https://www.ft.com/content/8cb5d0c6-f201-
      11e5-9f20-c3a047354386; and "Port News: Rosyth Dockyard's Goliath
      crane arrives," *Ships Monthly*, April 28, 2011, at https://shipsmonthly.
      com/news/port-news-rosyth-dockyards-goliath-crane-arrives/. For
      background on ZPMC, see Kate O'Keeffe and Chun Han Wong, "U.S.
      Sanctions Chinese Firms and Executives Active in Contested South
      China Sea," *Wall Street Journal*, August 26, 2020, at https://www.wsj.

com/articles/u-s-imposes-visa-export-restrictions-on-chinese-firms-and-executives-active-in-contested-south-china-sea-11598446551.

580   Jeanne Whalen, "U.S. slaps trade sanctions on more Chinese entities, this time for South China Sea island building," *Washington Post*, August 26, 2020, at https://www.washingtonpost.com/business/2020/08/26/china-entity-list-islands/. See "DOD Releases List of Additional Companies, in Accordance with Section 1237 of FY99 NDAA," *U.S. Department of Defense*, August 28, 2020, at https://www.defense. gov/Newsroom/Releases/Release/Article/2328894/dod-releases-list-of-additional-companies-in-accordance-with-section-1237-of-fy/; and "Qualifying Entities Prepared in Response to Section 1237 of the National Defense Authorization Act for Fiscal Year 1999 (PUBLIC LAW 105–261)," *U.S. Department of Defense*, August 28, 2020, at https:// media.defense.gov/2020/Aug/28/2002486689/-1/-1/1/LINK_1_1237_ TRANCHE-23_QUALIFYING_ENTITIES.PDF.

581   Conor Kennedy, "Ramping the Strait: Quick and Dirty Solutions to Boost Amphibious Lift," *China Brief*, July 16, 2021, at https://jamestown. org/program/ramping-the-strait-quick-and-dirty-solutions-to-boost-amphibious-lift/; and Andrew Tate, "Exercise demonstrates PLA Army Aviation ability to use commercial ships as temporary flight decks," *Janes*, August 21, 2020, at https://www.janes.com/defence-news/ news-detail/exercise-demonstrates-pla-army-aviation-ability-to-use-commercial-ships-as-temporary-flight-decks.

582   "Beijing-controlled Enterprises Little Hindered by U.S. Sanctions Aimed at Specific Subsidiaries," *Pointe Bello*, November 2020, at https://www. pointebello.com/insights/beijing-controlled-enterprises-little-hindered-by-us-sanctions.

583   The author would like to acknowledge and thank to Pointe Bello's Cecilia Joy Perez for her tutorial on ZPMC and its presence in the United States. For insights into ZPMC's operations, see "NWSA welcomes four ZPMC Super-Post Panamax cranes as part of terminal modernization," *Port Technology*, June 15, 2021, at https://www. porttechnology.org/news/nwsa-welcomes-four-zpmc-super-post-panamax-cranes-as-part-of-terminal-modernisation/; "Cranes for LBCT wharf, Long Beach, the U.S. were shipped," *ZPMC*, February 24, 2021, at https://www.zpmc.com/news/cont.aspx?id=233; "Port of Oakland's largest terminal gets three giant cranes in fall," *Port of Oakland*, June 18, 2020, at https://www.portofoakland.com/seaport/port-of-oaklands-largest-terminal-gets-three-giant-cranes-in-fall/; "ZPMC USA Expands Coast-to-coast," *Maritime Logistics Professional*, July 11, 2018, at https://www.maritimeprofessional.com/news/zpmc-expands-coast-coast-319480; and "ZPMC boosts cranes to work big ships at Port of Los Angeles," *Freight Waves*, November 18, 2016, at https://www.

freightwaves.com/news/zpmc-boosts-cranes-to-work-big-ships-at-port-of-los-angeles.

584   "ZPMC USA Expands Coast-to-coast," *Maritime Logistics Professional*, July 11, 2018, at https://www.maritimeprofessional.com/news/zpmc-expands-coast-coast-319480; and "ZPMC boosts cranes to work big ships at Port of Los Angeles," *Freight Waves*, November 18, 2016, at https://www.freightwaves.com/news/zpmc-boosts-cranes-to-work-big-ships-at-port-of-los-angeles.

585   "Beijing-controlled Enterprises Little Hindered by U.S. Sanctions Aimed at Specific Subsidiaries," *Pointe Bello*, November 2020, at https://www.pointebello.com/insights/beijing-controlled-enterprises-little-hindered-by-us-sanctions.

586   Cecilia Joy Perez, @ceci_joy, *Twitter*, 3:41 PM, August 26, 2020, at https://twitter.com/ceci_joy/status/1298707049346404354.

587   John Adams, "John Holland's Chisholm Road Prison Security Tender Closed," *Security, Electronics, and Networks*," July 28, 2020, at https://sen.news/2020/07/28/john-hollands-chisholm-road-prison-project-seeks-security/; "Chisholm Road Prison," *John Holland*, undated, accessed December 20, 2021, at https://www.johnholland.com.au/our-projects/chisholm-road-prison/; and "John Holland wins bid for Australian project with contract value of AUD 700 million," *CCCC International*, March 23, 2017, at http://en.ccccltd.cn/newscentre/businessupdate/201704/t20170414_52133.html.

588   See "Our Projects," *John Holland*, undated, accessed December 20, 2021, at https://www.johnholland.com.au/our-projects/.

589   See "Construction of Hutchison's container terminal, container yard and housing project at the port of Veracruz has been completed," *CCCC*, May 27, 2021, at http://en.ccccltd.cn/newscentre/CompanyNews2020/202105/t20210527_66391.html; Sam Chambers, "Mexico's president seeks to take back control of Veracruz port," *Splash*, August 19, 2020, at https://splash247.com/mexicos-president-seeks-to-take-back-control-of-veracruz-port/; "China harbor concludes first caisson," *Asipona Ensenada*, January 6, 2015, at https://www.puertoensenada.com.mx/engs/0000514/china-harbor-concludes-first-caisson; "ZPMC bags Lázaro Cárdenas deal," *World Cargo News*, March 27, 2013, at https://www.worldcargonews.com/news/zpmc-bags-laacutezaro-caacuterdenas-deal-27455; "Mexico: CHEC Wins Bid for Phase 1 of Manzanillo Container Terminal," *Dredging Today*, September 16, 2011, at https://www.dredgingtoday.com/2011/09/16/mexico-chec-wins-bid-for-phase-1-of-manzanillo-container-terminal/; and "Hutchison Port Holdings acquires overseas assets of International Container Terminal Services, Inc.," *Hutchison Whampoa Limited*, May 28, 2001, at http://www.hutchison-whampoa.com/en/media/press_each.

php?id=585. For background on Mexico's ports, see "Additional capacity added in maritime corridor Asia-China to Mexico is still not enough," *Mexico Daily Post*, August 22, 2021, at https://mexicodailypost. com/2021/08/22/additional-capacity-added-in-maritime-corridor-asia-china-to-mexico-is-still-not-enough/. For background on the Panama Canal, see Evan Ellis, "China's advance in Panama: An update," *Global Americans*, April 14, 2021, at https://theglobalamericans.org/2021/04/ chinas-advance-in-panama-an-update/; and "Milestones: 1997," *CK Hutchinson Holdings Limited*, undated, accessed December 21, 2021, at https://www.ckh.com.hk/en/about/milestones/?year=1997.

590   Leticia Casado and Manuela Andreoni, "CCCC expands its Latin America portfolio," *Dialogo Chino*, June 12, 2020, at https://dialogochino. net/en/infrastructure/35869-cccc-expands-in-latin-america/.

591   For example, see Daniel Michaels, "China's Growing Access to Global Shipping Data Worries U.S.," *Wall Street Journal*, December 20, 2021, at https://www.wsj.com/articles/chinas-growing-access-to-global-shipping-data-worries-u-s-11640001601.

592   Jiang and Luo, *Military-Civil Fusion*, p. 37.

593   Linda Hardesty, "Telefónica Selects Huawei for Virtual EPC Network in 13 Countries," SDX Central, January 30, 2017, at https://www.sdxcentral. com/articles/news/telefonica-selects-huawei-virtual-epc-network-13-countries/2017/01/; and "Telefónica selects Huawei to build large scale virtual EPC network in 13 countries as part of its UNICA program," *Telefónica*, January 30, 2017, at https://www.telefonica.com/en/ communication-room/telefonica-selects-huawei-to-build-large-scale-virtual-epc-network-in-13-countries-as-part-of-its-unica-program/.

594   "Telefonica, ZTE deploy vIMS in LatAm ahead of VoLTE rollout," *Comms Update*, December 20, 2016, at https://www.commsupdate.com/ articles/2016/12/20/telefonica-zte-deploy-vims-in-latam-ahead-of-volte-rollout/ .

595   For example, see Evan Ellis, "Testimony before the US-China Economic and Security Review Commission: China's Diplomatic and Political Approach in Latin America and the Caribbean," *U.S. China Economic and Security Review Commission*, May 20, 2021, at https://www.uscc. gov/hearings/china-latin-america-and-caribbean.

596   Juan Pedro Tomas, "ZTE to deploy vIMS network for Telefónica in Latin America," *RCR Wireless*, December 20, 2016, at https://www. rcrwireless.com/20161220/americas/zte-telefonica-latin-america-tag23.

597   "Who wields power? China's co-ownership of NGCP brought with it serious national security concerns," *Daily Tribune*, June 21, 2021, at https://tribune.net.ph/index.php/2021/06/21/who-wields-power/; and Patricia Lourdes Viray, "China 'in charge of nuts and bolts' of

Philippine power grid, Hontiveros claims," *Philstar*, December 9, 2019, at https://www.philstar.com/headlines/2019/12/09/1975666/china-in-charge-nuts-and-bolts-philippine-power-grid-hontiveros-claims.

598   Patricia Lourdes Viray, "China 'in charge of nuts and bolts' of Philippine power grid, Hontiveros claims," *Philstar*, December 9, 2019, at https://www.philstar.com/headlines/2019/12/09/1975666/china-in-charge-nuts-and-bolts-philippine-power-grid-hontiveros-claims.

599   James Griffiths, "China can shut off the Philippines' power grid at any time, leaked report warns," *CNN*, November 26, 2019, at https://www.cnn.com/2019/11/25/asia/philippines-china-power-grid-intl-hnk/index.html.

600   "The Board of Directors," *NGCP*, undated, accessed December 21, 2021, at https://www.ngcp.ph/profile#management.

601   "Eskom and State Grid Corporation of China to co-operate on strategies," *People's Daily*, July 6, 2016, at http://en.people.cn/n3/2016/0706/c90000-9082214.html; and "The Board of Directors," *NGCP*, undated, accessed December 21, 2021, at https://www.ngcp.ph/profile#management.

602   Geoffrey Wade, "The State Grid Corporation of China: Its Australian engagement and military links," *The Interpreter*, December 17, 2015, at https://www.lowyinstitute.org/the-interpreter/state-grid-corporation-china-its-australian-engagement-and-military-links.

603   For illustrative examples, Leticia Casado and Manuela Andreoni, "CCCC expands its Latin America portfolio," *Dialogo Chino*, June 12, 2020, at https://dialogochino.net/en/infrastructure/35869-cccc-expands-in-latin-america/; and James Griffiths, "China can shut off the Philippines' power grid at any time, leaked report warns," *CNN*, November 26, 2019, at https://www.cnn.com/2019/11/25/asia/philippines-china-power-grid-intl-hnk/index.html. See also "Eskom and State Grid Corporation," *People's Daily*.

604   "Beijing's *backdoors* into infrastructure and technology have a name … and a far-reaching purpose," *Pointe Bello*, February 2020, at https://www.pointebello.com/insights/reserved-interfaces.

605   "Beijing's *backdoors*," *Pointe Bello*.

606   Aaron L. Friedberg, "An Answer to Aggression: How to Push Back Against Beijing," *Foreign Affairs*, September/October 2020, at https://www.foreignaffairs.com/articles/china/2020-08-11/ccp-answer-aggression; and Aaron L. Friedberg, "Competing with China," *Survival*, June–July 2018, pp. 7–64.

607   For a cogent argument that the CCP is using big data to undermine U.S. security, see Matt Pottinger and David Feith, "The Most Powerful Data Broker in the World Is Winning the War Against the U.S.," *New*

York Times, November 30, 2021, at https://www.nytimes.com/2021/11/30/opinion/xi-jinping-china-us-data-war.html.

608 Garnaut, "Engineers of the Soul."

609 Garnaut, "Engineers of the Soul."

610 Ren and Zhao, *Strategic Support*, pp. 118–119. Note that Ren and Zhao draw their quote from this document: PLA General Political Department, *A Selection of Xi Jinping's Important Observations on National Defense and Military Buildup* [习近平关于国防和军队建设重要论述选编] (Beijing: Liberation Army Press, 2014), p. 51.

611 Ren and Zhao, *Strategic Support*, p. 211.

Chapter Twelve: World Empire

612 From "The Theory and Practice of Oligarchical Collectivism," in Orwell, *1984*, p. 193.

613 Victoria Vogrincic, "China's Heightened Space Presence in the Heart of Argentina's Patagonian Desert," *China Focus*, November 19, 2020, at https://chinafocus.ucsd.edu/2020/11/19/chinas-heightened-space-presence-in-the-heart-of-argentinas-patagonian-desert/; and Cassandra Garrison, "China's military-run space station in Argentina is a 'black box'," Reuters, January 31, 2019, at https://www.reuters.com/article/us-space-argentina-china-insight/chinas-military-run-space-station-in-argentina-is-a-black-box-idUSKCN1PP0I2.

614 Jean-Pierre Cabestan, "China's Djibouti naval base increasing its power," *East Asia Forum*, May 16, 2020, at https://www.eastasiaforum.org/2020/05/16/chinas-djibouti-naval-base-increasing-its-power/; and Joshua Berlinger, "Satellite photos reveal underground construction at Chinese military base," *CNN*, August 1, 2017, at https://www.cnn.com/2017/07/26/asia/china-military-base-djibouti-photos/index.html.

615 Ryan Browne, "Chinese lasers injure US military pilots in Africa, Pentagon says," *CNN*, May 4, 2018, at https://www.cnn.com/2018/05/03/politics/chinese-lasers-us-military-pilots-africa/index.html.

616 Sam LaGrone, "AFRICOM: Chinese Naval Base in Africa Set to Support Aircraft Carriers," *USNI News*, April 20, 2021, at https://news.usni.org/2021/04/20/africom-chinese-naval-base-in-africa-set-to-support-aircraft-carriers.

617 Michael Rubin, "Beware China's Inroads into the Atlantic," *National Interest*, June 26, 2019, at https://nationalinterest.org/feature/beware-chinas-inroads-atlantic-64391; and Aaron Mehta, "How a potential

China-built airport in Greenland could be risky for a vital US Air Force base," *Defense News*, September 7, 2018, at https://www.defensenews. com/global/europe/2018/09/07/how-a-potential-chinese-built-airport-in-greenland-could-be-risky-for-a-vital-us-air-force-base/.

618   Warren P. Strobel, "U.A.E. Shut Down China Facility Under U.S. Pressure, Emirates Says," *Wall Street Journal*, December 9, 2021, at https://www.wsj.com/articles/u-a-e-confirms-it-halted-work-on-secret-chinese-port-project-after-pressure-from-u-s-11639070894; and Michael M. Phillips, "China Seeks First Military Base on Africa's Atlantic Coast, U.S. Intelligence Finds," *Wall Street Journal*, December 5, 2021, at https://www.wsj.com/articles/china-seeks-first-military-base-on-africas-atlantic-coast-u-s-intelligence-finds-11638726327.

619   Michael Rubin, "Beware China's Inroads into the Atlantic," *National Interest*, June 26, 2019, at https://nationalinterest.org/feature/beware-chinas-inroads-atlantic-64391; and Aaron Mehta, "How a potential China-built airport in Greenland could be risky for a vital US Air Force base," *Defense News*, September 7, 2018, at https://www.defensenews. com/global/europe/2018/09/07/how-a-potential-chinese-built-airport-in-greenland-could-be-risky-for-a-vital-us-air-force-base/.

620   Office of the Secretary of Defense, "2021 Report on Military and Security Developments Involving the People's Republic of China," *Department of Defense*, November 3, 2021, pp. 130–131, accessible online at https://www.defense.gov/News/Releases/Release/Article/2831819/dod-releases-2021-report-on-military-and-security-developments-involving-the-pe/

621   Bill Gertz, "Ports, bases to strengthen China's power: Beijing aims for global dominance with commerce, military network," *Washington Times*, January 5, 2022, A9.

622   *Study Doctrine on Xi Jinping Thought on Chinese Socialism in a New Age* [习近平新时代中国特色社会主义思想学习纲要] (Beijing: CCP Propaganda Department, 2019), p. 210.

623   Song Zhongping, "With nearly 600 overseas military bases, US falsely claims China is 'building a new string of pearls'," *Global Times*, January 4, 2022, at https://www.globaltimes.cn/page/202201/1245047.shtml.

624   Ren and Zhao, *Strategic Support*, p. 215.

625   Ren and Zhao, *Strategic Support*, p. 215.

626   Ren and Zhao, *Strategic Support*, p. 216.

627   Ren and Zhao, *Strategic Support*, p. 216.

628   Ren and Zhao, *Strategic Support*, p. 100.

629   Jiang and Luo, *Military-Civil Fusion*. Note that the book is part of a series of teaching materials on Xi Jinping's Strong Military Thought

(习近平强军思想系列教材). It is labeled "internal teaching materials, handle and store with caution (内部教材注意保管)."

630   Jiang and Luo, *Military-Civil Fusion*, pp. 205–208.

631   Jiang and Luo, *Military-Civil Fusion*, p. 57.

632   Jiang and Luo, *Military-Civil Fusion*, p. 57.

633   Jiang and Luo, *Military-Civil Fusion*, p. 14.

634   Jiang and Luo, *Military-Civil Fusion*, p. 14.

635   Jiang and Luo, *Military-Civil Fusion*, p. 187.

636   Jiang and Luo, *Military-Civil Fusion*, p. 187.

637   Jiang and Luo, *Military-Civil Fusion*, p. 188.

638   Jiang and Luo, *Military-Civil Fusion*, p. 198.

639   Jiang and Luo, *Military-Civil Fusion*, p. 198.

640   Jiang and Luo, *Military-Civil Fusion*, p. 129.

641   Jiang and Luo, *Military-Civil Fusion*, p. 130.

642   Jiang and Luo, *Military-Civil Fusion*, p. 130.

643   Jacqueline Deal, "China could soon outgun the U.S.," *Politico*, May 27, 2021, at https://www.politico.com/newsletters/politico-china-watcher/2021/05/27/china-could-soon-outgun-the-us-493014.

644   Deal, "China could soon outgun the U.S."

645   James E. Fanell, "China's Global Naval Strategy and Expanding Force Structure: Pathway to Hegemony," *Testimony before the Permanent Select Committee on Intelligence*, May 17, 2018, accessible online at https://docs.house.gov/Committee/Calendar/ByEvent.aspx?EventID=108298.

646   Fanell, "China's Global Naval Strategy."

647   For background, see Rosemary Gibson and Janardan Prasad Singh, *China Rx: Exposing the Risks of America's Dependence on China for Medicine* (Amherst, NY: Prometheus Books, 2018). See also Rosemary Gibson, "China has cornered the market on antibiotics, so the U.S. must rebuild its manufacturing capacity," *Market Watch*, April 28, 2021, at https://www.marketwatch.com/story/china-has-cornered-the-market-on-antibiotics-so-the-u-s-must-rebuild-its-manufacturing-capacity-11619640612; and Chuin-Wei Yap, " Pandemic Lays Bare U.S. Reliance on China for Drugs," *Wall Street Journal*, August 5, 2020, at https://www.wsj.com/articles/how-the-u-s-ceded-control-of-drug-supplies-to-china-11596634936.

648   Ralph Jennings, "Zoom Gets More Popular Despite Worries About Links to China," *Voice of America*, October 24, 2021, at https://www.voanews.com/a/zoom-gets-more-popular-despite-worries-about-links-to-china/6282120.html; and Eduard Kovacs, "Keys Used to Encrypt

Zoom Meetings Sent to China: Researchers," *Security Week*, April 3, 2020, at https://www.securityweek.com/keys-used-encrypt-zoom-meetings-sent-china-researchers.

649   Nardy Baeza Bickel, "In this season of giving, watch out for harmful chemicals in plastic toys," *Michigan News*, December 13, 2021, at https://news.umich.edu/in-this-season-of-giving-watch-out-for-harmful-chemicals-in-plastic-toys/.

650   Eva Dou, "China's Xinjiang cotton is banned in the U.S. but still making it to store shelves, report says," *Washington Post*, November 17, 2021, at https://www.washingtonpost.com/world/asia_pacific/china-xinjiang-cotton/2021/11/17/fcfe320e-37a3-11ec-9662-399cfa75efee_story.html.

651   "Publishers push back titles as shipping delays cause 'unprecedented' challenge," *The Bookseller*, December 9, 2021, at https://www.thebookseller.com/news/shipping-delays-continuing-impact-publication-dates-1292302; Michael Seidlinger, "Looking for Answers to Supply Chain Challenges," *Publisher Weekly*, October 7, 2021, at https://www.publishersweekly.com/pw/by-topic/industry-news/manufacturing/article/87567-looking-for-answers-to-supply-chain-challenges.html; and "In China's publishing business, you have to duck and dive," *The Economist*, July 17, 2021, at https://www.economist.com/china/2021/07/15/in-chinas-publishing-business-you-have-to-duck-and-dive.

652   Jim Milliot, "Publishers Continue the Battle Against Book Tariffs," *Publisher's Weekly*, November 22, 2019, at https://www.publishersweekly.com/pw/by-topic/industry-news/bookselling/article/81829-publishers-continue-the-battle-against-book-tariffs.html.

653   Oliver Telling, "British publishers censor books for western readers to appease China," *Financial Times*, March 15, 2022, at https://www.ft.com/content/63cbf209-656f-4f99-9ee3-722755c228ed.

654   "How China Is Secretly Changing Everyone's Maps," *China Uncensored*, January 29, 2020, at https://www.youtube.com/watch?v=yBE7I8QIpw4. See also "China issues new set of regulations on maps," *The State Council of The People's Republic of China*, December 14, 2015, at http://english.www.gov.cn/policies/latest_releases/2015/12/14/content_281475253904932.htm.

655   "Taiwan: Lion Dance," *Super Wings*, October 25, 2015, Season 1, Episode 41/42 (Television Show). The author watched this show sometime around 2018. As of March 15, 2022, it had been removed from Amazon. Other episodes were renumbered accordingly. For original episode list, see https://en.wikipedia.org/wiki/List_of_Super_Wings_episodes. Ji Yuqiao, "Cartoon 'Super Wings' originally produced in South Korea has been suspended in China for using wrong maps," *Global Times*, March 2, 2021, at https://www.globaltimes.cn/page/202103/1217103.shtml.

656 "The U.S. Business," *WH Group*, undated, accessed December 15, 2021, at http://www.wh-group.com/html/bp_usa.php.

657 "Corporate Profile," *WH Group*, undated, accessed December 15, 2021, at http://www.wh-group.com/html/about.php.

658 Stone Fish, *America Second*, pp. 101–174.

659 German Lopez, "American Self-censorship: U.S. institutions are increasingly silencing themselves to win access to China," *New York Times*, February 20, 2022, at https://www.nytimes.com/2022/02/20/briefing/china-us-censorship.html.

660 Marc Edelman, "Kanter Freedom's NBA Ouster Has Parallels To NFL's Apparent Kaepernick Boycott," *Forbes*, February 22, 2022, at https://www.forbes.com/sites/marcedelman/2022/02/22/kanter-freedoms-nba-ouster-feels-eerily-similar-to-nfls-kaepernick-boycott/?sh=46b259eb2962.

661 Drake Bennett, "The Metaverse Gives China a New Digital Playground to Censor," *Bloomberg*, December 10, 2021, at https://www.bloomberg.com/news/newsletters/2021-12-10/china-metaverse-offers-new-digital-playground-for-censorship.

662 Hamilton and Ohlberg, *Hidden Hand*, pp. 119–138, 226–248.

663 Ross Anderson, "When China Sees All," *The Atlantic*, September 2020, at https://www.theatlantic.com/magazine/archive/2020/09/china-ai-surveillance/614197/.

664 Anderson, "When China Sees All."

665 Jonathan Hoffman, "Why do some Muslim-majority countries support China's crackdown on Muslims?" *Washington Post*, May 4, 2021, at https://www.washingtonpost.com/politics/2021/05/04/why-do-some-muslim-majority-countries-support-chinas-crackdown-muslims/; and Tamara Qiblawi, "Muslim nations are defending China as it cracks down on Muslims, shattering any myths of Islamic solidarity," *CNN*, July 17, 2019, at https://www.cnn.com/2019/07/17/asia/uyghurs-muslim-countries-china-intl/index.html.

666 Doug Jones, "Pope Francis' Silence on China," *The Jesuit Post*, April 19, 2021, at https://thejesuitpost.org/2021/04/pope-francis-silence-on-china/; "Cardinal Zen says Pope Francis being 'manipulated' on China," *CRUX*, March 2, 2020, at https://cruxnow.com/church-in-asia/2020/03/cardinal-zen-says-pope-francis-being-manipulated-on-china.

667 Stone Fish, *America Second*, pp. 53–59.

668 Hamilton and Ohlberg, *Hidden Hand*, pp. 249–265; Sophie Richardson , "China's Influence on the Global Human Rights System," *Human Rights Watch*, September 14, 2020, at https://www.hrw.org/news/2020/09/14/chinas-influence-global-human-rights-system#; and Tung Cheng-Chia

and Alan H. Yang, "How China Is Remaking the UN In Its Own Image," *The Diplomat*, April 9, 2020, at https://thediplomat.com/2020/04/how-china-is-remaking-the-un-in-its-own-image/.

669 Erin Hale, "Taiwan Ranks Among Top 10 Democracies in Annual Index," *Voice of America*, February 11, 2022, at https://www.voanews.com/a/taiwan-ranks-among-top-10-democracies-in-annual-index-/6438806.html.

670 "China's Hidden Capital Flight Surges to Record High," *Bloomberg News*, October 11, 2019, at https://www.bloomberg.com/news/articles/2019-10-11/china-hidden-capital-flight-at-a-record-in-2019-iif-says.

671 See Wolf, "Homeland Security and the China Challenge."

672 Christopher Wray, "Countering Threats Posed by the Chinese Government Inside the U.S.," *FBI News*, January 31, 2022, at https://www.fbi.gov/news/speeches/countering-threats-posed-by-the-chinese-government-inside-the-us-wray-013122; Kristina Davis, "San Diego civilian defense contractor accused of being compromised by Chinese spy," *San Diego Union-Tribune*, October 5, 2021, at https://www.sandiegouniontribune.com/news/courts/story/2021-10-05/san-diego-contractor-chinese-spy; and Susanna Kim, "Convictions for Trade Secret Sales a 'Shot Heard Around the World', *ABC News*, March 7, 2014, at https://abcnews.go.com/Business/convictions-trade-secret-sales-shot-heard-world/story?id=22816693.

673 Pete Williams, "FBI Director Wray says scale of Chinese spying in the U.S. 'blew me away'," *NBC News*, February 1, 2022, at https://www.nbcnews.com/politics/politics-news/fbi-director-wray-says-scale-chinese-spying-us-blew-away-rcna14369.

674 Derek Scissors, "A Stagnant China in 2040, Briefly," *American Enterprise Institute*, March 2020, at https://www.aei.org/research-products/report/a-stagnant-china-in-2040-briefly/.

Chapter Thirteen: Measuring Success

675 Yuval Noah Harari, *Sapiens: A Brief History of Humankind* (New York: Harper Perennial, 2015), p. 292.

676 For an excellent discussion on national and generational toughness, see Dan Carlin, *The End Is Always Near: Apocalyptic Moments from the Bronze Age Collapse to Nuclear Near Misses* (New York: Harper Collins, 2019), pp. 1–14.

677   Note the $500 billion estimate is highly simplistic, conservative, and still might understate true spending. It is based on an assumption that the Stockholm International Peace Research Institute's 2019 estimate still holds true – that China spends around 40 percent more than officially stated. Another $150 billion was added to account for purchasing power parity, per the CSIS observation that: "When adjusted for purchasing power parity (PPP), China's 2019 defense expenditure rises by well over $100 billion." For background, see See John Grady, "Mystery Shrouds Chinese Defense Spending," *USNI News*, October 26, 2021, at https://news.usni.org/2021/10/26/mystery-shrouds-chinese-defense-spending; and Matthew P. Funaiole and Brian Hart, "Understanding China's 2021 Defense Budget," *CSIS*, March 5, 2021, at https://www.csis.org/analysis/understanding-chinas-2021-defense-budget. Because aggregate numbers are probably grossly inaccurate and misleading in terms of actual fighting capability, some analysts have examined procurements, a metric that sheds light on which side has the most advanced combat force in total inventory value, see Jacqueline Deal, "China could soon outgun the U.S.," *Politico*, May 27, 2021, at https://www.politico.com/newsletters/politico-china-watcher/2021/05/27/china-could-soon-outgun-the-us-493014.

678   This expression draws from Garnaut, "Engineers of the Soul."

679   "Human Development Report 2020: The next frontier, Human Development and the Anthropocene," *United Nations Development Program*, December 15, 2020, at http://hdr.undp.org/en/2020-report.

680   "2021 World Press Freedom Index: Journalism, the vaccine against disinformation, blocked in more than 130 countries," *Reporters Without Borders*, undated, accessed January 17, 2022, at https://rsf.org/en/2021-world-press-freedom-index-journalism-vaccine-against-disinformation-blocked-more-130-countries.

681   "2021 World Press Freedom Index," *Reporters Without Borders*, undated, accessed January 17, 2022, at https://rsf.org/en/ranking.

682   "2021 Round-Up," *Reporters Without Borders*, undated, accessed January 20, 2022, at https://rsf.org/en.

683   "Countries and Territories: Global Freedom Scores," *Freedom House*, undated, accessed January 17, 2022, at https://freedomhouse.org/countries/freedom-world/scores.

684   "Global Freedom Scores," *Freedom House*.

685   "Promoting U.S. Leadership," *Freedom House*, undated, accessed January 17, 2022, at https://freedomhouse.org/issues/promoting-us-leadership.

686   "2020 Country Reports on Human Rights Practices: China (Includes Hong Kong, Macau, and Tibet)," *U.S. Department of State Bureau of Democracy, Human Rights, and Labor*, undated, accessed January 17,

2022, at https://www.state.gov/reports/2020-country-reports-on-human-rights-practices/china/.

687 "2020 Human Rights: China," *U.S. Department of State Bureau of Democracy, Human Rights, and Labor*.

688 "2020 Human Rights: China," *U.S. Department of State Bureau of Democracy, Human Rights, and Labor*.

689 *World Report 2022* (New York: Human Rights Watch, 2022), p. 159, accessible online at https://www.hrw.org/world-report/2022.

690 Peng Yin, et al., "The effect of air pollution on deaths, disease burden, and life expectancy across China and its provinces, 1990–2017: an analysis for the Global Burden of Disease Study 2017," *The Lancet*, September 1, 2020, at https://www.thelancet.com/article/S2542-5196(20)30161-3/fulltext.

691 Donna Lu, "Air pollution in China may have caused millions of deaths since 2000," *New Scientist*, September 21, 2020, at https://www.newscientist.com/article/2254967-air-pollution-in-china-may-have-caused-millions-of-deaths-since-2000/#ixzz7IFfZS90x.

692 "China's air pollution harms its citizens and the world," *U.S. Embassy Georgia*, November 24, 2020, at https://ge.usembassy.gov/chinas-air-pollution-harms-its-citizens-and-the-world/.

693 "China's air pollution," *U.S. Embassy Georgia*.

694 Gabriel Collins and Andrew S. Erickson, "China's Climate Cooperation Smokescreen: A Roadmap for Seeing Through the Trap and Countering with Competition," *Rice University's Baker Institute for Public Policy*, September 21, 2021, p. 10, accessible online at https://www.bakerinstitute.org/research/chinas-climate-cooperation-smokescreen/.

695 Hal Brands, "China is running out of water and that's scary for Asia," *Bloomberg Opinion*, December 29, 2021, accessible online at https://www.aei.org/op-eds/china-is-running-out-of-water-and-thats-scary-for-asia/. See also Chris Buckley and Vanessa Piao, "Rural Water, Not City Smog, May Be China's Pollution Nightmare," *New York Times*, April 11, 2016, at https://www.nytimes.com/2016/04/12/world/asia/china-underground-water-pollution.html.

696 Blumenthal, *The China Nightmare*, p. 100.

697 Gabriele Collins and Andrew S. Erickson, "U.S.-China Competition Enters the Decade of Maximum Danger: Policy Ideas to Avoid Losing the 2020s," *Rice University's Baker Institute for Public Policy*, December 2021, p. 8, accessible online at https://www.andrewerickson.com/2021/12/u-s-china-competition-enters-the-decade-of-maximum-danger-policy-ideas-to-avoid-losing-the-2020s/.

698   Michael Beckley and Hal Brands, "What Will Drive China to War?"
       The Atlantic, November 1, 2021, at https://www.theatlantic.com/ideas/
       archive/2021/11/us-china-war/620571/.

699   Beckley and Brands, "What Will Drive China to War?"

700   Ren and Zhao, *Strategic Support*, p. 213.

701   See Garnaut, "Engineers of the Soul."

702   For background, see Robert Service, *Comrades! A History of World
       Communism* (Cambridge, MA: Harvard University Press, 2007).

703   *The Fundamentals of Xi Jinping Thought*, pp. 359–397. See also
       Xi Jinping Thought: A Study Guide; *Study Doctrine on Xi Jinping
       Thought*; CCP Central History and Literature Research Academy, eds.,
       *Selected Works of Xi Jinping on Great Power Diplomacy with Chinese
       Characteristics* [习近平关于中国特色大国外交论述摘编] (Beijing:
       Central Publishing House, 2019); and Zhao and Xian, *Great Power
       Diplomacy*, pp. 21–43.

Chapter Fourteen: Portents

704   Marx and Engels, *The Communist Manifesto*, p. 29.

705   Thomas P. Ehrhard, "Treating the Pathologies of Victory: Hardening
       the Nation for Strategic Competition," *Heritage Foundation*, October
       30, 2019, at https://www.heritage.org/military-strength-topical-
       essays/2020-essays/treating-the-pathologies-victory-hardening-the-
       nation-strategic.

706   For pathbreaking studies on how this is playing out in Europe, see
       Toshi Yoshihara and Jack Bianchi, "Uncovering China's Influence in
       Europe: How Friendship Groups Coopt European Elites," *Center for
       Strategic and Budgetary Assessments*, July 1, 2020, at https://csbaonline.
       org/research/publications/uncovering-chinas-influence-in-europe-how-
       friendship-groups-coopt-european-elites; Gerry Groot, "The CCP's
       Grand United Front abroad," *Sinopsis*, September 24, 2019, available
       at https://sinopsis.cz/en/the-ccps-grand-united-front-abroad/; Didi
       Kirsten Tatlow, "Mapping China-in-Germany," *Sinopsis*, October 2,
       2019, available at https://sinopsis.cz/en/mapping-china-in-germany/;
       and Jichang Lulu, "Repurposing Democracy: The European Parliament
       China Friendship Cluster," *Sinopsis*, November 26, 2019, available at
       https://sinopsis.cz/wp-content/uploads/2019/11/ep.pdf.

707   The following section draws from (a somewhat dated) conference paper.
       See Ian Easton, "Wither American Strategy? The Future of U.S. Policy

toward the Indo-Pacific," *Japan Institute of International Affairs*, October 25, 2017, available online at https://www.jiia.or.jp/column/column-295. html. It has been lightly modified.

708   Garnaut, "Engineers of the Soul."

709   Robert D. Kaplan, *Hog Pilots, Blue Water Grunts: The American Military in the Air, at Sea, and on the Ground* (New York: Random House, 2007), p. 384.

710   See Mark Stokes, "Chinese Authoritarian Influence in the United States," in Hsu Szu-chien and J. Michael Cole, eds., *Insidious Power: How China Undermines Global Democracy* (Manchester, UK: Camphor Press, 2020), pp. 43–81; Hamilton and Ohlberg, *Hidden Hand*; Larry Diamond and Orville Schell, eds., "China's Influence and American Interests: Promoting Constructive Vigilance," *Hoover Institution*, November 29, 2018, at https://www.hoover.org/research/chinas-influence-american-interests-promoting-constructive-vigilance; and J. Michael Cole, "Chinese Propaganda: Coming Soon to a Conference Near You," *The Diplomat*, September 23, 2015, at http://thediplomat.com/2015/09/chinese-propaganda-coming-soon-to-a-conference-near-you/. This assertion is also based on the author's private discussions with think tankers, graduate students, university professors, and researchers in Boston, Princeton, San Diego, and Washington, DC

711   See Gershaneck, *Media Warfare*; Gershaneck, *Political Warfare*; Joske, "Picking Flowers, Making Honey"; Hamilton, *Silent Invasion*; and Anne-Marie Brady, "Magic Weapons: China's political influence activities under Xi Jinping," *Wilson Center*, September 18, 2017, at https://www.wilsoncenter.org/article/magic-weapons-chinas-political-influence-activities-under-xi-jinping; and Mark Stokes and Russell Hsiao, *The People's Liberation Army General Political Department: Political Warfare with Chinese Characteristics* (Arlington, VA: Project 2049 Institute, October 2013), at http://www.project2049.net/documents/PLA_General_Political_Department_Liaison_Stokes_Hsiao.pdf.

712   See Mark Stokes, "Chinese Authoritarian Influence in the United States," in Hsu Szu-chien and J. Michael Cole, eds., *Insidious Power: How China Undermines Global Democracy* (Manchester, UK: Camphor Press, 2020), pp. 43–81; Clive Hamilton and Maeike Ohlberg, *Hidden Hand: Exposing How the Chinese Communist Party is Reshaping the World* (Toronto, Canada: Optimum Publishing International, 2020); Larry Diamond and Orville Schell, eds., "China's Influence and American Interests: Promoting Constructive Vigilance," *Hoover Institution*, November 29, 2018, at https://www.hoover.org/research/chinas-influence-american-interests-promoting-constructive-vigilance; and J. Michael Cole, "Chinese Propaganda: Coming Soon to a Conference Near You," *The*

Diplomat, September 23, 2015, at http://thediplomat.com/2015/09/chinese-propaganda-coming-soon-to-a-conference-near-you/.

713 See Stone Fish, *America Second*.

714 Peter Mattis, "The Center of Chinese Influence: The Chinese People's Political Consultative Conference," in Hsu Szu-chien and J. Michael Cole, eds., *Insidious Power: How China Undermines Global Democracy* (Manchester, England: Camphor Press, 2020), p. 38.

715 Bethany Allen-Ebrahimian, "China Built an Army of Influence Agents in the U.S.," *Daily Beast*, July 18, 2018, at https://www.thedailybeast.com/how-china-built-an-army-of-influence-agents-in-the-us. See also Bethany Allen-Ebrahimian, "Why U.S. giants keep caving to China," *Axios China*, December 21, 2021, at https://www.axios.com/why-us-giants-keep-caving-to-china-d2768f92-02bf-42e9-86d7-1430d7f3a700.html; Bethany Allen-Ebrahimian and Zach Dorfman, "Suspected Chinese spy targeted California politicians," *Axios China*, December 8, 2020, at https://www.axios.com/china-spy-california-politicians-9d2dfb99-f839-4e00-8bd8-59decodaf589.html; Bethany Allen-Ebrahimian, "China tried to get World Bank to fund surveillance in Xinjiang," *Axios China*, December 11, 2019, at https://www.axios.com/china-world-bank-xinjiang-ai-huawei-surveillance-263c5753-1cb8-4366-aad3-c9be9b285fa5.html; and Bethany Allen-Ebrahimian, "This Beijing-Linked Billionaire Is Funding Policy Research at Washington's Most Influential Institutions," *Foreign Policy*, November 28, 2017, at https://foreignpolicy.com/2017/11/28/this-beijing-linked-billionaire-is-funding-policy-research-at-washingtons-most-influential-institutions-china-dc/.

716 Steven Pinker, *Enlightenment Now: The Case for Reason, Science, Humanism, and Progress* (New York: Penguin Books, 2018).

717 Zhao and Xian, *Great Power Diplomacy*, p. 118.

718 Garnaut, "Engineers of the Soul."

719 For a fascinating discussion on this phenomenon and its implications, see Anders Corr, *The Concentration of Power: Institutionalization, Hierarchy, and Hegemony* (Ottawa, Canada: Optimum Publishing, 2021).

720 "Human Intelligence in the Digital Age – Speech by Richard Moore, Chief of the UK's Secret Intelligence Service," *IISS*, November 30, 2021, at https://www.iiss.org/events/2021/11/human-intelligence-digital-age.

721 Gabriel Scheinmann, "The U.S. Should Want a Cold War With China," *Wall Street Journal*, February 10, 2022, at https://www.wsj.com/articles/the-us-should-want-a-cold-war-with-china-xi-jinping-taiwan-geopolitics-military-confrontation-competition-biden-democracy-11644510051.

Chapter Fifteen: New Horizons

722 Quote drawn from Steven Pinker, *Enlightenment Now*, p. 347.

723 Miles Yu, "The meaning of Taiwan," *Taipei Times*, January 10, 2022, at https://www.taipeitimes.com/News/editorials/archiv es/2022/01/10/2003771062.

724 Garnaut, "Engineers of the Soul."

725 Garnaut, "Engineers of the Soul."

726 Thomas G. Mahnken, "Cost-Imposing Strategies: A Brief Primer," *Center for New American Security*, November 2014, pp. 7–8.

727 Peter Mattis, "From Engagement to Rivalry: Tools to Compete with China," *Texas National Security Review*, August 2018, p. 88, accessible online at https://tnsr.org/2018/08/from-engagement-to-rivalry-tools-to-compete-with-china/.

728 Tobin, "Xi's Vision," p. 163.

729 Tobin, "Xi's Vision," p. 163.

730 Toshi Yoshihara and Jack Bianchi, *Seizing on Weakness: Allied Strategy for Competing With China's Globalizing Military* (Washington, DC: Center for Strategic and Budgetary Assessments, 2021), p. 103, available online at https://csbaonline.org/research/publications/seizing-on-weakness-allied-strategy-for-competing-with-chinas-globalizing-military.

731 Yoshihara and Bianchi, *Seizing on Weakness*, p. 104

SELECTED BIBLIOGRAPHY

Books in Mandarin

The Fundamentals of Xi Jinping Thought on Chinese Socialism in a New Era (习近平新时代中国特色社会主义思想基本问题). Beijing: CCP Central Committee Central Party School Press, 2020.

Study Doctrine on Xi Jinping Thought on Chinese Socialism in a New Era (习近平新时代中国特色社会主义思想学习纲要). Beijing: CCP Propaganda Department, 2019.

Xi Jinping Thought on Chinese Socialism in a New Era: A Study Guide (习近平新时代中国特色社会主义思想学习问答). Beijing: CCP Central Propaganda Department, 2021.

CCP Central History and Literature Research Academy, ed. *Selected Works of Xi Jinping on Great Power Diplomacy with Chinese Characteristics* (习近平关于中国特色大国外交论述摘编). Beijing: Central Publishing House, 2019.

Fang Yugang, and Liu Jizhong, eds. *The Basis for Building the People's Military: The Strong Military Spirit* (人民军队建军之本强军之魂). Beijing: National Defense University, 2018.

Guo Fenghai, and Li Haitao, eds. *The Main Contradictions Facing Our Nation's Society in This New Era* (新时代我国社会主要矛盾). Beijing: National Defense University Press, 2018.

Jiang Luwu, and Luo Yongguang, eds. *Realizing the Deep Development of Military-Civil Fusion in Our Overall Setup* (形成军民融合深度发展格局). Beijing: National Defense University Press, 2018.

Ren Tianyou, and Zhao Zhouxian, eds. *Strategic Support for Achieving the Great Chinese Resurgence* (实现中华民族伟大复兴的战略支援). Beijing: National Defense University Press: 2018.

Xi Jinping. *The Governance of China* (谈治国理政). Beijing: Foreign Language Press, October 2014.

——. *The Governance of China, Volume Two* (谈治国理政，第二卷). Beijing: Foreign Language Press, October 2017.

——. *The Governance of China, Volume Three* (谈治国理政，第三卷). Beijing: Foreign Language Press, April 2020.

Xi Jinping Thought on Chinese Socialism in a New Era: A Study Guide (习近平新时代中国特色社会主义思想学习问答). Beijing: CCP Central Propaganda Department, 2021.

Zhao Ziyu, and Xian Fengli, eds. *Great Power Diplomacy with Chinese Characteristics* (中国特色大国外交). Beijing: National Defense University Press, 2018.

Laws, Articles, and Government Reports in Mandarin

"Build Up a Strong Public Health System and Provide Powerful Support for Protecting the People's Health (构建起强大的公共卫生体系为维护人民健康提供有力保障)." *People's Daily*, June 3, 2020.

"CCP Politburo Office Releases Notification of 'Central Talent Work Coordination Small Group View Regarding Implementation of Plan to Recruit High-level Overseas Talents' (中共中央办公厅转发'中央人才工作协调小组关于实施海外高层次人才引进计划的意见'的通知)." CCP News Net, June 20, 2012.

"China's Actions to Fight the COVID-19 Pandemic (抗击新冠肺炎疫情的中国行动)." PRC State Council Information Office, June 7, 2020.

"Chinese Communist Party Center Releases: 'Opinion on Deepening Talent Development Reform System and Mechanisms' [中共中央

印发：'关于深化人才发展体制机制改革的意见']." Ministry of Science and Technology, January 17, 2017.

"Counter Spy Law of the People's Republic of China (中华人民共和国反间谍法)." PRC Ministry of National Defense, December 7, 2017.

"Curriculum Vitae of the Chairman of the PRC State and PRC Central Military Commission (中华人民共和国主席、中华人民共和国中央军事委员会主席简历)." Xinhua, March 17, 2018.

"The Decision of the CCP Central Committee on Several Major Issues Regarding Insisting on and Improving the System of Socialism with Chinese Characteristics and Advancing the Modernization of the State Governance System and Its Governance Capabilities (中共中央关于坚持和完善中国特色社会主义制度推进国家治理体系和治理能力现代化若干重大问题的决定)." *CCP News*, November 6, 2019.

"Deeply Implementing Comprehensive State Security, Strongly Building a Legal Organization System for State Security (深入贯彻落实总体国家安全观 大力健全国家安全法律制度体系)." Xinhua, December 4, 2019.

"Explained: The Long-Term Planning Doctrine for Developing Military Talent Before 2020 (解读：2020年前军队人才发展规划纲要)." *Liberation Army Daily*, August 13, 2014.

"How Did We Achieve This Rare Earths Trump Card? (是什么成就了稀土这张王牌)." Xinhua, June 6, 2019.

"Interim Law for Managing Program Resources and Budgets of Culture and Famous Talents Project and 'Four-in-One Group' Talent Program (文化名家暨"四个一批"人才工程项目资助及经费管理暂行办法)." CCP Propaganda Department, Document No. 17, 2014.

"Interim Measures to Recruit Overseas High-level Talents (引进海外高层次人才暂行办法)." Central Organization Department, Document No. 28, 2008.

"Internet Security Law of the People's Republic of China (中华人民共和国网络安全法)." Office of the CCP Central Cyberspace Affairs Commission, November 7, 2016.

"Made in China 2025 (中国制造2025)." PRC State Council, May 8, 2015.

"Margaret Chan Appointed to High Ranking Tsinghua Cadre Position, Tedros Congratulates and Thanks Chairman Xi's Leadership (陳馮富珍任職清華高幹,譚德塞道賀也謝習主席領導)." Radio Free Asia, April 3, 2020.

"Master Plan to Develop and Build Zhongguancun into a National Indigenous Innovation Demonstration Zone (2016–2020) [中关村国家自主创新示范区发展建设规划（2016–2020）]." Leading Small Group of Zhongguancun National Indigenous Innovation Demonstration Zone, August 18, 2016.

"National Planning Doctrine for Mid-to-Long Term Talent Development, 2010–2020 (国家中长期人才发展规划纲要(2010- 2020年)发布)." Xinhua, June 6, 2010.

"Reference List for National Recruitment of High-level Overseas Talents (国家引进海外高层次人才参考目录)." CCP Central Organization Department, Document No. 60, December 19, 2016.

"September 21, 1988: Deng Xiaoping Proposes Establishing a New International Political Order (1988年9月21日 邓小平提议建立国际政治新秩序)." Central People's Government of the People's Republic of China, September 6, 2007.

"Standardization Law of the People's Republic of China (中华人民共和国标准化法)." Standardization Administration of the People's Republic of China, November 8, 2017.

"State Intelligence Law of the People's Republic of China (中华人民共和国国家情报法)." PRC National People's Congress, June 27, 2017.

"State Security Law of the People's Republic of China (中华人民共和国国家安全法)." PRC Ministry of National Defense, April 7, 2017.

"13th Five-Year National Plan for Science and Technology Innovation ('十三五'国家科技创新规划)." PRC State Council, July 28, 2016.

"Today, How Should We Protect the 'Lifeblood of National Defense'? (今天，我们该如何保护'国防血液'?)." *National Defense News*, January 22, 2015.

"Today the One Belt, One Road Health Cooperation and 'Health Silk Road' Beijing Communique Was Released (一带一路"卫生合作暨"健康丝绸之路"北京公报今日发布)." *People's Daily*, August 18, 2017.

"Touched by the Fatherland's Love for Hong Kong: An Exclusive Interview with CCPCC's Margaret Chan (心系祖国情牵香港——专访全国政协常委陈冯富珍)." *CCPCC News*, July 12, 2019.

"Written Interview with Zhuang Rongwen, Director of the State Network Information Office and Chairman of the World Internet Conference, on his Concept Document 'Working Hand in Hand to Construct a Community of Common Destiny Online' (国家互联网信息办公室主任、世界互联网大会组委会主席庄荣文就发布《携手构建网络空间命运共同体》概念文件接受书面采访)." Office of Central Cyberspace Affairs Commission, October 17, 2019.

"Xi Jinping Gives Important Directive on Deepening Reforms of Talent Development Systems and Mechanisms (习近平就深化人才发展体系机制改革作出重要指示)." Xinhua, May 6, 2018.

"Zhongguancun National Indigenous Innovation Demonstration Zone: Action Plan (2017–2020) for Cultivating Artificial Intelligence Industry (中关村国家自主创新示范区人工智能产业培育行动计划2017–2020年)." Zhongguancun Science Park, September 30, 2017.

Bai Jie. "Ceaselessly Insisting on and Perfecting an Independent, Sovereign and Peaceful Foreign Policy to Realize the Great Rejuvenation of the Chinese Race and to Create a Beautiful Future for Mankind: Exclusive Interview with Deputy Foreign Minister Le Yucheng (坚持和完善独立自主的和平外交政策，为实现中华民族伟大复兴、开创人类美好未来不懈努力——专访外交部副部长乐玉成)." Xinhua, January 6, 2020.

Chen Peiyong. "And Just Like That, He Lit Up the World: Marxism's Vast Influence, Current Value, and the Development of This Age (就这样在世界闪耀——马克思主义的深远影响、当代价值与时代发展)." *Central Discipline Inspection Committee News*, May 3, 2018.

Li Zhengfen. "Zhongguancun Core Area: Exploring Military-Civil Fusion 'the Haidian Way' (中关村核心区： 探索军民融合'海淀模式')." *China High Tech*, December 11, 2017.

Ma Xiaowei. "Deepen International Cooperation in the Pandemic Fight, Jointly Build a Community of Common Health for all Mankind (深化抗击疫情国际合作,共筑人类卫生健康共同体)." *Qiushi*, April 16, 2020.

Wang Yi. "Guided by Xi Jinping Thought on Foreign Affairs, Push Forward the Construction of a Community of Common Destiny for all Mankind Amid Global Cooperation to Fight the Pandemic (王毅： 以习近平外交思想为指引 在全球抗疫合作中推动构建人类命运共同体)." *Qiushi*, April 15, 2020.

Xi Jinping. "Absolutely Winning an All-Around Middle Class Society and Struggling for the Grand Victory of Socialism with Chinese Characteristics in a New Age (决胜全面建成小康社会夺取新时代中国特色社会主义伟大胜利)." *People's Daily*, October 18, 2017.

——. "Bring Forth Powerful Technologies for Winning the Guerilla War against the Pandemic (习近平： 为打赢疫情防控阻击战提供强大科技支撑)." *Qiushi*, March 15, 2020.

"Insist on and Improve the System of Socialism with Chinese Characteristics and Advance the Modernization of the State Governance System and Its Governance Capabilities (坚持和完善中国特色社会主义制度推进国家治理体系和治理能力现代化)." *Qiushi*, January 1, 2020.

——. "Speech at the General Assembly to Commemorate the 200th Anniversary of Karl Marx's Birth (在纪念马克思诞辰200周年大会上的讲话)." Xinhua, May 4, 2018.

——. "Unite and Cooperate to Fight the Pandemic: Work together to Build a Community of Common Health for all Mankind (团结合作战胜疫情共同构建人类卫生健康共同体)." Xinhua, May 18, 2020.

——. "Unity and Cooperation are the Most Powerful Weapons for the International Community's Victory in the War Against the Pandemic (团结合作是国际社会战胜疫情最有力武器)." *Qiushi*, April 15, 2020.

——. "Working Together to Construct a Community of Common Destiny for All Mankind (共同构建人类命运共同体)." *Qiushi*, January 18, 2017.

——. "Working Together to Fight and Overcome the Pandemic (携手抗疫共克时艰)." *People's Daily*, March 27, 2020.

Xinhua Editorial Board. "Why Marxism is Capable of Staying Young Forever (马克思主义为什么能永葆青春)." *Xinhua*, May 4, 2018.

Zhuang Rongwen. "Building an Internet Superpower, a Thought Weapon and Guidebook for Action (网络强国建设的思想武器和行动指南)." Xinhua, February 1, 2021.

Books in English

Allison, Graham. *Destined for War: Can America and China Escape Thucydides's Trap?* New York: Houghton Mifflin Harcourt, 2017.

Blanchette, Jude D. *China's New Red Guards: The Return of Radicalism and the Rebirth of Mao Zedong.* New York: Oxford University Press, 2019.

Blumenthal, Dan. *The China Nightmare: The Grand Ambitions of a Decaying State.* Washington, DC: American Enterprise Institute Press, 2020.

Bougon, François. *Inside the Mind of Xi Jinping.* London, UK: Hurst, 2018.

Brown, Kerry. *CEO, China: The Rise of Xi Jinping.* New York: I.B. Tauris, 2016.

Carlin, Dan. *The End Is Always Near: Apocalyptic Moments from the Bronze Age Collapse to Nuclear Near Misses.* New York: Harper Collins, 2019.

Cliff, Roger. *China's Military Power: Assessing Current and Future Capabilities.* New York: Cambridge University Press, 2015.

Colby, Elbridge A. *The Strategy of Denial: American Defense in an Age of Great Power Conflict*. New Haven: Yale University Press, 2021.

Corr, Anders. *The Concentration of Power: Institutionalization, Hierarchy, and Hegemony*. Ottawa, Canada: Optimum Publishing, 2021.

Courtois, Stephane, Nicolas Werth, Jean-Louis Panne, Andrzej Paczkowski, Karel Bartosek, and Jean-Louis Margolin. *The Black Book of Communism: Crimes, Terror, Repression*. Cambridge, MA: Harvard University Press, 1999.

Doshi, Rush. *The Long Game: China's Grand Strategy to Displace American Order*. New York: Oxford University Press, 2021.

Economy, Elizabeth C. *The Third Revolution: Xi Jinping and the New Chinese State*. New York: Oxford University Press, 2018.

Economy, Elizabeth C. *The World According to China*. Medford, MA: Polity Press, 2022.

Eftimiades, Nicholas. *Chinese Intelligence Operations*. Lexington KY: CreateSpace, 1994.

Engerman, David C. *Know Your Enemy: The Rise and Fall of America's Soviet Experts*. New York: Oxford University Press, 2009.

Erickson, Andrew S., ed. *Chinese Naval Shipbuilding: An Ambitious and Uncertain Course*. Annapolis, MD: Naval Institute Press, 2016.

Erickson, Andrew S., Lyle J. Goldstein, and Carnes Lord. *China Goes to Sea: Maritime Transformation in Comparative Historical Perspective*. Annapolis, MD: Naval Institute Press, 2009.

Erickson, Andrew S., and Lyle J. Goldstein, ed. *Chinese Aerospace Power: Evolving Maritime Roles*. Annapolis, MD: Naval Institute Press, 2011.

Erickson, Andrew S., and Ryan D. Martinson, eds. *China's Maritime Gray Zone Operations*. Annapolis, MD: Naval Institute Press, 2019.

Feigenbaum, Evan A. *China's Techno-Warriors: National Security and Strategic Competition from the Nuclear to the Information Age*. Stanford, CA: Stanford University Press, 2003.

Friedberg, Aaron L. *A Contest for Supremacy: China, America, and the Struggle for Mastery in Asia*. New York: W.W. Norton, 2011.

Gaddis, John Lewis. *The Cold War: A New History*. New York: Penguin, 2005.

Gershaneck, Kerry K. *Media Warfare: Taiwan's Battle for the Cognitive Domain*. Washington, DC, Center for Security Policy, 2021.

———. *Political Warfare: Strategies for Combating China's Plan to "Win without Fighting"*. Quantico, VA: Marine Corps University Press, 2020.

Gertz, Bill. *Deceiving the Sky: Inside Communist China's Drive for Global Supremacy*. New York: Encounter Books, 2019.

Gibson, Rosemary, and Janardan Prasad Singh. *China Rx: Exposing the Risks of America's Dependence on China for Medicine*. Amherst, New York: Prometheus Books, 2018.

Haddick, Robert. *Fire on the Water: China, America, and the Future of the Pacific*. Annapolis, MD: Naval Institute Press, 2014.

Hamilton, Clive. *Silent Invasion: China's Influence in Australia*. London: Hardie Grant Books, 2018.

Hamilton, Clive, and Maeike Ohlberg. *Hidden Hand: Exposing How the Chinese Communist Party is Reshaping the World*. Toronto, Canada: Optimum Publishing International, 2020.

Harari, Yuval Noah. *Sapiens: A Brief History of Humankind*. New York: Harper Perennial, 2015.

Hsu Szu-chien, and J. Michael Cole, eds. *Insidious Power: How China Undermines Global Democracy*. Manchester, UK: Camphor Press, 2020.

Kaplan, Robert D. *Hog Pilots, Blue Water Grunts: The American Military in the Air, at Sea, and on the Ground*. New York: Random House, 2007.

Kennedy, Scott, ed. *Global Governance and China: The Dragon's Learning Curve*. New York: Routledge, 2018.

Kokas, Aynne. *Hollywood Made in China*. Oakland, CA: University of California Press, 2017.

Lam, Willy Wo-Lap. *Chinese Politics in the Era of Xi Jinping*. New York: Routledge, 2015.

——, ed. *Routledge Handbook of the Chinese Communist Party*. New York: Routledge, 2018.

Lee, Kai-Fu. *AI Superpowers: China, Silicon Valley and the New World Order*. New York: Houghton Mifflin Harcourt, 2018.

Li Xiaobing. *A History of the Modern Chinese Army*. Lexington, KY: University Press of Kentucky, 2007.

Lovell, Julia. *Maoism: A Global History*. New York: Vintage Books, 2020.

Mahnken, Thomas G., ed. *Competitive Strategies for the 21st Century: Theory, History, and Practice*. Stanford, CA: Stanford Security Studies, 2012.

——, ed. *Net Assessment and Military Strategy: Retrospective and Prospective Essays*. New York: Cambria, 2020.

Mann, James. *The China Fantasy: Why Capitalism Will Not Bring Democracy to China*. New York: Penguin, 2007.

Marx, Karl, and Frederick Engels. *The Communist Manifesto*. New York: International Publishers, 1848.

Mattis, Peter, and Matthew Brazil, *Chinese Communist Espionage: An Intelligence Primer*. Annapolis Maryland: Naval Institute Press, 2019.

McGregor, Richard. *The Party: The Secret World of China's Communist Rulers*. New York: Harper Perennial, 2010.

——. *Xi Jinping: The Backlash*. Sydney, Australia: Penguin Random House, 2019.

McReynolds, Joe, ed. *China's Evolving Military Strategy*. Washington, DC: Jamestown Foundation, 2017.

Minnick, Wendell, ed. *Chinese C4I/EW Vol. 1*. Middletown, DE: CreateSpace, 2022.

——, ed. *Chinese C4I/EW Vol. 2*. Middletown, DE: CreateSpace, 2022.

——. *Chinese Fixed-Wing Unmanned Aerial Vehicles*. Middletown, DE: CreateSpace, 2016.

——. *Chinese Space Vehicles and Programs*. Middletown, DE: CreateSpace, 2016.

——. *Directory of Foreign Aviation Companies in China*. Middletown, DE: CreateSpace, 2014.

Navarro, Peter. *Crouching Tiger: What China's Militarism Means for the World*. Amherst, NY: Prometheus Books, 2015.

Orwell, George. *1984*. New York: Signet Classics, 1950.

Osnos, Evan. *Age of Ambition: Chasing Fortune, Truth, and Faith in the New China*. New York: Farrar, Straus and Giroux, 2014.

Pillsbury, Michael. *China Debates the Future Security Environment*. Washington, DC: National Defense University Press, 2000.

——. *The Hundred-Year Marathon: China's Secret Strategy to Replace America as the Global Superpower*. New York: Henry Holt, 2015.

Pinker, Steven. *Enlightenment Now: The Case for Reason, Science, Humanism, and Progress*. New York: Penguin, 2018.

Ringen, Stein. *The Perfect Dictatorship: China in the 21st Century*. Hong Kong: Hong Kong University Press, 2016.

Rogin, Josh. *Chaos Under Heaven: Trump, Xi, and the Battle for the 21st Century*. New York: HMH Books, 2021.

Rolland, Nadege. *China's Eurasian Century?: Political and Strategic Implications of the Belt and Road Initiative*. Washington, DC: National Bureau of Asian Research, 2017.

Ross, John Grant. *You Don't Know China: Twenty-two Enduring Myths Debunked*. Manchester, UK: Camphor Press, 2014.

Saunders, Phillip C., Arthur S. Ding, Andrew Scobell, Andrew N.D. Yang, and Joel Wuthnow. *Chairman Xi Remakes the PLA: Assessing Chinese Military Reforms*. Washington, DC: National Defense University Press, 2019.

Schweizer, Peter. *Red-Handed: How American Elites Get Rich Helping China Win*. New York: Harper, 2022.

Sciutto, Jim. *The Shadow War: Inside Russia's and China's Secret Operations to Defeat America*. New York: Harper, 2019.

Service, Robert. *Comrades! A History of World Communism*. Cambridge, MA: Harvard University Press, 2007.

Shambaugh, David, ed. *China & the World.* New York: Oxford University Press, 2020.

Smith, Marion, and Murray Bessette, eds. *Truth, Memory, Justice: One Hundred Years After the Bolshevik Revolution.* Washington, DC: Academia Press, 2019.

Spalding, Robert. *Stealth War: How China Took Over While America's Elite Slept.* New York: Portfolio/Penguin Press, 2019.

Stokes, Mark A. *China's Strategic Modernization: Implications for the United States.* Carlisle, PA: Strategic Studies Institute, 1999.

Stone Fish, Isaac. *America Second: How America's Elites Are Making China Stronger.* New York: Alfred A. Knopf, 2022.

Swaine, Michael D., and Ashley J. Tellis. *Interpreting China's Grand Strategy: Past, Present, Future.* Washington, DC: RAND Corporation, 2000.

Taylor, M. Fravel. *Active Defense: China's Military Strategy since 1949.* Princeton, New Jersey: Princeton University Press, 2019.

Tellis, Ashley J., Alison Szalwinski, and Michael Wills. *Strategic Asia 2020: U.S.-China Competition for Global Influence.* Washington, DC: National Bureau of Asian Research, 2020.

Thiel, Peter. *Zero to One: Notes on Startups or How to Build the Future.* London, UK: Virgin Books, 2014.

Ward, Jonathan D.T. *China's Vision of Victory.* Washington, DC: Atlas, 2019.

Wuthnow, Joel. *Chinese Diplomacy and the UN Security Council: Beyond the Veto.* New York: Routledge, 2013.

Wuthnow, Joel, Arthur S. Ding, Phillip C. Saunders, Andrew Scobell, and Andrew N.D. Yang. *The PLA Beyond Borders: Chinese Military Operations in Regional and Global Context.* Washington, DC: National Defense University Press, 2021.

Yoshihara, Toshi, and James R. Holmes. *Red Star Over the Pacific: China's Rise and the Challenge to U.S. Maritime Strategy*, Second Edition. Annapolis, MD: Naval Institute Press, 2018.

ACKNOWLEDGEMENTS

This book was only possible because I had a great deal of help and a wonderful home in which to write. I owe a special debt of gratitude to the Project 2049 Institute's founder and chairman, Randy Schriver, who gave me the opportunity to be part of the amazing team he built. Randy sat down for several interviews that enriched these pages, and he penned the foreword.

Richard Armitage pushed me to tackle big analytic challenges outside my comfort zone and supported this project idea from the very start. John Gastright Jr. led our think tank through the long pandemic lockdown with unflagging enthusiasm and kept team morale high. Mark Stokes was an endless font of wisdom, inspiration, and fun. It's an honor to work with such a prescient analyst and maverick mentor.

My colleagues and friends Colby Ferland and Eric Lee carefully read the manuscript, corrected my many mistakes, and gave me fantastic feedback on style. Jennifer Hong kindly reviewed drafts and coached me on strategic communications. Surya Narayanan went above and beyond the call of duty to help me hunt down typos. Grace Young led a group of young scholars to collect data, including Margaret Baughman, Joseph Ross, Sherman Tylawsky, Jae Chang, and Maryanne Liu. Grace also worked overtime to produce amazing drawings for the book.

Louis Martin-Vézian gave top-notch assistance to this book by collating and visualizing data and creating maps and infographics. He's the only young analyst I know who can make every deadline with ample room to spare while traveling the world and balancing competing demands on his time and talents, all while making it appear effortless.

Over the course of research, Dan Blumenthal, Wallace Gregson, Paul Giarra, Andrew May, Anders Corr, Dan Tobin, Aaron Friedberg, Patrick

Jenevein, Ivan Kanapathy, Greg Levesque, Emily Weinstein, Ceci Joy Pérez, and Emily David all provided much-needed tutorials and sounding boards, while offering their expert insights. James Proud, Miles Yu, and Charles Morrison each read the book and stunned me with their encouragement and generous assistance.

I am deeply grateful to Jacqueline Newmyer Deal, Gabo Alvarado, Toshi Yoshihara, Matt Pottinger, Dan Tobin, and Peter Mattis, who all provided reviews and comments on various drafts of the manuscript, making for a much-improved final cut. They all had better and more important things to do, but took the time to talk to me and share their perspectives.

Camphor Press and Eastbridge Books have been an absolute delight to work with. This is my second book with them. John Grant Ross, the sage editor-in-chief, made final revisions a blast by using a blend of humor and the Socratic method to draw out ideas and test my (sometimes faulty) assumptions. Michael Cannings, the language and history buff with an eye for marketing, blew me away with his cover design, planning skills, and guidance through the publishing process. Mark Swofford copyedited and provided professional counsel on everything from Mandarin romanization to the technical rules governing various mediums of expression.

Others who made this book possible would not thank me to reveal their names and generosity. I am in awe of their selfless dedication to the creation and dissemination of knowledge that benefits American public education. If you like this book, the credit belongs to those listed above (and some who are unlisted). If you disagreed and/or saw mistakes, I am entirely responsible, not only for the translations, analysis, and findings presented, but also for the style in which they were delivered.

ABOUT CAMPHOR PRESS

Camphor Press is an independent publisher focused on English-language books about East Asia. Founded in Taiwan in 2014 with a mission to provide a platform for important writing about the region, the press is rooted in the principles of free expression and opposition to censorship.

The Eastbridge imprint of Camphor Press (under which this book is published) is a home for both deeply-researched scholarly works and books in translation.

ABOUT THE PROJECT 2049 INSTITUTE

The Project 2049 Institute is a nonprofit research organization focused on promoting American values and security interests in the Indo-Pacific region. We specialize in open-source research using Chinese-language sources to inform policy debate and advance public education. Our core mission is to create and disseminate knowledge that makes the region more peaceful and prosperous.

The Project 2049 Institute is located in Arlington, Virginia, and was co-founded in 2008 by the Honorable Randall Schriver and Lt Col Mark Stokes (USAF, ret.). We are a 501(c)(3) tax-exempt organization. Independent and non-partisan, our research is focused on bolstering human rights and national security.

ABOUT THE AUTHOR

Ian Easton is a Senior Director at the Project 2049 Institute, where he studies defense and security issues involving the People's Republic of China. Previously, Easton was a visiting fellow at the Japan Institute for International Affairs, a China analyst at the Center for Naval Analyses, and a researcher for the Asia Bureau of Defense News. He has testified before the U.S.-China Economic and Security Review Commission and given talks at the U.S. Naval War College, U.S. Army JAG School, Japan's National Defense Academy, Taiwan's National Defense University, and Germany's Command and Staff College. Easton holds an M.A. in China Studies from National Chengchi University in Taiwan and a B.A. in International Studies from the University of Illinois Urbana-Champaign. He studied Mandarin at Fudan University in Shanghai and National Taiwan Normal University in Taipei.

Made in the USA
Middletown, DE
16 November 2023

42917734R00199